JC599.M4 E88 2008
Estévez.

Human ri
trade i
200

Human Rights and Free Trade in Mexico

Human Rights and Free Trade in Mexico

A Discursive and Sociopolitical Perspective

Ariadna Estévez

palgrave
macmillan

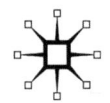

HUMAN RIGHTS AND FREE TRADE IN MEXICO
Copyright © Ariadna Estévez, 2008.

All rights reserved.

First published in 2008 by
PALGRAVE MACMILLAN™
175 Fifth Avenue, New York, N.Y. 10010 and
Houndmills, Basingstoke, Hampshire, England RG21 6XS
Companies and representatives throughout the world.

PALGRAVE MACMILLAN is the global academic imprint of the Palgrave Macmillan division of St. Martin's Press, LLC and of Palgrave Macmillan Ltd. Macmillan® is a registered trademark in the United States, United Kingdom and other countries. Palgrave is a registered trademark in the European Union and other countries.

ISBN-13: 978–0–230–60655–5
ISBN-10: 0–230–60655–5

Library of Congress Cataloging-in-Publication Data

Estévez, Ariadna.
    Human rights and free trade in Mexico : a discursive and sociopolitical perspective / Ariadna Estévez.
        p. cm.
    Includes bibliographical references and index.
    ISBN 0–230–60655–5
        1. Human rights—Mexico. 2. Free trade—Social aspects—Mexico.
  I. Title.

JC599.M4E88 2008
323.0972—dc22
                                                             2007047140

A catalogue record for this book is available from the British Library.

Design by Newgen Imaging Systems (P) Ltd., Chennai, India.

First edition: June 2008

10 9 8 7 6 5 4 3 2 1

Printed in the United States of America.

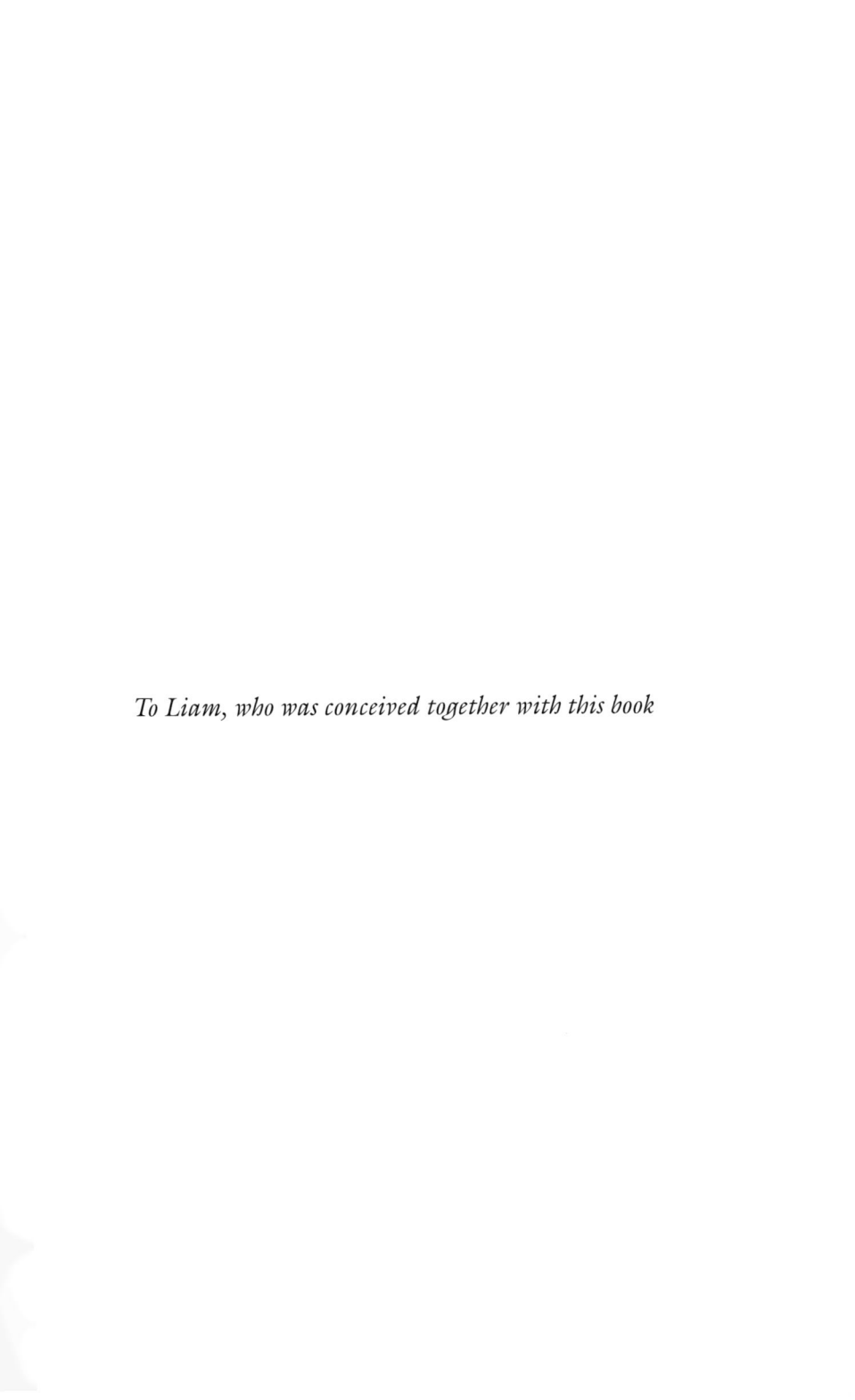

To Liam, who was conceived together with this book

Contents

List of Tables ix

Acknowledgments xi

Introduction: A Discursive and Sociopolitical Approach to Free Trade and Human Rights 1

Part I

Introduction 31

1 The Neoliberal Paradox: Conservative Economic Change and the Rise of Democratic Politics 33

2 The Emergence of Human Rights Discourse in Mexico 55

3 The Exhaustion of Transition to Democracy Discourse: Human Rights Discourse Enters Anti-free Trade Struggles 75

Part II

Introduction 99

4 Constructing Free Trade Worldviews with Human Rights Discourse 105

5 The Construction of Identities and Specific Agendas with Human Rights Discourse 133

6 Articulating Anti-free Trade Struggles with Human Rights Discourse 155

Conclusions	187
Notes	195
Bibliography	229
Interviews	251
Index	253

List of Tables

1. Categories derived from the theory of hegemonic articulation used in the analysis of discursive practices   100
2. Differences between NGOs and SMOs   102
3. Subject positions and agendas with human rights articulation   152
4. Chronology of increasing human rights articulation in the Hemispheric Social Alliance   165
5. Chronology of the first and second stages of the Democratic Clause Project   183
6. Differences between the Hemispheric Social Alliance and the Democratic Clause Project   185

Acknowledgments

I would like to express my deepest gratitude to my professor and friend Zdenek Kavan for his support, guidance, friendship, and knowledge of fine wines that were immensely helpful throughout the writing of this book. I am particularly thankful for his willingness to read endless drafts and his constantly insightful comments.

I am also indebted to Dr. Tim Havard for going through the entire draft several times to make sure my English was legible enough. I must also thank him for translating quotes and parts of the interviews.

Last, I would like to thank Dr. Neil Stammers, whose friendship and critical view of my work has always been helpful, especially when the wine was flowing.

I would also like to include a special mention for the Center for Research on North America (the National Autonomous University of Mexico) for their support while putting this book together.

Finally, these acknowledgments would not be complete without special thanks for my interviewees, the Free Trade Mexican Action Network, the Miguel Agustín Pro Juárez Human Rights Center, and the Fray Francisco de Vitoria Human Rights Center, for sharing their experience and knowledge.

Introduction

A Discursive and Sociopolitical Approach to Free Trade and Human Rights

The terms of free trade in Mexico have led to, among other things, deterioration in the environment, small-scale agricultural production, working conditions, wages, and the living standards of women and indigenous peoples. While organizations from the various social movements concerned with these issues have worked at the national and transnational levels with groups from other movements, this has generally occurred within the limits of agents' own particular discourses and the only point they have managed to agree on is their discontent with the impact of free trade. In this context, the difficulties involved in the negotiation of goals and agendas could be considered an expression of the reaffirmation of particularity derived from the transformations of late capitalism and the result of the fragmented nature of postmodern societies (Arditi 1991, Gabardi 2001, Harvey 1989, Laclau 1990).

More recently, social gents have begun to use the language and mechanisms of human rights in order to organize collective action against those free trade-related issues that directly affect the majority of Mexicans. In the name of human dignity they have participated in both national and international joint political action combining strategic civil and political rights claims and economic, social, and cultural rights demands. This strategic combination serves the purpose of demanding participation in policy design and decision-making related to trade as well as state and corporate accountability.

This phenomenon is related to an important issue in the sociopolitical study of globalization: the politics of human rights and, more specifically, the potentiality of human rights discourse to contribute to transnational collective action. While most studies in this field focus on the strategies deployed by social movements in order to influence global social change, they pay little attention to more sociological concerns, such as the agency-related and structural issues producing these struggles and the construction of identities and worldviews through the use of human rights discourses. This study aims to fill this gap by arguing that Mexican social movements operating at the transnational level use human rights discourses in order to establish common ground in their struggle against the unfair terms of free trade. While this study does not suggest that the idea that human rights have political potential for collective action is new,[1] it does offer a new perspective on such thinking by means of a discourse analysis that considers the way human rights were adopted as a discourse for political struggle and how human rights language is used by social agents.

This discourse analysis focuses on the issue of human rights potentiality for collective action in specific sites—Mexico in this case—that in turn generates instances of transnational collective action and thus of contingent universals. In particular it uses a discursive approach to assess the potentiality of human rights discourse for bringing together social agents while establishing a link between the construction of agent identities and global structural change. This approach allows for the simultaneous analysis of structural and subjective issues and considers the joint action undertaken by organizations as discursively constructed.

The originality of this perspective can be identified in its consideration of the sociopolitical potentiality of human rights discourses in the specific case of Mexico and its treatment of an issue that in general has not been the subject of in-depth studies. While it is true that some studies of the political potentiality of human rights discourse in Mexico exist, these are either concerned with the impact of human rights struggles for norm-change (Keck and Sikkink 1998a), or are limited in scope due to an exclusive focus on the rights of political citizenship (Foweraker 1990, Foweraker and Landman 2000). In the first group there is Keck and Sikkink's study of the human rights movement in Mexico and Argentina. Here, the authors demonstrate that governmental human rights policies emerge in response to the presence of human rights networks and can therefore lead to changes in human rights practices (Keck and Sikkink 1998a). A sociological focus on the use of human rights discourse for the organization of collective action is not included in this study.

Foweraker's empirical work on the construction of citizenship and "popular movements" in Mexico is restricted exclusively to civil and political citizenship rights (Foweraker 1990, Foweraker and Landman 2000). For Foweraker, social movements are those dealing with citizenship rights whereas those addressing economic and social issues are popular movements because they ground their collective action in "demands," which he does not consider to be rights. He claims that "Whatever the virtues of these rights [economic, social, cultural, and collective rights] (and there are many), they do not qualify as integral to the discourse of rights..." (Foweraker and Landman 2000:14). In addition to the work of Keck and Sikkink and Foweraker there is also an empirical study by Williams (2001) which deals with shifts in the character of protest and social movement formation as a consequence of economic change, in particular the introduction of free trade-related distributive policies. However, rights—apart from citizenship rights allowing public protests—are not a primary concern of her examination.

Regarding transnational collective action in general, existing studies focus on the use of human rights for effecting change in human rights norms. Recent literature studying the use of human rights for collective action in globalization tends to examine human rights from the perspective of normative theory in international relations. Using insights from the American School of Social Movement Theory,[2] this literature argues that transnational social movements are a key factor in norm creation and change and contends that civil society actors are central to the contemporary establishment and expansion of human rights as norms. By encouraging norm-making through political processes, civil society contributes to social change (Brysk 2002, Brysk 2005, Gready 2003, 2004, Keck and Sikkink 1998b, Khagram, Riker, and Sikkink 2002, Risse 2000, Risse, Ropp, and Sikkink 1999, Thomas 2001). It also contributes to the establishment of a system of global governance based on justice (Falk 2000).

This perspective is inscribed in the increasing interest of scholars from the fields of international relations, sociology, and politics in transnational collective action and human rights. The specific study of human rights in transnational collective action argues that social agents advocate norms in framing processes, that is, activists frame their issues in human rights terms and therefore they either contribute to the creation of new norms or the reform of existing ones (Khagram, Riker, and Sikkink 2002, Gready 2004, 2003). They also highlight the importance of exploiting political opportunities presented to them in order to influence norm reform (Khagram, Riker, and Sikkink 2002, Keck and Sikkink 1998b, Gready 2004). They acknowledge the role of structural issues in shaping frames, especially when explaining the current move toward addressing economic and social rights and locating duty in private actors (Brysk 2005). However, there is a tendency in this literature to see movements as autonomous agents of change as the authors pay almost no attention to international and national structural change in the shaping of strategies—Thomas even argues that communist rule weakened as a consequence of social movement action rather than as a combination of factors: economic reform encouraged by Gorbachev together with social pressure (Thomas 2001:6–7).

In the light of the literature discussed above, this study offers fresh insight into the study of human rights and social movements in the specific case of the struggle against free trade in Mexico by offering a discourse analysis that includes both analytical and empirical elements. Here, I shall explain the steps taken to conduct this examination. First, I will discuss the discursive framework, which builds on a sociopolitical and Latin American understanding of human rights discourse and poststructuralist views of collective action and discursive practices. I shall accordingly discuss each of these parts and describe how they relate to the chapter outline, after discussing why it is important to study human rights strategies against free trade.

Why Study Human Rights Strategies against Free Trade?

This study does not suggest that trade is itself a violation of human rights; it suggests that free trade rules—or the lack of them—clash with many of the cornerstones of international human rights discourse, such as state duty and legal enforcement for the protection of labor, the environment, minorities, and so on. In the specific case of Mexico, free trade has become central to economic policy. In fact, Mexico has adopted free trade in a highly orthodox way, starting with the unilateral elimination of tariffs on exports and imports in 1987. Between 1993 and 2003 it signed 11 free trade agreements involving 44 countries.[3] The North America Free Trade Agreement (NAFTA) is by far the most important trade agreement, because in 2003 Mexico's exports to the United States alone represented 88.2 percent of the total (146,802.7 million dollars of a total of 165,355.2). Imports represented 61.81 percent of the total (105,685.9 million dollars of a total of 170,958.2).[4] For free trade enthusiasts, Mexico offers a success story because it has liberalized trade massively and obtained sustained export growth as a consequence—this in itself is considered a development goal (United Nations Development Program 2005). According to the United Nations Development Program (UNDP), Mexico is responsible for over half of Latin America's exports of manufactured goods. It has sustained export growth rates of roughly 26 percent concentrated in high value-added technology sectors such as cars and electronics—the so-called *maquiladora* industry.

Civil society challenges this idea of success by pointing out that the trade surplus is mostly due to petroleum and *maquiladora* production, which are prior to, and independent from, trade agreements (Arroyo Picard et al. 2003).[5] In addition, since Mexico is a low value-added producer of high-value added products, that is, it is an exporter of manufactured goods assembled with imported components, this type of export sector fails to forge links with the local economy and communities. Furthermore, it provides minimal skills and technology transfers (United Nations Development Program 2005). According to the Mexican Action Network on Free Trade (RMALC, the Spanish acronym for Red Mexicana de Acción Frente al Libre Comercio) this kind of manufacturing has led to the collapse of national industries and the UNDP considers it a weak industrial policy.

According to the UNDP, in order for free trade to be a successful development strategy, it has to be, ironically, not that free. The recipe for trade success according to the UNDP includes privileging a state-planned industrial and technology policy over the use of cheap labor and the production of primary goods as "comparative advantages." This state-led policy should guarantee technology transfer, regulate foreign investment, restrict imports, and provide incentives. In addition, the state has to manage openness in a way that aids rather than destroys economic sectors such as small-scale agriculture. It should also rely on social and environmental regulation (United Nations Development Program 2005).

For social movements, good trade policy has to avoid implementation of the principles and provisions discussed above, which have had a negative social impact. The terms of the trade agreements signed by Mexico have prevented the country from intervening in the planning and implementation of policy. Furthermore, these terms have prevented Mexico from regulating labor, protecting the environment and the agricultural sector, and controlling the performance of corporations. These arguments underpin the strategies of social movements using human rights discourses to oppose free trade.

Apart from the macro level of impact described above, trade policy has a direct influence on microeconomics: income, women, agriculture, labor, and the environment. First, regarding income, inappropriate trade policy has allowed the Mexican government to rely on low wages as a comparative advantage. From the early stages of liberalization, the Mexican government has relied on maintaining low wages and weak collective bargaining rights as a comparative advantage (interview with Alberto Arroyo, 2004). Nevertheless, this strategy has ultimately proved unsuccessful because there are always countries offering even lower wages, such as China (United Nations Development Program 2005). The UNDP believes that, in addition to this, wages are stagnant partly because exports are from low value-added sectors, such as the *maquiladora* industry. At the end of the day, it is stagnant wages, more than unemployment, which account for the decision of millions of Mexicans to emigrate to the United States (Novelo Urdanivia 2004:225).[6]

Low wages can also be used to explain the increasingly unequal distribution of income, which is one of the major problems in contemporary Mexico. This situation has been exacerbated by free trade since the poor cannot compete with imports and the rich take advantage of the opportunities presented by exports (United Nations Development Program 2005, Programa de las Naciones Unidas para el Desarrollo 2002). The UNDP's Human Redevelopment Report, Mexico, 2002, highlights inequality as a massive development problem in Mexico by examining the income gap between the poor, the poorest, and the wealthiest. While the individual wealth of 13 people in the country is estimated at one billion dollars each, 23.5 million Mexicans from a total population of 100 million cannot cover their basic needs. While each of these 13 billionaires earns 1.9 million dollars a day, the poorest survive on one dollar a day. According to the UNDP framework, almost 46 percent of Mexican homes are considered to be poor, as their per capita income is less than two dollars a day. Only 10 percent of Mexican homes have earnings of 26 dollars a day. Average per capita income nationally is six dollars a day, and only 40 percent of Mexicans earn more than the average income; economic growth per capita averaged only a fraction over 1 percent from 1990 to 2003 (Programa de las Naciones Unidas para el Desarrollo 2002).

Second, women's rights are particularly affected by employment conditions because they account for 58 percent of people employed in *maquiladoras*. Most women are concentrated in the textile industry, which is one of the sectors with the lowest wages together with the food sector; while male employees are concentrated in the manufacturing sector—predominantly machinery and tools—which offer better paid jobs (2002 WB study quoted in Red Género y Economía et al. 2003). In addition, although they do not emigrate to the United States as frequently as men, women face many problems when their partners leave their homes, such as irregular income (Mexicans in the United States send money on a very irregular basis) and have to take charge of the household, which includes the performance of unpaid domestic work (Red Género y Economía et al. 2003).

Third, lack of control over policy also has consequences for agriculture. A major problem is that the richer countries continue to protect their agricultural production. This prevents poorer countries from competing due to their inability to subsidize production, which in turn leads to their products being more expensive. In the case of Mexico, state failure to support the agricultural sector is a major problem. The agricultural sector entered into crisis in the late 1960s, but the elimination of subsidies from the early 1980s through structural adjustment programs, legal reforms eliminating community land ownership, and the liberalization of agricultural products in asymmetric conditions such as those of NAFTA has practically destroyed the sector in Mexico. While U.S. farmers receive subsidies amounting to 120 dollars per hectare annually and farm some 29 hectares each, their Mexican counterparts receive approximately 45 dollars annually to farm an average of 1.8 hectares each (Arroyo Picard et al. 2003).[7] In addition, agricultural production in Mexico is less "competitive" due to factors secondary to farming itself, such as higher costs for fuel, electricity, and marketing (Arroyo Picard et al. 2003).

The Hemispheric Social Alliance claims that a major problem in the decline of the agricultural sector is that the Mexican government either incorrectly negotiated terms for the elimination of import tariffs, or has not used the protection allowed under the terms of such agreements as NAFTA. As a result, while Mexico imported 8.8 million metric tons of grain and oilseed in 1993, by 2002, such imports had increased to 20 million metric tons, representing an increase of over 100 percent (Arroyo Picard et al. 2003:27). "The situation with meat, tropical fruits, and other products is similar," Arroyo indicates, "These imports have replaced national products, increasing rural unemployment. In addition, part of the country's infrastructure has been destroyed" (Arroyo Picard et al. 2003:27). In relation to this, one of the biggest agricultural tragedies generated by free trade under NAFTA is Mexico's dependency on the import of maize, which is culturally central to the Mexican diet. Maize imports have increased sixfold since 1994 (United Nations Development Program 2005). However, even more worrying is Mexico's increasing loss of food sovereignty, as it has spent 78 billion dollars on food imports over the last ten years (Arroyo Picard et al. 2003). This situation is leading to the progressive destruction of the sector. From 1991 to 2002, employment in the agricultural sector decreased from 8.2 million jobs to 7.2 million. It is likely that unemployment in this sector contributed to the increase of jobs in the informal economy, which passed from 33.7 percent of total jobs in 1992, to 42.8 percent in 2002 (Oficina del Alto Comisionado de las Naciones Unidas para los Derechos Humanos en México 2003:78).

Fourth, failure to enforce the law has had a negative impact on workers' collective bargaining power. The Mexican government has maintained control over trade unions in order to prevent protests directed at the policy of low wages and the attraction of foreign direct investment via loose labor regulation. The government promises investors that workers will be members of unions affiliated to the national and corporatist Mexican Workers' Confederation (CTM, the Spanish acronym for Confederación de Trabajadores de México) and prevents the formation of independent unions. It also uses the labor courts (controlled by executive power, rather than judicial power, through the Employment Secretariat) to make independent unions illegal or to ensure they lose legal suits against employers (Villalba 2004). This policy has led to the persecution and even murder of independent union leaders, as well as the illegal closure of factories in which independent unions have managed to win control of the collective labor agreement.

There are numerous cases of independent unions harassed by the government throughout the 1990s and the first decade of the twenty-first century. For example, in 1991 the corporatist trade union was responsible for the death of a worker and injuries to several others during a referendum at the Ford Motor Company's Cuautitlán factory. Here employees were to vote for the trade union that would assume responsibility for negotiation of the collective labor agreement—the choices were the corporatist, CTM-affiliated union, and an independent union set up by workers after the corporatist union agreed to a reduction of workers' benefits with the employer. The independent union lodged a complaint with labor authorities, which ruled against workers. They appealed the decision, but the company delayed procedures for a year, providing the Ford Motor Company with the opportunity to fire 800 workers supporting the independent union. In the end, and because the case became publicized, labor authorities ruled in favor of workers' demands for a new vote.

A more recently publicized case was that of the Euzkadi workers. In December 2001, German Continental Tires (Hulera Euzkadi) closed down one of its two plants without proper authorization from Mexican authorities as established in labor law. The plant that closed down was located in the state of Jalisco, where workers had an independent union. The company did not close its plant in San Luis Potosí State, where the union is affiliated to the CTM. When workers called a strike to challenge the illegality of the closure, the government supported the German corporation by arguing, without legal support, that the strike was "not applicable" (Ortega and Solís 1990).

Finally, regarding the environment, failure to enforce the law has also led to environmental dumping—the bending or even elimination of laws protecting the environment. For instance, in 1995 the state government awarded the U.S. forestry company Boise Cascade the concession and exclusive rights to purchase and exploit timber in Costa Grande in Guerrero. This is an area plagued by poverty and environmental laws lax enough to permit the loss of 38 percent of the forest (86,000 hectares out of a total of 226,203) between 1992 and 2000. In 1998, a group of farmers in Petatlán, Guerrero state, realized that water had become scarce in the region and that this was due to deforestation. In response to this, they organized themselves to protect the forest against the environmental pillaging of Boise Cascade, which suspended its operations that year as a result of pressure from farmers. However, the state government used the claim that armed groups were operating in the area to justify the deployment of troops and the abuse of locals. A well-known case of such abuse was the arbitrary detention, torture, solitary confinement, and imprisonment of Rodolfo Montiel and Teodoro Cabrera, local farmers active in the defense of the environment. Their case was taken up by environmental and human rights groups and resulted in their release in 2001 (Cienfuegos and Carlsen 2003).

In addition, the lack of environmental regulation of corporations under NAFTA has led to environmental vulnerability in local communities, as the case of Metalclad shows. Metalclad is a U.S.-based company that was awarded 15.6 million dollars in damages from the municipal government of Guadalcázar, San Luis Potosí. The municipality had refused to issue the company a permit to run a toxic waste depot because of its justified concerns for the health of the local population (Bejarano González 2003).

Also linked to the lack of environmental regulation is the case of patents. Under the World Trade Organization (WTO) agreement on patents and copyright, large multinational laboratories, and even small companies based in rich countries, are patenting methods of harnessing the planet's biological wealth adopted and perfected by indigenous peoples over thousands of years. One example is the case of a type of bean known as *Enola*. In 1994, Larry Proctor, the owner of Pod-Ners, a small seed production company based in the United States, purchased in Sonora, Mexico, a package with many different types of beans. He chose the yellow ones, planted them, and let them grow. After mixing several generations of the bean, he managed to produce a bean that he considered different to the original, and he subsequently requested a patent in the United States that he called *Enola* after his wife. This patent covers any variety of yellow beans, and the patent owner demands royalties for every kilo of yellow beans imported into the United States (La Neta 2005).

In summary, Mexico has been very enthusiastic in liberalizing trade by signing free trade agreements. However, the terms of these agreements have had massive social and environmental consequences because the state has failed to establish a national policy that encourages local industrial and agricultural sectors. In addition, the government has chosen deregulation of the environment and labor as a comparative advantage.

Human Rights Discourse: A Sociopolitical and Latin American Understanding

In order to analyze how human rights are used in collective action against the human rights violations resulting from free trade policy, I argue that it is necessary to define human rights as a nonessentialist and ongoing discursive construction. This is not only because such a view is coherent with a discursive analysis of collective action, but also because a view of human rights grounded on social practices rather than morals and metaphysics fits the dynamics of human rights discourse construction in Latin America.

It is widely accepted that more than 500 years after colonization and almost 200 years after independence from Spain and Portugal, a largely Catholic and Westernized Latin America does not have a major problem with accepting a mainstream modern and secular discourse such as human rights. Asian and African scholars have conducted theoretical examinations of human rights, suggesting the need for a cultural dialogue that includes the views of the Muslim or Hindu worlds or the importance of community (Baxi 2002, Donnelly 2002, Nyamu-Musembi 2002, Sen 1999). Latin American human rights scholarship on the other hand has quietly accepted the cultural relevance of mainstream human rights discourses (Beuchot 1993, Fix-Zamudio 1982). Consequently, the contribution of Latin American scholars to the discourse of human rights has been limited and largely overshadowed by the contributions of European, mostly Spanish theorists, such as Peces-Barba (Peces-Barba, Asís Roig, and Barranco Avilés 2004, Peces-Barba and Universidad Carlos III de Madrid 1995).

Most Latin American philosophy scholars argue that Latin American human rights discourse begins its construction in the sixteenth century, with the theological work of missionaries in New Spain such as Fray Bartolomé de las Casas, Francisco de Vitoria, and Vasco de Quiroga. These missionaries defended and reaffirmed the dignity of indigenous populations and demanded their social welfare based on scholastic ideas of the human person (Carozza 2003, Beuchot 1993, 2005, De la Torre Rangel 1994). However, given the region's tradition of social struggle, and social and political thought linked to these struggles, this book argues that a Latin American human rights understanding would have to be built on the interaction of European-based intellectual traditions and social struggles.

Here we challenge the position adopted by the majority of Latin American human rights scholars by proposing a genealogical and intertextual view of human rights that serves to recover the region's major contribution to the field. This contribution is based precisely on bottom-up struggles for human rights and the region's intellectual traditions, including structuralist discourses rarely linked to human rights. Consequently, in this section I shall first offer justification for a regional understanding of human rights based on social struggles rather than purely European politico-legal philosophy. Following this, I shall discuss the theoretical framework devised to help recover these and other Latin American struggles contributing to the construction of contemporary human rights discourse. This will help forward the methodological basis for a human rights conceptualization that is specific to Latin America. Finally, building on the idea that human rights should be understood in the context of intellectual tradition and social struggles, I will offer a definition of human rights discourse that responds to the Latin American experience.

Justifying a Latin American Conceptualization of Human Rights

Today, the idea that human rights are the product of European liberalism is a familiar one. Put simply, human rights are defined as entitlements emerging from either a universal human nature based on the possession of reason or the morality emerging from having said reason. These alleged natural rights to life, liberty, and property, which were first conceived in seventeenth-century England, developed later throughout Europe as entitlements to legal security and political liberty. Relativist approaches to human rights—especially those generated by anthropology scholarship—have accused human rights proponents of making human rights appear as universal, when in fact they represent a singular view of the world, the Western view, as expressed in liberalism (An-Na'im 1995, Wilson 1997).

Even Latin American scholars attempting to identify the region's original contribution to human rights thought tend to find this in the intellectual contributions made to the Western tradition of modern thought. Beuchot, for instance, shares the view of Carozza that the Latin America contribution to human rights discourse can be found in the theological and Aristotelian defense of indigenous people's human dignity. This defense was advanced by such thinkers as De las Casas, Vitoria and Quiroga and it is closely linked to liberal notions of human worth. While de las Casas and Vitoria built on Aristotelian and Christian ideas of the human person in order to support a proposal for the human dignity and freedom of indigenous people, De Quiroga demanded indigenous welfare and proposed educative and health policies to protect them (Beuchot 2000). In a similar way, given the fact that the 1917 Mexican Constitution was the first expression of French contractualism to include social entitlements, it is quite easy to identify major contributions to human rights discourse in Latin America, although most of these constitutional rights are in fact ineffective.[8]

Argentinean-Mexican philosopher Enrique Dussel argues that the thought of De las Casas, Quiroga, and Vitoria should be considered part of early non-Eurocentric Latin American thinking. He claims that while these theologians were Spanish and their theoretical resources European (scholastic humanism), their ethical-philosophical question was concerned with the right of Europeans to dominate, occupy, and manage these recently "discovered" cultures. This concern, he says, was lost in the philosophy of the centuries to come, when Europeans universalized their particularities via philosophy (Dussel 2006). Although I generally agree with these arguments in terms of the history of ideas, these ideas have to do more with the Enlightenment version of human rights than with human rights as we know them today, rights that use the Universal Declaration of Human Rights (DUDH) as a starting point.

It is for this reason that I also disagree with Beuchot's suggestion that a philosophical foundation for human rights from a Latin American perspective is necessary. He proposes, along the lines of mainstream European legal arguments for the metaphysical and moral foundations of human rights, to see them founded in a human nature based on reason and providing the morals to legitimate the needs that lead to their recognition (Beuchot 1993). The Latin American contribution here is the construction of the human dignity underlying such foundations, which is based on an allegedly specific Latin American scholasticism.

I argue that both sixteenth-century Spanish scholasticism and Beuchot's proposal are not consistent with Latin American reality. Both are related to liberal philosophy and juridical practice, which has little to do with Latin America's history of human rights construction. In the light of this, I propose that a truly Latin American notion of human rights should be founded in the region's social struggles and their feedback with Latin American thought based on the region's social reality. For this, I shall follow the arguments of Indian legal theorist Upendra Baxi (Baxi 2002) and Mexican-Argentinean liberation philosopher Enrique Dussel (Dussel 2007). Baxi argues that both foundationalist and relativist ideas of human rights that attribute human rights authorship exclusively to European thinkers or liberal thought in general lead us to the false belief that human rights are "the gift of the West to the rest" (Baxi 2002:24–27). Such ideas, he claims, ignore non-Western traditions of thought that anticipate and reinforce contemporary ideas of human rights. This is because we tend to see a continuum in the evolution of human rights thinking and practice, when in fact liberal understandings of rights have been contested by social movements since the formulation of the International Bill of Rights.

Therefore, Baxi distinguishes between the emergence of "modern human rights" and "contemporary human rights" with the former emerging from Enlightenment thought, excluding the poor and the colonized, and carrying with it three major assumptions that systematically exclude most peoples of the world. The first of these assumptions is the idea of an allegedly universal human nature that conceives the individual (always a "man") as an autonomous subject with the capacity to transform the world if his rights are recognized and are used to impose limits on the state. As some schools of feminist thought have pointed out, when considering its tendency toward overdetermination and its construction as a way to preclude the possibility of significant subjectivities, the idea of a universal human nature undermines diversity and leads to a failure to acknowledge needs and differences arising from social and economic inequalities and cultural and gender differences. Feminists claim, for example, that universal human nature in fact refers to a very specific kind of person: young, white, heterosexual male and with property (Chinkin 1999, Chinkin et al. 1997, Ramsay 1997).

Second, there is the idea of the "individual" that has emphasized individualistic constructions of the individual (detached from community) and ontological individualism (the assertion that only individual interests, wants, and preferences exist). Both these notions are linked to the idea of the universal individual and have overemphasized negative liberty. Both methodological individualism and ontological individualism have led to an underdevelopment of mechanisms of enforcement for human rights related to wider social issues, such as economic, social, and cultural rights, hence limiting the production of texts concerning these rights (Woodiwiss 2002). Finally, there is the alleged separation between public and private spheres that leaves the household and the market outside state influence and consequently excludes problems related to these spheres (Clapham 1993). This separation has had a negative effect on approaches to women's rights and responses to violations of rights resulting from economic activity. However, the feminist challenge to this led to the recognition of sexual and domestic violence as violations of the human rights of women. In addition, the increasing number of challenges to corporate activity has led to the formulation of the idea of corporate responsibility in human rights.

In contrast to these limitations of modern human rights, contemporary human rights display two particular characteristics according to Baxi. First, there is resistance to the assumptions and actual human rights violations coming from dominant human rights discourses. Second, there is an increasing inclusion of different kinds of subjects and negotiations between nongovernmental organizations (NGOs) and governments at the United Nations (UN). This has led to the recognition of the rights of women, migrants, indigenous peoples, gays and lesbians, refugees, children, etc. (Baxi 2002:24–41). Such political trends have challenged and overcome the limitations of liberal human rights discourse. For this reason it is impossible to talk about a continuum in human rights thinking and therefore contemporary human rights are fundamentally different from modern human rights.

Furthermore, Baxi claims that in their contemporary version human rights become an "insurrectionary practice," which he defines thus: "Through myriad struggles and movements throughout the world, 'human rights' become an arena of transformative political practice that disorients, destabilizes, and at times even helps destroy deeply unjust concentrations of political, social, economic, and technological power" (Baxi 2002:10). Baxi's examples are movements for decolonization, ecological integrity, and women's rights. Further examples of contemporary human rights would be the struggles for social, democratic, and collective rights in Latin America over the last 30 years, such as the movements for land and services in Brazil, for democracy in the Southern Cone, and indigenous rights in Mexico and Ecuador.

For his part, and in a similar vein, when reflecting on Latin American thought in general, Dussel argues that Latin American scholars have to start an "epistemological decolonization" by reconstructing concepts and theories in isolation from European thinking. He rejects ideas of postmodernism and proposes a transmodern epistemological process that comprises, but does not start from, modern European thought. Dussel claims that it is necessary to look at a "world philosophy"—as opposed to Western-centered "universal philosophy"—that demonstrates an understanding of several notions currently monopolized by Eurocentric epistemologies. One such notion could be human rights, which, he argues, exists in most cultures. In fact, individual human rights should be seen as a liberal "ontological defamation" (Dussel 2007).

From a Latin American perspective, a transmodern and decolonized epistemology reframing a variety of concepts including human rights would have to begin in the region's social reality, more specifically, in the lessons of its major revolutions: the populist movements of Perón and Cárdenas; the Cuban socialist revolution; the Chilean democratic revolution for human rights; the Sandinista revolution for democratic socialism; the Zapatista movement for indigenous rights and democracy; and the Bolivarian revolutions headed by the presidents of Bolivia, the first indigenous president in the region, Evo Morales, and Venezuela, Hugo Chávez. "With the region's reality, we are ahead in philosophical thinking," says Dussel, who is one of the major proponents of the philosophy of liberation (Dussel 2007).

In the light of Baxi's and Dussel's calls for a contemporary and decolonized conceptualization of human rights, an understanding specific to Latin America is therefore better framed by the notion of contemporary human rights than by the idea of modern rights and demands independence from European legalism that derived rights from liberal philosophy. In a strict sense, these foundations do not reflect the Latin American tradition of social struggle underlying the region's intellectual traditions. While not denying the contribution of sixteenth-century Spanish religious thinking, Latin American liberal legalism, and liberal political thinking, it is fair to say that this contribution is to the modern rather than the contemporary view of human rights expressed as an exclusionary constitutionalism. Following the lead of Baxi and Dussel, a Latin America-specific understanding of human rights cannot rest on an assimilation of European thought. It must provide a synthesis of social movement practice and the intellectual constructions supporting them, including traditions rarely linked to human rights such as liberation theology.

Genealogy and Intertextuality of Human Rights Discourse

In order to conceptualize human rights in such a way that the experience and intellectual traditions of social struggles such as those described above are used to form the basis of this conceptualization, the ideas of genealogy and intertextuality prove very useful. These concepts help to establish both the historical specificity of a discourse and its continuous construction within sociopolitical struggles and tend to serve the interests of these struggles. In the first place and with respect to genealogy, Michel Foucault in his initial studies—those looking at medicine and psychiatry (Foucault 1977)—described discourses as "autonomous systems of rules that constitute objects, concepts, subjects and strategies, thereby governing the production of scientific statements," which in turn determine what can be said and known about a given discipline (Howarth 2000:9). Later, in his works dealing with sexuality (Foucault 1985, 1988, 1998) and the history of punishment, Foucault borrowed from Nietzsche to develop a more complex and power-related idea of discourse that he came to see as "'tactical elements or blocks operating in the field of force relations.' From this perspective, discourses are the means for different forces to advance their interests and projects, while also providing 'points of resistance for counter-strategies to develop'" (Howarth 2000). In this way Foucault distinguished between discourse and nondiscursive practices, such as institutions and techniques, and was interested in the processes by which discourse and discursive practices relate to each other, for example, the relation power/knowledge (Foucault 1988, 1998). By adopting such a perspective, Foucault developed the basis for a genealogical method of discourse analysis that traced the emergence and formation of subjects, objects, concepts, and strategies in specific contexts within power relations.

Based on this understanding of discourse, human rights as an insurrectionary practice could be understood as a discursive formation, the genealogy of which could be traced in Latin America as a whole, or in each region or country. Genealogy could help identify the power relations leading to the development of human rights and how these became a site for political, social, economic, and cultural disputes. At the same time, genealogy could reveal the contribution of local knowledge to the construction of concepts and strategies according to context-specific needs—in this case, Latin American structuralist thinking.[9]

In the second place, if human rights are seen as a discursive formation, they are constructed according to specific historical contexts and social needs. This means that objects, subjects, concepts, and strategies are neither fixed nor determinate but undergoing constant construction due to their relations and the emergence of counter-strategies. However, the question remains as to how, precisely, this construction comes about. I argue that this is possible thanks to intertextuality and the political legitimacy of human rights texts.

Baxi argues that intertextuality, a term drawn from literary criticism and literary theory but widely adopted in Critical Legal Studies,[10] refers to the way texts are never completely new or self-evident but formed by the conjunction of previous texts and their particular social contexts. Texts have to be understood in their own social and historical context, but also as incorporating present readings and contexts. The intertextual character of all texts, including legal texts, is asserted by scholars of Critical Legal Studies who claim that legal texts carry a surplus of meaning created by the fact that the meaning of a text is never self-evident but dependant on past and future readings and rewriting (Rosenfeld 1998). For Baxi, the values and instruments related to human rights can be considered texts ready to be reread and reinterpreted (Baxi 2003). For instance, the Universal Declaration of Human Rights (UDHR) refers to natural rights and Enlightenment philosophy, but its construction has to be understood in the context of the Second World War. In turn, the UDHR informs the Convention for the Elimination of All Forms of Discrimination against Women (CEDAW) that was formulated in the 1970s, a historical period when the women's movement was very active.

The precise form in which social agents engage in the intertextality of human rights can be seen in the work of African legal scholar Celestine Nyamu-Musembi, in particular her work on the "actor-oriented perspective of human rights." She argues that human rights instruments are used for historically and geographically specific constructions of human rights that usually expand the rubric of rights and are later taken to the international level.[11] Nyamu-Musembi analyzes how, in their daily work, local intellectuals and activists interpret major debates in human rights in the light of international human rights law and mechanisms of defense. These debates include universality versus particularism; individualism versus collectivities; the status of economic, social, and cultural rights (ESCRs); and the accountability of non-state actors. She concludes that people's individual interpretations widen the scope of certain rights for, while theoretical and philosophical debates continue, in practice people have effectively moved beyond these debates. She claims that "looking for the meaning of rights from the perspective of those claiming them transforms defined normative parameters of human rights debates, questions established conceptual categories and expands the range of claims that are validated as rights" (Nyamu-Musembi 2002:1).

Both Baxi's idea of the intertextuality of human rights and Nyamu-Musembi's notion of the actor-oriented perspective of human rights are commonly applied to legal defense and jurisprudence construction.[12] However, based on a genealogical view of human rights as an insurrectionary practice, I contend that these concepts can also be applied to political interpretations of human rights in negotiations with the state or international institutions in two fundamental ways. First, in advocacy and the lobbying of policy proposal, legal texts can be interpreted politically to formulate a particular claim that carries the symbolism of the human rights texts without necessarily having to take the case to court. Second, it could be applied in the production of a legitimate claim without this claim necessarily being established as a legal right, which is an approach consistent with the process of jurisprudence. The legitimacy of human rights claims is based on the surplus of political meaning carried by the discourse, a point I shall discuss in more detail below.

A Latin American Understanding of Human Rights

In the light of this discussion, genealogy and intertextuality contribute to a Latin American understanding of human rights that revindicates the region's principal contributions to international discourse in complementary ways. First, viewing human rights as a discursive formation allows for a genealogical analysis that serves to trace both the particular power relations leading to specific disputes within human rights discourse and the role of Latin American thought in shaping these struggles and, by extension, specific human rights struggles. Second, from an actor-oriented perspective of human rights, intertextuality allows for an understanding of how human rights texts and values can be interpreted and reinterpreted to forward the demands of new subjects of rights as well as a consideration of how social agents widen the scope of rights in both courts and politics. This raises ethical questions that are resolved at the political level.

Based on this discussion it is now possible to offer a conceptualization of human rights from the Latin American perspective. Human rights can be understood as a discursive formation using values and instruments that are intertextual. Understood in this way, human rights can be reinterpreted in the context of social struggles in order to lobby demands and construct new human rights entitlements in the legal and political arenas. Human rights are therefore legal-political linguistic constructions that could be used by people suffering social exclusion and violence. Since discourses assign meaning to physical facts, human rights as used by the powerless constitute a discourse that both assigns meaning to human suffering and provides the necessary tools for contesting the causes (socioeconomic inequality, discrimination) and the expressions (state violence, repression, exclusion) of such suffering. Understood in this way, human rights become an important "insurrectionary practice" (Baxi 2002:10).

Important Questions Arising from this Approach

It has to be acknowledged that in its attempt to rescue the region's specific sociopolitical contribution to international human rights discourse, this Latin American understanding of human rights as an insurrectionary practice could raise some important questions regarding the moral basis of human rights discourse and the risks of overpoliticization. In the first place, if the conceptualization of human rights does not reside on moral foundations, we may be opening the door for everyone, including the powerful and governments, to use the discourse to advance their own instrumental ends. If the morality of an alleged universal human nature is no longer underpinned by ethics what could take their place? In addressing these questions, Costas Douzinas argues that when human rights are not used for assigning meaning to suffering or empowering people against oppression, they are no longer a critique of law but the legislation of one's desires (Douzinas 2000). For his part, Baxi claims that human rights constitute a discourse that imposes limits on the powerful, whether these be state or private actors engaged in abuse, and that anything beyond this scope cannot form the basis for a human rights struggle (Baxi 2002).

In spite of this theoretical objection, human rights are still used by the powerful to advance their claims; take, for example, the case of some writings that claim corporations have human rather than instrumental rights (Addo 1999a). This means that human rights still represent a site for power disputes. I contend, therefore, that the solution to the ethical question posed above has to be political rather than theoretical, and consequently human rights can still be used in the politics of social movements. Human rights discourse is viable for emancipatory struggles because it carries a surplus of political meaning and this surplus is expressed in two ways. First, it is expressed in the legitimacy of human rights law. Human rights law provides a moral backup to the demands expressed through social struggles since states have made an international commitment to respect and promote them and human rights are now an important source of legitimacy (Brysk 2005, Falk 2000, Schmitz and Sikkink 2002). Second, the human rights agendas of social movements and their mobilization do not simply refer to a set of abstract ideas but to a project aimed at tackling real human suffering. The struggle for the respect of human rights in any given conflict is therefore not a struggle for some metaphysical qualification of people but for people themselves, for the conditions that guarantee their human dignity. It is not simply about respect for the ideals of human dignity, equality, and duty per se, but the establishment of conditions that lead to a situation in which those ideals are in fact fulfilled.[13]

In the second place, if a Latin American conceptualization of human rights argues for the permanent expansion of the discourse, is there not a risk of an overproduction of rights? This question has been raised by human rights supporters and detractors alike. Such question has even inspired scholars to establish a core of rights, which they call basic rights (Shue 1980), human rights proper (Rawls 1999), and universal human rights (Talbott 2005). Answers to the question are polarized. While some believe that converting needs into rights leads to a loss of effectiveness, others claim that rights languages empower people who suffer domination, poverty, and violence.[14] I argue that overproduction should not happen if the ideas of intertextuality

(Baxi 2003) together with the historical logic of legitimating new rights (Dussel and Senent de Frutos 2001) are accepted.

First, most rights, including those recognized very recently such as the right to development and the collective rights of indigenous peoples are simply variations of the human rights recognized and declared in the International Bill of Rights. For instance, the right to development is a variation of the right to determination with specific emphasis on economics, while indigenous peoples' rights are a variation of cultural rights. This means that new rights are the product of intertextuality, in the sense discussed previously: new rights refer to existing rights in new contexts. However, already existing rights may appear to be new because they refer to new legal subjects, people whose specific needs and features are not yet included in a legal system.

This takes us to the second point of the discussion, that of the process of legitimating new rights. Dussel claims that new rights emerge as new subjects reclaim them (Dussel and Senent de Frutos 2001). Reflecting specifically on human rights within the state, Dussel argues that in a given political system the "prevailing law system" plays the specific role of constructing a formal reference or the institutionalization of the duties and rights that all members of the political community must obey. There is a problem, though, if certain citizens are excluded, although not intentionally, from the entitlement of new rights that the system does not yet include:

> Citizens who see themselves as the subjects of new rights consider themselves victims, inevitably suffering the negative effects of the body of the law or political actions which at best are non-intentional...The victims of a "prevailing law system" are those "without rights" (or those that don't yet have institutionalized, recognized or applicable rights). It is therefore a matter of the dialectic of the political community with the "rule of law," conducted on behalf of the many emerging groups without rights which are the victims of existing economic, cultural, military, etc. systems (Dussel and Senent de Frutos 2001:151).

For this reason, Dussel claims that a list of human rights cannot be set a priori, in the way naturalists attempt to establish them. For Dussel, it is obvious that a historical relationship exists between the legal system and individuals and that it is impossible to think of such a system without citizens who demand rights within new contexts, "Material negativity (misery, pain, humiliation, violence suffered, etc.) indicates that a situation in which people are 'without rights' represents a black 'hole' within the 'legal system'" (Dussel and Senent de Frutos 2001:153). In a strict sense:

> ..."rule of law" is an historic condition and represents the...evolutionary path of history, which is manifested as the growing tradition in the legal world of a political community that uses the macro-institutionality of the State. Those "without-rights-yet," when struggling for the recognition of a new law, represent the creative-historical, innovative moment of the body of human law. In this way we avoid falling into the trap of the dogmatism of natural law (a metaphysical foundationalist solution that is no longer acceptable) and neither do we fall victim to relativism (all laws are valid for having been imposed by force at a given time) or mere contingencialism (there are no universal principles) but rather use the conciliation of a non-functionalist universality that demonstrates that "new" rights are universally demanded (whether by a culture or by humanity according to the corresponding degree of historical consciousness) of the political community in the state of their historical evolution and growth (Dussel and Senent de Frutos 2001:152).

Dussel's reflection on "those with no rights," the victims of the "prevailing legal system" within a political system, can be applied to the discussion of the appearance of new rights within the international system. While there are limits to the expansion of international human rights discourse, these cannot be imposed from above. Limits are effectively established by the intertextuality of the existing International Bill of Human Rights and the emergence of new subjects of rights in the sense proposed by Dussel.

Having clarified these two important questions, it is fair to say now that human rights as an insurrectionary practice could inform a Latin American perspective of human rights that facilitates collective action, especially in terms of constructing the contingent unity of social agents.

Human Rights Discourse and the Contingent Unity of Social Subjects

In order to establish how human rights as an insurrectionary practice emerged and has served to unify social struggles against free trade in Mexico, I shall use a framework that builds on three different post-structuralist methodologies for discourse analysis: genealogy, hegemonic articulation, and interpretative repertoires. First, genealogy as described above is the basis for the research strategy deployed here, since a genealogical examination will help to establish simultaneously the emergence of human rights as an insurrectionary practice and how human rights as an insurrectionary practice in turn came to unify different subjects in the struggle against free trade.

Second, in order to examine how human rights unify different social agents in contemporary struggles against free trade in Mexico, I shall employ insights from E. Laclau's notion of *hegemonic articulation* and adapt them for a sociolinguistic discourse analysis.[15] Hegemonic articulation will help to establish how human rights bring different social agents together in a unified but still plural struggle against free trade. Laclau and Mouffe argue that the structural transformations ushered in by late capitalism have led to new forms of social protest and solidarity in both postindustrial and poor countries.[16] They claim that the plural and fragmented nature of contemporary societies leads to a complex and growing proliferation of subjectivities and a strong affirmation of particularity. This is because, in their view, subjects can identify with as many discourses as they want and then occupy different *subject positions* defined by those discourses. They are not defined by some essential relationship between the mode of production and a social class as in traditional Marxism (Torfing 1999:148–152). In their opinion, social fragmentation is not necessarily an obstacle for achieving emancipation since plurality is a requisite for the establishment of democratic politics (Laclau 1996:15–16). However, some notion of unity is still necessary for emancipatory politics.

In order to assess how the plurality of social subjects can join for emancipation, Laclau and Mouffe developed the idea of hegemonic articulation. Articulation means the temporary, nonessential unity of social agents through the construction of nodal points of meaning that partially define how sociopolitical agents frame their struggle (Laclau and Mouffe 2001). Laclau calls these privileged points of meaning *empty signifiers*, with an empty signifier referring to the "name" of that contingent articulation (Laclau 2005). Using insights from antidescriptivism, Laclau claims that a name creates a new object. Consequently, an empty signifier does not refer to an object that has descriptive features associated with that word, but to the particular system informed by the different social agents articulated by the use of that name (Laclau 2006). In this study, human rights will be the empty signifier fixing meaning in the hegemonic articulation against free trade, that is, human rights will be the discourse assigning meaning and thus bringing together different social agents in a single but still plural struggle against free trade.[17] While examining the genealogy of human rights as an insurrectionary practice in Mexico, I shall also study how human rights originally emerged as an empty signifier.

Third, in order to examine how social agents employ human rights discourse in order to construct a sense of sameness in a human rights articulation against free trade, I shall analyze discursive practices using Wetherell and Potter's notion of interpretative repertoires together with Laclau's categories of hegemonic articulation, empty signifier, and subject positions as described above. Wetherell and Potter are interested in the context of discourses rather than their abstract meanings. This is why they rely on Foucault's view of discourses, that is, the historically determined bodies of knowledge, whereby people become subjects and are regulated through the kinds of identities assumed in discourse (Wetherell and Potter 1992:79). They acknowledge, though, that such a view of discourse dismisses its function as social practice as it overlooks the implications of referring to bodies of knowledge in specific social contexts.

Accordingly, they have developed the idea of repertoires that refers to discourses in the poststructuralist tradition but focuses on how these are used to sustain different social practices and to construct a realistic effect in everyday speech (Wetherell and Potter 1992:95). Wetherell and Potter define interpretative repertoires as "discernible clusters of terms, descriptions and figures of speech often assembled around metaphors or vivid images. In more structuralist language we can talk of these things as systems of signification and as the building blocks used for manufacturing versions and performing particular actions... Interpretative repertoires are pre-eminently a way of understanding the content of discourse and how that content is organized" (Wetherell and Potter 1992:90–91).

Furthermore, interpretative repertoires are "a methodology that simultaneously emphasizes the constitution of subjects and the ideological work of discourse. It focuses on the specific construction of realism produced by discourses, their placement in a sequence of discourse, and their rhetorical organization. It refers to the ways talk and texts are organized that make any particular reality appear solid—effects derived from categorization and particularization, the use of combinations of vivid and systematically vague formulations, the mobilization of various narrative techniques, constructions involving consensus and corroboration, and various basic rhetorical forms such as lists and contrasts" (Wetherell and Potter 1992:95).

I shall therefore examine which interpretative repertoires social agents mobilize when articulating with human rights as an empty signifier in order to achieve temporary unity. In addition, there will be a consideration of the repertoires social agents use to construct their views of free trade, subject positions, and common agendas when articulation uses human rights as an empty signifier.

To sum up briefly, while carrying out a genealogical analysis of the emergence of human rights as an insurrectionary practice and eventually as an empty signifier articulating struggles against free trade in Mexico, I shall also analyze how agents construct a sense of sameness in their discursive practices through the use of human rights discourse. This analysis requires a focus on how subjects construct subject positions, hegemonic projects, and common agendas and a consideration of interpretative repertoires, representing a more language-centered poststructuralist discourse approach.

Structure of the Book

This book is conceived as a simultaneous examination of the structural/subjective and discursive issues allowing Mexican social movements to use human rights discourse for the construction of joint agendas and organization of collective action against free trade. It considers both the construction of human rights discourse and its use for framing demands in the social field. The simultaneous application of a genealogical examination and a more language-centered discourse analysis suggests that this book addresses two complementary issues: the emergence and development of human rights discourse and how human rights discourses are employed in current struggles against free trade. These issues are dealt with in the book's two parts.[18]

Part one addresses the emergence and development of human rights as an insurrectionary practice in anti-free trade struggles. Consistent with the idea of a Latin American conceptualization of human rights, the next two chapters offer a genealogy of human rights discourse in Mexico. They therefore address different issues useful for establishing a specific understanding of human rights discourse, the scope of this discourse and how human rights came to function as an empty signifier articulating agents opposing free trade. Accordingly, chapter one addresses the context of the emergence of human rights as an insurrectionary practice. It discusses the structural issues that allowed for democratic discourses, including human rights, to be used by social movements.

Chapter two identifies the period when human rights emerged as an insurrectionary practice, a period dating back to the 1980s when the Mexican social left incorporated democratic discourses into mobilization strategies. At this time democratic thinking met traditional Latin American structuralist discourses, especially liberation theology, to form a holistic human rights discourse. However, this holistic discourse increasingly ignored structural concerns, as human rights became an object of the predominantly political understanding of transition to democracy. Chapter three argues that in the 1990s human rights became a discourse in its own right but was heavily influenced by transition to democracy, which was effectively reduced to electoral issues. Free trade could not be established as a subject of human rights discourse because this subordination systematically prevented the development of nonlegalistic and more political-economic approaches. It wasn't until democracy exhausted itself as a discourse in the human rights and anti-free trade movements that free trade could become a focus of human rights discourse.

Part two of the book discusses how human rights are employed as an insurrectionary practice in anti-free trade struggles, that is, how they are used by social agents to construct human rights understandings that bring them together to form a common agenda against free trade. This part examines in detail the empirical differences between social subjects and how they construct worldviews, subject positions, and agendas. Consequently, based on the idea that by the beginning of the twenty-first century, human rights have expanded their scope to include socioeconomic issues, chapters four and five address both the subjective and structural implications of conceiving human rights as an empty signifier. Chapter four establishes the implications of using human rights as an empty signifier by examining three interrelated issues. First, it presents the specific free trade issues clashing with human rights principles and the ways the texts of human rights discourse are used in response to them. These responses make human rights a relevant tool of opposition to those terms of free trade having a negative impact on people and the environment. It goes on to examine how social subjects, building on the available texts, construct their own understandings of free trade when fixing meaning with human rights discourse. Building on the idea that human rights identities are different for different agents, chapter five goes on to discuss how subject positions influence the construction of agendas, especially in terms of the specific human rights subjects chosen for such purposes.

Chapter six goes on to examine how human rights have served as an empty signifier in two specific articulations: the Hemispheric Social Alliance (HSA), an intersector and region-wide articulation opposing the forthcoming Free Trade Area of the Americas (FTAA), and an articulation against the Agreement on Economic Partnership, Political Co-ordination and Co-operation between the Mexican Government and the European Union (Global Agreement), which shall be referred to in the present study as the Democratic Clause Project (DCP).

Finally, the Conclusion establishes the pros and cons of understanding human rights as an insurrectionary practice and the implications of examining human rights hegemonic articulation by looking at discursive practices.

Part I

Introduction

Human rights discourse is not a given, it develops differently in local, national, and regional contexts. While historians of "universal human rights" insist on tracing the birth of human rights to seventeenth-century England and following their development through the French, American, and Industrial revolutions, the different understandings and uses of human rights discourses in Europe and Latin America suggest different lines of development. On the one hand, the emergence of natural rights in Europe in the seventeenth century and their development through natural law and bourgeois interests have led to them being conceived in relation to questions of liberty and as being market-oriented. This could explain why European and American anti-free trade activists see human rights discourse principally reflecting Western interests. On the other hand, rights discourses in Latin America emerged with Constitutionalism after the period of Independence (nineteenth century) and human rights as such did not appear until the second half of the twentieth century. Furthermore, unlike constitutional rights, which were formulated by the liberal elites, UN-declared human rights became a political discourse advancing the democratic and social agendas of social movements.

I contend that these different paths of development are not the product of chance as they have been defined by the constitutive relationship between subject and structure in specific historical contexts. Part one of this book traces the structural and subjective issues providing the conditions for the development of human rights discourse in Mexico and their suitability for social rather than democratic struggles such as the anti-free trade movement. Such a genealogical analysis follows A. Woodiwiss' employment of the genealogical method for problematizing the emergence of international human rights discourse.

Woodiwiss has examined the emergence and development of UN human rights discourse and in the process has problematized the institutional negligence of ESCRs by studying four interrelated elements.

The first of these elements is the objects discourses refer to. The emergence and development of objects can be analyzed when looking at the official sites where they are problematized, the experts and professionals who decide what becomes an object, and the actual things discourses refer to. Second, concepts that are the intellectual constructs used to speak about objects. This includes the order in which concepts were developed, the methodologies used to determine their legitimacy as instances of knowledge, and how these translate in the specific case of the objects under discussion. Third, the ways in which statements about objects are made. This includes an examination of precisely who the qualified speakers are, the sites where statements can be made, and the specific ways objects are spoken about. Finally, strategies that refer to the ways constructs are combined and thematized. They include how action is directed according to the definition of modes of enunciation and the conceptual framework developed to address the objects (Woodiwiss 2002:152–153, 2003).

Part one of the book will therefore problematize the structural and subjective issues allowing for the development of human rights discourse in Mexico from the 1980s to the early 2000s.

Chapter 1

The Neoliberal Paradox: Conservative Economic Change and the Rise of Democratic Politics

Constitutional or so-called fundamental rights appeared in Mexico in the nineteenth century as a consequence of the introduction of liberal thought. In contrast, human rights as declared in international law developed in Mexico in the context of a serious economic crisis that affected the whole of Latin America in the 1980s. During this crisis international financial institutions interfered in national politics and imposed a conservative economic discourse that had an overwhelmingly negative impact on people's welfare and contributed to the establishment of new methods of collective action. The discourse introduced by these institutions was neoliberalism.

This chapter examines how the discursive arrangements for the political economy prevailing in the country since the late 1940s collapsed, leading to the recomposition of the social field that in turn allowed for the adoption of democratic discourses, including the discourse of human rights. Accordingly, this chapter will first discuss how neoliberal discourse emerged and how these new arrangements later dislocated existing corporatist politics and allowed for the multiplication of social agents and the introduction of pluralistic social politics.

THE RISE OF NEOLIBERAL DISCOURSE

Neoliberal discourse, also known as "new conservatism" in Western democracies, replaced the discourse of the Welfare State in rich countries and developmentalism in poorer countries, such as those of Latin America. Developmentalism emerged in Latin America as a critique of modernization theory and employed a series of assumptions concerning Latin America's place in the world economy that demanded the state control the economic as well as the political and social spheres in order to achieve development. Developmentalism, which generated different types of repressive regimes in the region, swept through most Latin American countries from the late 1940s to the late 1960s. It had "a certain Keynesian flavor as it entailed a major increase in government expenditure for development purposes but it went even further as it regarded the state as the crucial agent for economic, social and political change" (Kay 1989). It was discursively conceived by the Structuralist School of Development, which originated at the Economic Commission for Latin America and the Caribbean (ECLAC) and had a major influence in the region through its writings, speeches, press reports, technical advice, and training for top civil servants (Kay 1989). Up to the 1970s, the Mexican economy relied on the developmentalism industrialization policy of import substitution.

Import-substitution policy was based on the idea that from the time they were colonized by Spain, France, and Portugal, Latin American countries had been performing the role of producers of primary products for the international economy. In this view, policy was needed to help peripheral countries switch from what they called outward-looking development to an inward-directed policy. Through the employment of an import-substitution industrialization policy, the state focused on helping local industry to develop, providing it with subsidies and imposing import quotas on foreign firms. In this way products that would otherwise have been bought from industrialized countries, such as supplies for road construction, water, and electricity, could be manufactured locally. In addition, the state maintained low wages in urban centers by offering subsidies for basic foods, imposing price controls, and nationalizing economically strategic industries such as oil. Finally, there was state support for an overvalued exchange rate that kept inflation low, made exports very expensive and imports cheap, thereby facilitating the import of machinery (Green 1995:16–17).[1]

By this time, international trade was regulated according to the General Agreement on Trade and Tariffs (GATT). This was the basis for the postwar trade regime and provided the framework for seven rounds of global tariff reduction that successively reduced tariffs around the world—while there were 80 countries participating in the Kennedy Round (1960–1983), by the Uruguay Round (1986–1993) most countries were participating (Held et al. 1999:164). It was not until the 1980s that developing countries were strongly "encouraged" by the IMF and the WB to liberalize their economies, including trade (Held et al. 1999:167, Tussie and Woods 2000:56–57). However, in this period:

> ...trade was shaped by a particular combination of liberalization and protection. Trade patterns were reinforced by capital flows and the freer mobility of capital relative to other factors of production. Yet, while capital intensive goods experienced greater dynamism and enjoyed the benefit of deeper tariff reductions, labor intensive goods remained relatively protected, with below average tariff reductions as well as a greater incidence of non-tariff regulations (Tussie and Woods 2000:58).

By the end of the 1970s, these arrangements entered into crisis following the collapse of Keynesian economics in the North. Keynesian discourse was unable to provide an answer for the specific problem presented to industrialized societies, namely, simultaneous inflation and stagnation (Johnson and Johnson 1978). For its part, Mexico experienced a debt crisis that was provoked by two interrelated events. One, it was unable to cope with rises in oil prices, the costs of arms supplies, and the accumulation of wealth by elites. Two, the recession in Western countries led to a rise in interest rates. Mainstream economists concluded that internal public policy was the cause of the debt crisis and development failure (Green 1995, Kaplan 2002).

In both the North and the South a new discourse was used to prescribe a cure for the problem: neoliberalism/new conservatism, which was based on an eclectic reinterpretation of neoclassical economics through the monetarist quantity theory of money—a focus on how money enters the economy (injection effects) and how this has an impact on relative prices and investment in particular sectors. Neoclassical liberal economic discourse was based on liberty and individual rights with respect to property, professional activity, and access to goods. This discourse relied heavily on the ideas of Adam Smith, who argued that individuals naturally tended toward a desire for liberty, work, and trade. If individuals are free to pursue their desires, the natural tendency will be toward the establishment of markets, a mechanism that conciliates interests and leads to the common good—the laissez-faire doctrine. Neoclassicals believe that the state's role is limited to defending the country in wartime, guaranteeing security and performing economic activities that the private sector refuses to perform (public goods) (Clarke 1988, Gilpin 2001, Palan 2000, Villarreal 1993:111).

Milton Friedman, one of the most important proponents of economic neoliberalism, reinterpreted these principles in his book *Free to Choose*, borrowing Hayek's libertarian ideas. Friedrich von Hayek considers liberty and freedom to be the same thing, "the condition of men in which coercion of some by others is reduced as much as possible in society...The task of a policy of freedom must therefore be to minimize coercion or its harmful effects, even if it cannot eliminate it completely" (Hayek 1960:11–12). He does differentiate *liberty* from *liberties* stating that the first is a general condition while the second is a set of exceptions in a regime where all is prohibited apart from that, which is explicitly permitted (Hayek 1960:19). Building on Kant, Austrian liberalism,[2] and the Anglo-Saxon liberal tradition, Hayek rejected state intervention but was in favor of the establishment of general rules for the protection of the individual and property in order to guarantee effective competition. This has served as the basis for much liberal criticism of Hayek, who was willing to accept a level of coercion of individual liberty through the application of law, which he saw as a spontaneous system originating in individual action. In his work on liberty, he relies heavily on English constitutionalism and praises very highly the idea of the rule of law.

Friedman borrows from Hayek's idea of freedom to construct state intervention in economics and welfare as a totalitarian measure assaulting freedom, and to construct state regulation for the protection of capital and property as necessary state intervention that, paradoxically, guarantees a free society. This combination is what makes Freidman's economics "eclectic." The differences between classic economics and Austrian liberalism are epistemological. Austrian liberalism asserts that the private experience of the individual is the only foundation for knowledge of the world and that actions of individuals should be understood only by reference to their knowledge, beliefs, perceptions, and expectations. Hayek stated that the only means to obtain data in the social sciences is through the attitudes, values, and opinions of individuals (Gray 1998, Shand 1990). However, he disagreed with Mises' subjectivism in that economic theories are well-established truths that need no empirical evidence to be tested—he believed that only some parts of economic theory were a priori and most of it was testable (Gray 1998). Gray points out that in fact Hayek's subjectivism made him skeptical of monetary theory and the policy of Friedman just as he was skeptical of those of Keynes. Both propose an aggregate approach that is opposed to Austrian liberalism. While Keynesians suggest restoring economic activity through an increase in aggregate power, neoliberals suggest that a successful stabilization of the general price level would coordinate economic authority (Gray 1998).[3]

Furthermore, in order to define the role of government in a society where members want "the greatest possible freedom to choose as individuals," Friedman used Hayek's ideas to reinterpret, in a very contradictory fashion, Adam Smith's notion of state duties. Smith's duties include, protecting society from the violence and invasion of other independent societies; the duty of protecting individuals from other individuals (administration of justice); and public works. Classical economics seeks the maximization of individual interest, equality, and freedom, and focuses on the market, which is seen as a self-organizing mechanism in that it conciliates interests and leads to the common good. However, it does leave room for state intervention in cases of "market imperfection," although it does not provide the theoretical means for assessment (Shand 1990).

In Hayek's reinterpretation these duties came to mean the duty to protect individuals from the coercion of other individuals, without excessive use of those coercive powers—the military and police forces; the duty to facilitate voluntary exchanges by adopting general economic and social rules, particularly for securing private property rights. Defined in these terms, the revamped version of Smith's state duties eliminates the notion of security. However, it does not abolish state intervention. Rather, it replaces direct economic and welfare intervention with regulation, so that policing and security for capital become the main goals in an allegedly noninterventionist state. As for state intervention in welfare, Friedman rejects it—and in fact demonizes it—on the grounds of the alleged harmful effects that equality has on freedom, and claims that people benefit more from the privileging of freedom over equality.

To sum up these ideas briefly, whilst trying to eliminate the political from the economic, Friedman in fact made neoliberalism a political discourse because he justified a form of state intervention that favored a select few to the detriment of the majority who were left with no social security. Consequently, this discursive shift has not meant less intervention but a different kind of intervention disguised as noninterventionist policy. Keynesian policies were replaced by policies intended to liberalize economies and impose the neoliberal reinterpretation of state duties in classical economics for the discursive construction of a system that is supposed to maximize freedom through preventing state coercion but that in fact is a new form of state intervention that replaces an old one in response to global processes. Chang sees the contradictions in Friedman's eclectic combination of intellectual traditions precisely in his virulent attack on state economic and social intervention while making regulation for the operation of free markets and the protection of capitals and property appear a noninterventionist measure (Chang 2002).

While in rich countries neoliberalism thus conceived by the monetarists was introduced via Margaret Thatcher in the United Kingdom and Ronald Reagan in the United States, in developing countries neoliberal discourse was imposed through the WB and the IMF. These institutions made further loans conditional on the progressive transformation of national economies that needed to abandon their focus on import-substitution and replace it with an export-led focus. This transformation was carried out in three stages: stabilization, structural adjustment, and trade liberalization (Green 1995). First, stabilization was aimed at "stabilizing" macroeconomic indicators, such as inflation, through the reduction of public expenditure, the raising of interest rates, and the control of wages (Green 1995). Second, structural adjustment programs included a list of radical measures: the cleaning up and stabilizing of public finances; inflation control; rigid monetary, credit, and fiscal policies; renegotiation of foreign debt; tax reform (reducing income tax, eliminating capital tax, privileging of the wealthy, and reinforcing value-added tax); a slimming of the state by firing staff, selling off industries, abandoning social welfare, as well as the abandonment of its promotion and orienting role; and privatization (Kaplan 2002:684).[4] Finally, financial institutions ordered the privileging of exports and encouraged the private sector to export, eliminating import-substitution policies that allowed for the cohesion of corporatist organizations.

This progressive enforcement of neoliberal policy had consequences for social arrangements that in turn had both a negative and positive impact. One aspect of this positive impact was democratization of the social field.

Neoliberalism and the Weakening of Corporatism

The early implementation of neoliberal discourse had very serious effects on the lives of the working and middle classes in Mexico and consequently on the corporatist arrangements supporting the authoritarian regime. Broadly defined, corporatism is a system of interest representation whereby organizations are appointed or created by the state that allows them to monopolize representation in exchange for allowing the state to control the election of leaders and the articulation of political demands (Malloy 1977, Stevens 1977).

In Mexico the institutional realm of corporatism was created in 1939 during the presidency of Lázaro Cárdenas. For many Mexicans who recall Cárdenas as the savior of the state oil industry—which was nationalized in 1938—he was a nationalist concerned with the interests of workers and peasants. Whatever his intentions were, though, "he ironically created a structure that for the most part has benefited the interests of the middle classes and the wealthy," and extended rather than restructured the state because these politics relied on leadership, centralization, money, and reward (Camp 1996:153). Within the ruling party he set up three nationwide corporatist confederations: the Farmers' National Confederation (CNC, the Spanish acronym for Confederación Nacional Campesina), which grouped farmer organizations; the Workers' Confederation of Mexico (CTM, the Spanish acronym for the Confederación de Trabajadores de México), which gathered together trade unions; and the National Confederation of Popular Organizations (CNOP, the Spanish acronym for the Confedcración Nacional de Organizaciones Populares), which grouped all the remaining social organizations representing neither farmers nor workers (i.e., street vendors). President Cárdenas set up a fourth sector: the military. However, his successor as president, General Manuel Avila Camacho, removed it because he did not want the Army to have a public political voice or the same status as the other sectors. However, the military still had an important share of resources through informal channels. In addition, because the civilian elite set up military schools, they were always subordinated to the party and therefore to the president (Camp 1996).

Individuals belonging to corporatist organizations were forced to support the Institutional Revolutionary Party (PRI, the Spanish acronym for Partido Revolucionario Institucional)—in most elections the PRI had only a few more votes than those attributed to members of the three sectors.[5] The long-term consequences of the operation of the PRI's "electoral machinery" included skepticism regarding the formal outcome of elections and the discourse of liberal democracy in general. As a result, no serious opposition party was able to establish itself, save the National Action Party (PAN, the Spanish acronym for Partido Acción Nacional), which always stood for clean elections and liberal values.

PRI-style corporatism encouraged *clientelism*, which is a set of informal ties through which goods and services are granted not as rights generated by citizenship, but in exchange for political favors and loyalty. Even though the state-organized corporatist structure made independent social mobilization very difficult, such mobilization was not impossible. Nevertheless, independent expressions usually had to face cooptation or, if they failed to accept political favors in exchange for loyalty, repression. Many movements ended up having to accept rewards. J. Fox describes very well how the Mexican corporatist structure works:

> Integral to the Mexican state's "success" is its skilful use of the carrot-and-stick technique. Typical government responses to popular movements for social reform and democracy have combined partial concessions with repression, conditioning access to material gains on political subordination. Nor does the state always wait to be pressured; its remarkable capacity for pre-emptive measures continues to surprise seasoned observers. One cannot understand Mexico's long-standing relative political stability without looking at both sides of the coin. The state does sometimes give-in—to some people, some of the time—although usually with strings attached. Some of Mexico's rulers specialize in such bargaining, operating, however, in the shadow of their colleagues' capacity for fierce repression if the negotiations break down. This camouflage is a key component of what Mario Vargas Llosa called "the perfect dictatorship" (Fox 1995:188).[6]

Until the mid-1980s, when the neoliberal project was launched, corporatist politics had important implications for the national political economy because they helped to secure the Mexican developmentalist state and thus sociopolitical stability. Developmentalism merged well with corporatism, which was justified by the argument that the state had to establish corporatist relationships because it had failed to simultaneously integrate societal actors and to sponsor development. The state faced the problem of "integrating a multiplicity of societal interests into a decision making structure that guarantees a minimum of political stability and allows decision makers to launch development oriented policies" (Malloy 1977:6).

This corporatist machinery entered into crisis with the implementation of neoliberal policies in the 1980s for, while wages plummeted, subsidies of food and other basic goods were cut and investment in social services was dramatically reduced, the corporatist trade unions as well as farmer and popular organizations gathered in the CTM, the CNC and the CNOP failed to defend the interests of their constituencies. Rather than defend these interests, leaders used their monopoly of representation to support neoliberal policies and to control social protest (Tamayo 1990).

Corporatist politics weakened further as President Miguel de la Madrid (1982–1988) was no longer channeling money and state patronage to trade union and farmer leaders due to the shortage of government resources for those areas under neoliberal policies. This weakened the link between the state and workers and farmers, and slowly started the process of dismantling—or reforming—the corporatist relationship between unions and farmers organizations and the state.[7] Accordingly, spaces for negotiation were lost and workers and farmers no longer held the monopoly of representation granted by the state in 1938. Tuda Rivas argues, however, that the dissolution of the axis of corporatism granted autonomy to formerly subordinated corporatist structures, such as *caciques*, who seized the power handed over by the state, thus intensifying corporatism at sub-national levels and within specific groups (Tuda Rivas 2005). Nevertheless, things were not the same, as the Fray Francisco de Vitoria Human Rights Center puts it:

> In fact, the adjustments could not have been exclusively economic. Mexico also had to reconfigure itself in terms of social and political relations and one of the most serious modifications was that related to the disarticulation or reduction of state corporatist policy to its minimum possible expression and the subsequent dismemberment and reduced profile of unions and sectors. The logic behind this movement, through which the governing group separated the social base from its legitimacy, is related to the need to privatize all aspects of national life where possible and increasingly concentrate all decisive political spaces in an ever smaller group of leaders sympathetic to the interests of consortiums where economic power is concentrated (Centro de Derechos Humanos "Fray Francisco de Vitoria" 1997:41).

The catalyst for the transformation of the social left was the 8.1 Richter-scale-earthquake that destroyed thousands of homes and buildings in Mexico City on September 19, 1985, a date that also marked the third year of the De la Madrid administration. As half of the city lay in ruins and the government response was inadequate, people started to organize themselves to help the victims, remove bodies trapped beneath debris, and obtain aid for the thousands of homeless. The earthquake therefore served as a catalyst for the independent organization of identities previously repressed by corporatist politics, especially women and *colonos* (community leaders demanding urban services).

In addition, a few days after the quake itself, female workers from textile sweatshops, people who became homeless, and physicians from a collapsed hospital were the first groups to mobilize in order to complain about the lack of supervision of materials used in the construction of the collapsed buildings. They also denounced corruption, labor conditions, the lack of control over security measures, and the lack of building maintenance. Shortly after, these spontaneous mobilizations were transformed into grassroots organizations and popular movements (Alvarez Enríquez 2002).

Commenting on these mobilizations, Carlos Monsiváis (Monsiváis 2000) wrote:

> At the center are the lessons of the quakes of 1985. Thanks to this great communal experience an unknown (and unexpected) force revealed the enormous rewards that collective effort can bring. The omnipresence of the state quickly and peacefully deactivated most of the initiatives taken, trusting only the magnitude of resources available and the inevitable disarticulation of the efforts of the masses. But not even the power of a state that conveniently erases such communal accomplishments could eliminate the cultural, political, and psychological consequences of those four or five days during which brigades and rescue teams, among the rubble and the desolation, felt responsible for their own actions and in charge of the new city that was clearly emerging in front of their very eyes. Although in the strictest sense, during the period of the earthquake the only movements emerging were those formed by the homeless, for hundreds of thousands of others it strengthened the will to act, to consider the minor and major consequences of individual action within collective action. The experience of the earthquake gave the term "civil society" an unexpected credibility.[8]

In the long run this spontaneous solidarity became organized outside the sphere of state-controlled unions and farmer and social groups; it marked the reactivation of social movements with their demands for housing, land, and urban services addressed to the state.[9] These movements directed material demands to the state for improving living conditions (housing, health services, education, land) but not in a clientelist way as they sought to politically influence state policymaking rather than exchange loyalty for material needs (Alvarez Enríquez 2002, Centro de Derechos Humanos "Miguel Agustín Pro Juárez" 1992b).

In the long term these movements failed to change the direction of economic policy but certainly shook the bases of corporatist politics because they challenged existing forms of relating to the state.

The extent of this change is, however, the subject of debate. On the one hand there were some optimistic scholars, like Monsiváis and Foweraker, who believe that popular movements changed social movement politics. Foweraker claims that: "They challenged clientelism because their strategic initiatives, and especially their search for political alliances built around horizontal networks of leadership and solidarity, have made the use of clientelism very ineffective" (Foweraker 1990:17). On the other hand there were the pessimists, like Hellman, who believe that these movements are as prone to clientelism as all movements. She argues that:

> ...these movements (are)...deeply enmeshed in clientelistic patterns from which they escape only very rarely. Although the emergence of a new movement may challenge the old PRI-linked networks based on local caciques, it undermines the control of the caciques *only* by replacing the old networks with alternative channels that, generally speaking, are also clientelistic in their mode of operation (Hellman 1994:128).

The importance of this, however, is that the 1985 earthquake in Mexico City served as a catalyst for increasing discontent with neoliberal policies and as an opportunity for independent actors to organize themselves outside corporatist limits. The sense of solidarity created as a result of the earthquake became a new space for independent politics. In short, the new independent organizations challenged state control over social movements and thus contributed to the multiplication of social identities and the construction of new discourses for collective action.

Economic Change and the Reorganization of Mexican Society: The Rise of Democratic Politics

The rise of neoliberal discourses and the subsequent dislocation of corporatist politics served to create scenarios that in turn served as the political ground for the adoption of, first, the discourse of transition to democracy and, second, human rights. The first scenario was the multiplication of social actors and the second the increased channeling of social conflict into electoral politics.

The Multiplication of Social Actors

If the 1985 earthquake served as a catalyst for organization outside the crisis-hit corporatist structure, the 1988 presidential election represented the moment when this new independent form of organization matured. This can be seen in the way it facilitated the multiplication of new sociopolitical actors with the creation of a broad movement around the figure of Cuauhtémoc Cárdenas and how, in the process, structural adjustment programs came to be implemented. As economists within the neoliberal elite came to occupy top positions in the federal government from 1982 onward, the ruling PRI had split into two groups.

The first group was formed by those relying on neoliberal discourse and attempting to liberalize economics without liberalizing politics. In the process, these neoliberals were effectively removing the discursive pillars of the PRI, that is, the social achievements of the 1910 Mexican Revolution (social rights recognized in the Federal Constitution). The second group was formed by those with diametrically opposite goals: the prioritizing of national economic interests and a democratization of the internal election process for the PRI's presidential candidate.[10] As Tamayo points out, neoliberal discourse required the dismantling of the Mexican state, which had its origins in the 1910 Revolution, and its replacement by a "modern" state (Tamayo 1990:124).

As the 1988 electoral process approached, a group of prominent PRI members left the party. This group was led by Cuauhtémoc Cárdenas, the son of Lázaro Cárdenas, the Mexican president who established corporatism and promoted socialist policies in the 1930s as well as nationalizing the oil industry. Cuauhtémoc Cárdenas built his own campaign on the governing elite's loss of legitimacy resulting from their renunciation of nationalism. He received the support of not only popular movements but also of workers and farmers from the CTM and CNC who were discontented with their leaders' unresponsiveness to the collapse of their living standards. These people rejected policies implemented by De la Madrid that undermined the traditional "social pact" based on patronage and cooperation/cooptation (Chand 2001, Tamayo 1990). Furthermore, apart from social movements, Cárdenas was also supported by highly trained social scientists who brought "democratic contents, symbols and demands into the picture" (Tuda Rivas 2005).

Although electoral law prevented the formation of new parties so close to the day of the elections, a small opposition party that had traditionally followed the PRI, the Authentic Party of the Mexican Revolution (PARM, the Spanish acronym for Partido Auténtico de la Revolución Mexicana), postulated Cárdenas as its candidate. The only candidate who refused support to Cárdenas was activist Rosario

Ibarra de Piedra, from the Workers' Revolutionary Party (PRT, the Spanish Acronym for Partido Revolucionario de los Trabajadores) who considered that would be betraying her socialist ideals if she supported him. The political left withdrew their own candidacies and supported Cárdenas who became the candidate of all opposition parties—except the right-wing PAN—united under the banner of the National Democratic Front (FDN, the Spanish acronym for Frente Democrático Nacional). He became a political phenomenon in part due to his family name: "Cuauhtémoc Cárdenas became the symbol, the redemptive myth, capable of reversing social decay, of resuming the abandoned path and promoting democratization, the defense of national sovereignty, and social equality" (Tamayo 1990:130).

Accordingly, voting was massive in 1988 but Cárdenas did not win, or if he did, his victory was not recognized by the PRI. There is widespread belief that Cárdenas won the election but that the PRI, which maintained complete control of the electoral system, manipulated the information and the data so their own candidate, Carlos Salinas de Gortari, emerged victorious. Because the state had absolute control over electoral institutions, and the final word in establishing the legality of electoral processes, it was impossible to determine whether Cárdenas had won or not. What mattered, in the end, was recognition by the PRI-government, the ultimate authority in deciding the validity of any electoral victory.

Independent from the results of the election, in the terms of this discourse analysis, the importance of the 1988 elections resides in the fact that it was the result of the conjunction of factors explained here: the emergence of urban social movements, the decay of corporatism due to neoliberal policies, and a split in the political elite. All of these factors facilitated the formation of a broad movement around Cardenas, which included independent organizations and corporatist organizations disillusioned with the PRI government. As can be seen, the movement was not formed around causes but around the symbolic figure of Cárdenas because individual movements were prepared to abandon their specific agendas and surrender their individuality to a "national project" (Tamayo 1990:131). Nevertheless, the movement received the support of social scientists handling democratic discourses. This last feature would have important consequences because social scientists were the people responsible for introducing democratic discourse into the manifesto drawn up by Cárdenas (Tuda Rivas 2005).

This movement, though, did not last long. The direct impact of the elections and Salinas' strategy of recovering support for his party irremediably damaged the movement. After the 1988 electoral fraud, popular movements and dissident organizations became increasingly weaker for two reasons. The first of these reasons was the active participation of popular organizations in the 1988 electoral process. As many activists were not entirely convinced of the benefits of elections as a means to overthrow authoritarian power, popular movements split after the election and weakened as a consequence. According to Alvarez, as important branches of urban movements decided to participate in the 1988 elections this meant:

> ...an unequivocal symptom of a process of change in collective action, in which many of them accepted the electoral route and designed a political strategy based on a relationship with institutions of the political system; the development of this process anticipated the tendency in popular movements to weaken as a recurrent modality for collective action, which would be defined in the nineties...(Alvarez Enríquez 2002:154–155).

Second, as mass mobilizations demanded the recognition of Cárdenas as president, the new government saw the need to reformulate its relationship with social movements by means of going back to clientelism, although in a different way than previously. Clientelism was achieved in two ways: by establishing a different form of corporatist relationship with dissident unions and farmer organizations (neocorporatism); and by offering organizations funding in exchange for support for "modernization." Economic liberalization demanded the state eliminate financial support for corporatist organizations and establish a form of unionism more in tune with business efficiency. Accordingly, PRI-style corporatism was replaced by a type of corporatism with a socioeconomic rather than a political objective. In this new relationship, unions were willing to accept labor flexibility in exchange for an increase in union bargaining power regarding the "external" conditions of workers. These included qualification requirements, the modernization of companies, productivity and product quality improvement, and new forms of labor organization (Bizberg 2003).[11]

As for farmers' organizations, Salinas employed a similar strategy. In 1989 he announced the setting up of the Permanent Agrarian Council (CAP, Spanish acronym for Consejo Agrario Permamente), which grouped most independent organizations and the corporatist CNC. Through this new body, organizations committed themselves to support the "modernization" of agriculture in exchange for loans and credits. In order to coopt independent farmer organizations, Salinas went as far as to incorporate the two most important leaders of the strong independent National Union of Farmer Organizations (UNORCA, Spanish acronym for Unión Nacional de Organizaciones Regionales Campesinas Autónomas) into his government. One of these leaders was appointed chairman of the enormous and corporatist CNC, and the other, deputy of the Agriculture Secretariat responsible for the lobbying of independent organizations. Through this move, Salinas managed to gain support for legal reforms necessary for the liberalization of agriculture—such as the elimination of collective land in constitutional Article 27 (Bizberg 2003).

The cooptation of popular movements through funding and support was achieved through *convenios de concertación* (consensus agreements) by which the government awarded them funding for various projects in exchange for political support of the government (Haber 1997, Hellman 1994:131). An example of this was the Committee for Popular Defense (CDP, acronym for Comité de Defensa Popular) in Durango, north-central Mexico, which was the first social organization to sign such a pact. The Comité managed to gain support from President Salinas for the funding of business projects, their opposition to the state governor, and registration as a political party. This party eventually became the Labor Party (PT, Spanish acronym for Partido del Trabajo) (Hellman 1994).[12] The funding of projects was largely carried out through the National Solidarity Program (Pronasol, Spanish acronym for Programa Nacional de Solidaridad), which also served as a response by the Salinas administration to the shift of grassroots movements toward the electoral arena. This tendency was first constructed after De la Madrid's electoral reforms since these reforms were used to induce movements to vote for the PRI once again (Hellman 1994).

Pronasol was designed to provide social welfare and infrastructure for people in extremely poor communities and relied on a discourse of community participation and co-responsibility between the state and citizens. As Hernández and Fox indicate, "Pronasol's political goal is to promote a direct link between the president and the local community, often bypassing local authorities and traditional political bosses. While Pronasol appears to decentralize, in practice it centralizes power within the presidency..." (Hernández and Fox 1995:206).[13]

Many observers regretted this and saw the demise of the once vibrant popular movements through a revamped farmer and worker neo-corporatism. This view was reinforced by the fact that in 1991 by-elections, the PRI managed to recover the congressional majority it lost in the 1988 elections, thanks to the impact of Pronasol, farmer cooptation, and union neo-corporatism. However, an alternative, albeit polemical, interpretation is also possible. The demise and progressive weakening of urban movements and the emergence of neo-corporatism and revamped clientelism could be seen as constituting the contradictory effects of neoliberal policies that kept Mexico in tune with the economic global trend through authoritarian means. This means that although old expressions weakened, new expressions emerged. NGOs started to multiply and changed their roles thus becoming a vibrant locus for political action. In the words of Álvarez Enríquez:

> In the collective vision offered by civil society towards the end of the 1980s we can see an evolution of autonomous social organization towards more diversified forms of collective action as well as the adoption of more institutionalized structures. The predominant form of social organization ceases to be that of assertive popular movements and space is shared with a civil associationism expressed in a wide variety of civil and citizen organizations inserted in extremely diverse camps of social and urban development and which express the diversity, and also to a great extent the complexity, of society in the capital (Alvarez Enríquez 2002:162).

Although NGOs were mostly a product of the 1970s, they mushroomed in the late 1980s and early 1990s for two reasons.[14] First, the spread and globalization of ideas of transition to democracy theory, which focused on elections as well as civic participation, encouraged people to organize around their group interests and at the same time opened up a space for the internationalization of Mexican social struggles (Concha Malo 1994b). This was facilitated by the development of global communications facilitating networking with foreign NGOs (Aguayo Quezada and Parra Rosales 1997, Chalmers and Piester 1996). Second, it was also due to the repression used to implement neoliberal policies and maintain corporatist support for the ruling party. Cárdenas "provided an alternative reference point to the kinds of popular movements that in the past might have thrown in their lot with the reformist wing of the PRI. To the extent that those movements remain outside of the co-optive grip of the official party, repression has been used more often than co-optation to impose social control" (Hellman 1994:127). This in turn led to a situation of systematic, and selective, repression that favored an increase in the number of human rights NGOs that were seen as the most effective means to organize against governmental abuse (Maldonado 2004). Eighty-nine of the 250 human rights NGOs operating in 1997 were established after 1988 (Aguayo Quezada and Parra Rosales 1997; Maldonado 2004).

On the other hand, as Salinas placed obstacles in the path of NGOs, these organizations united to defend themselves. In December 1989, in an attempt to broaden its tax base and to "impose some political controls on autonomous sectors" (Hernández and Fox 1995:200), the Ministry of Finance sent the Congress a new tax law initiative intended to treat "civil associations" as corporations. This initiative proposed, in its "Tax Miscellany," to change a paragraph in article 70 of the Income Tax Law to establish that civil associations were exempt from tax because of the nature of their work. The law reform would establish that NGOs had to pay 2 percent of their profits in tax (Aguayo Quezada and Parra Rosales 1997, Hernández and Fox). NGOs saw this as a threat to their philanthropic and development work and consequently drafted their own initiative for consideration by Congress. This initiative was ignored. Months later, officials from the Finance Ministry and NGOs signed an agreement that resolved the problem. Nevertheless, NGOs realized that they had to join forces in order to resist any future governmental repression. They called a national meeting in August 1990 that set up the Convergence of Civic Organizations for Democracy (Convergencia, which stands for Convergencia de Organismos Civiles por la Democracia), bringing together over 50 NGOs as well as grassroots organizations (Aguayo Quezada and Parra Rosales 1997, Hernández and Fox 1995).

After the establishment of Convergencia, NGOs articulated in order to advance specific issues while opening up democratic spaces. The most important of these were: the National Network of Civil Organizations "All Rights for All" (Red TDT, the Spanish acronym for Red Nacional de Organismos Civiles "Todos los Derechos para Todos"), which was set up in 1991 by over 50 human rights groups from all over the country in order to promote issues related to impunity and repression; the RMALC, which was founded in 1991 by independent trade unions and NGOs dealing with a variety of issues in order to demand the democratization of NAFTA negotiations; the Mutual Support Forum, which brought together grassroots organizations affiliated to the Catholic Church; the Citizen Movement for Democracy (MCD, the Spanish acronym for Movimiento Ciudadano por la Democracia) set up in 1992 for the defense of indigenous rights and promotion of transition to democracy; and Civic Alliance, which was set up in 1994 in order to promote electoral observation (Centro de Derechos Humanos "Miguel Agustín Pro Juárez" 1993a, 1993b, Chalmers and Piester 1996, Hernández Navarro 1994, Luján 2002).

As for the changing role of NGOs, this was effected after the 1988 electoral fraud. For years what they had basically done was provide assistance for grassroots organizations. From the 1970s to the late 1980s, NGOs "concentrated their efforts on popular education. Inspired by the pedagogy of Paulo Freire, they emphasized 'consciousness raising.' Any kind of service activity could serve as the entry point for this higher goal: literacy, basic education, health and hygiene, housing cooperatives, small-scale artisanry, or food distribution. In the discourse of the time, the prevailing goal called for the poor to discover their oppression and find a path to liberation. Within this context, NGOs offered a variety of services along the way, although their overall goal was educational" (Hernández and Fox 1995:192). Therefore by the late 1980s and early 1990s, NGOs were dealing with a wide array of issues related to different aspects of the movements they were aiming to support. For instance, development NGOs were supporting urban movements in housing demands; environmental NGOs were assisting farmers' grassroots organizations in issues related to rural development; women's groups were supporting women in post-1985 urban movements.

After the 1988 presidential elections this role changed, but not because they believed in Cárdenas: he was viewed with distrust and NGOs only joined the movement after the elections, during the period of antifraud mobilizations. This was partly in order to accompany the movements they supported, but also because they supported the ideas of transition to democracy and were deeply shocked by the electoral fraud. They began to reassess civic action, participation in elections, and general participation in public matters as a means to change the status quo (Hernández Navarro 1994:17). As a result, NGOs developed a more political role marked by autonomy rather than separation from the state, constructed a form of politics in which parties do not dominate processes, and promoted specialization in issues they backed politically (Chalmers and Piester 1996). This more political role, in conjunction with specialization, led to their increasing participation in democratic politics and their articulation around democracy. This was indeed the case of the first articulation against free trade.

Channeling Conflict to the Electoral Arena

Throughout the twentieth century the Mexican political system represented a special case in Latin America. Mexico's political uniqueness was described by transition to democracy scholars as a semi-authoritarian regime (Camp 1996), a partial democracy (Potter 2000), or a monistic democracy (Juan Linz, Glen Dealy, and Susan Purcell in Stevens 1977). Mexico's political regime is better described in terms of a mixture of all these conceptualizations, as each of them describes some of its features. In terms of decision-making processes it was semi-authoritarian because access to these processes was restricted—the executive branch would make most decisions while the legislative and judicial branches would be subordinated. However, access to these processes was greater than in authoritarianism and, more importantly, decision-makers changed regularly. In relation to electoral processes it was also a partial democracy, because while elections were held, they were organized in such a way that only certain candidates could be elected.

Opposition political parties existed but the electoral system was organized to ensure that they would neither win an election nor form a government. Liberties were also restricted, in particular, the rights to freedom of expression and access to alternative information, and independent associations and organizations critical of the state existed but were closely monitored. In relation to political participation it was a monistic democracy because pluralism was limited and popular mobilization was only carried out in support of the state. The peculiarity of the Mexican system during the last two-thirds of the twentieth century is encapsulated by the ability of the PRI to stay in power. The PRI, rather than a military elite or a communist centralized government, managed to establish a state-centered political system where power was concentrated in the executive branch and the totality of the political elite was produced by the same party. The peculiar features of the Mexican political system can be attributed to the centrality of the state and the presidential office, and to the corporatist structure of the party that allows the president to control the political, economic, and social arenas during his six-year term.

From the mid-1970s onward PRI presidents reversed this trend so they could remain in power. They tried to channel the organization of opposition and protest into the electoral arena in order to either limit spheres of struggle or to provide a safety valve in times of crisis. President José López Portillo (1976–1982) enforced an electoral reform that facilitated the registration of new opposition parties, gave small parties the right to sit on supervisory committees at elections, gave them campaign expenses and access to official TV and radio time, and provided financial support for parliamentary staff and party press. This reform reinforced PRI hegemony by guaranteeing its numerical superiority and did not prevent electoral fraud. Accordingly it had little impact on social activists outside party politics.

In the 1980s, with weakening of the corporatist structure as a consequence of progressive neoliberal policies, president De la Madrid resumed Lopez Portillo's plan of channeling social conflict toward the electoral arena by tolerating competition and enforcing more reforms. He tolerated intense electoral competition at the local level in 1983 and enforced his own electoral reform in 1986. This established that the winning party could not occupy more than 70 percent of the seats in the Chamber of Deputies; that 300 deputies were to be elected by relative majority; that proportional representation was to increase from 100 to 200 seats (making a total of 500 seats); that opposition parties could obtain 40 percent of seats without winning a single majority district; that the winning party could also have sufficient proportional representation to obtain an absolute majority; and that half of the seats in the Senate could be renewed every three, rather than six, years. These measures were not intended to change the status quo or to prevent electoral fraud, but made people in popular movements believe that elections, after all, could serve as an option—elections had traditionally been rejected by the left as a means of change, given their rejection of democracy in general and their experience with elections where the PRI always "won" (Aguayo Quezada and Parra Rosales 1997, Camp 1996, Chand 2001, Foweraker 1989, Tamayo 1990).

Aguayo argues that De la Madrid's continuation of Lopez Portillo's reform, or in his words, De la Madrid's "Democratic Spring," marked the beginning of party politics activism in the social left. De la Madrid acknowledged local electoral triumphs of the PAN in Chihuahua, Durango, and Aguascalientes, where the conservative Catholic Church and the business community became active in promoting the freedom to vote and directly challenged the PRI (Aguayo Quezada and Parra Rosales 1997). These triumphs led social activists to believe that elections could in fact serve as a real site for power struggles. However, it was not until the 1988 elections when the left was finally encouraged to vote, as Aguayo recalls:

> I subscribed to the logic that elections were a fraud, that they were completely useless. Therefore, since the 1970s, all my work as an academic, as a columnist and as an activist...was conditioned by the fact that I was not interested in elections at all. Like most people in NGOs...Most people from the social left, where I come from, were not interested in elections at all. In the 1980s a simultaneous revolution

took place, which is a fundamental change in the assumptions of the left. From training farmers, workers, etc. there was a move to the use of the vote as an instrument for change. In the past the belief was that in order to overthrow the PRI and authoritarianism, mass mobilization was necessary. In the 1980s the fundamental change became voting (Aguayo 2004).

The increased channeling of social conflict into the electoral arena and the social left's subsequent acceptance of elections as a site for power disputes was a major factor for democratic politics to emerge in Mexico. This in turn would allow for liberal discourses such as democracy and human rights to develop.

Conclusions

This chapter has identified the consequences of continuous economic change for the multiplication of social agents by describing its concrete expressions: the crisis of corporatist representation and the emergence of different forms of social organization. As corporatist organizations failed to provide solutions to the problems presented to workers and farmers, there was a move toward the independent organization of social groups and the shifting of social conflict toward the electoral arena.

The proliferation of sociopolitical actors together with the weakening of corporatism and the increasing interest in elections established the political basis for the development of liberal-inspired discourses such as democracy and human rights, as will be demonstrated in the next chapter.

Chapter 2

The Emergence of Human Rights Discourse in Mexico

Introduction

The discursive consequence of the rise of neoliberalism, the reorganization of society, and the weakening of corporatism in Mexico as discussed in the previous chapter was the emergence of human rights as a political discourse. Human rights—as opposed to constitutional rights—did not emerge as a legal discourse but as a political discourse for the organization of people outside the corporatist structure, especially those not represented by the political left and those interested in advancing transition to democracy in the country as a left-wing political project.

This chapter develops a genealogy that demonstrates how human rights emerged as a discourse. It highlights the role of conceptual frameworks in the setting-up of human rights discourse in order to establish how, in this specific case, the intellectual and political context led to the formation of a discourse that began as a social struggle and eventually became a legal and liberal discourse supporting Mexico's obsession with electoral democracy. It is divided into three parts. The first part addresses the regional intellectual and political context that made it possible for leftist activists in Mexico to begin talking about human rights. The second discusses the emergence of human rights issues and the conceptual frameworks informing an early version of human rights discourse. The third part will examine how these frameworks were interpreted and eventually led to a loss of holism.

Latin American Transition to Democracy and the Pragmatic Objectives of Human Rights Discourse

Human rights discourse emerged in Mexico as a sociopolitical rather than a legal discourse because a wider political and intellectual project was under way in Latin America: transition to democracy. Transition to democracy made human rights a strategic objective given the widespread use of repression in the region. Transition to democracy was in fact a pragmatic choice that served as a contrast to the political and intellectual traditions of the region. For decades Latin American activists and intellectuals had been very skeptical of, if not overtly opposed to, the liberal discourses of democracy. This was not only due to the dominance of Marxist-Leninist discourses, but also because in the context of the Cold War, liberal discourses were promoted by the U.S.-sponsored Alliance for Progress. This hemispheric program promoted by president J.F. Kennedy encouraged democracy and development via aid throughout the Latin American region as a way to prevent socialist contagion after the Cuban Revolution turned to socialism in 1961.

However, democracy ceased to be a demonized discourse for the Latin American left as a consequence of the impact of the coup d'etats in South America in the 1970s (Lesgart 2003, Roitman Rosenmann 2005). These events had a significant impact on left-wing political thought and action as the intellectual community began to question the effectiveness of structuralist discourses used to forward social analysis, in particular dependency theory.[1] The underlying idea was that revolution as a means of social and political change had provoked the anger of the ultra-right and had polarized social and political actors; for intellectuals, this necessitated a change in the production of knowledge and consequently of political action (Lesgart 2003:30, Roitman Rosenmann 2005). Intellectuals of the Latin American Council for Social Sciences (CLACSO, the Spanish acronym for Consejo Latinoamericano de Ciencias Sociales) began to look for new ways of conceiving politics in the region. Accordingly, they analyzed the characteristics of military regimes with their origins in the national security doctrine, which intellectuals began to refer to as bureaucratic-authoritarian systems,[2] in order to distinguish them from the old authoritarian regimes marked by corporatism as a means of preventing dissent and in an attempt to avoid socialist strategies that might anger the extreme right even more. They sought strategies that political actors could use to oppose military regimes without encouraging a mass armed movement designed to overthrow existing power (Lesgart 2003, Ruiz Contardo 2004). The natural answer was liberal democracy (Lesgart 2003:68).

Simply put, liberal democracy is conceived in the following manner: governments and legislatures are chosen directly or indirectly by periodic and free elections; choices can be made on the basis of political parties; there are sufficient civil liberties to make the right to choose effective; formal equality exists before the law; there is protection for minorities; and there is acceptance of the principle of maximum individual freedom (Macpherson 1977:11). The definition of democracy forwarded in transition to democracy was heavily individualistic and liberty oriented, not only due to this liberal definition but also because of the pragmatic explanation for the causes of democratization. In the beginning, intellectuals assessed the implications of civic culture, institution building, and the cycles of capitalism for the installation of democracy. Analyses showed that the disappearance of democracy coincided with times of economic crisis, especially in countries where industrialization had developed late and along the lines of transnationalization, such as those of the Southern Cone. Because the analysis had a negative implication and the main objective was to find theoretical alternatives, intellectuals decided to analyze democracy as an exclusively political category, detached from cultural and socioeconomic factors (Lesgart 2003:83–84). Transition theory thus constructed focused on social actors as the main factor for change and highlighted the role of political elites in democratic processes. Any structural cause was dismissed (Grugel 2002).

In the transition framework, democratization ceased to be analyzed in terms of the requisites for democracy and began to be assessed in terms of the possibilities of a country to pass from a nondemocratic and bureaucratic-authoritarian regime to a democratic one. The focus on political elites in transition theories is derived from the idea that these have to negotiate a pact that eventually leads to such a framework, although transition theories also leave room for non-pact-based transitions. The substantive features of democracy advanced by some scholars were reduced to the construction of "civil society" and "participation" in the process of democratization (Lesgart 2003:85–90).

Because it became an exclusively political concept, democracy was transformed into "political democracy," considered only in terms of institutions, procedures, and representation, and focused on the legal framework allowing for the transition from an authoritarian-bureaucratic regime to a democratic one, defined as a set of institutions and procedures. The reason for choosing this intellectual-political construct was heavily pragmatic since it fulfilled a dual purpose: intellectually it opposed the term authoritarianism and politically it allowed for the protection of individuals vis-à-vis the brutal repression of military juntas by advancing as strategic objectives the rule of law and human rights (Lesgart 2003:81). Political democracy implied a heavily liberal version of human rights, which only considered civil liberties and political rights defined in a foundational and legalistic way—human rights are inherent to human nature because of the possession of reason and precede the law, which in turn should guarantee them. Consequently, the focus of a political-democracy oriented human rights concept is the realization of the rule of law for the establishment of a truly democratic system, which is not necessarily a means but an end in itself.

It was in this regional intellectual and political context that transition to democracy arrived in Mexico. Mexico had not suffered the terrible situation leading to the elaboration of transition to democracy theory in South American countries—elections were still held and the human rights situation was not as serious as that in many Central and South American countries. However, its political situation was considered sufficiently bad to relate it to increasing authoritarianism and the subsequent need for a transition to democracy. In Mexico, transition to democracy had a very specific meaning: not the overthrow of a military regime but a change of party in the presidential office through democratic elections, which the PRI had at the time managed to retain for 60 years. In addition, since in Mexico democracy was a discourse identified not only with U.S. foreign policy but also with the political right represented by the PAN, the left maintained the principles of traditional structural analysis and established that free elections should not be an end in themselves. For the left, elections should be considered a means to achieving a government genuinely elected by the people not because this was good in itself but because a government emerging from the people would be willing to pursue the ideals of social justice and economic sovereignty.[3]

Consequently, Mexican intellectuals began to construct a political project that would lead Mexico to a transition from authoritarianism to a regime characterized by the holding of free elections. Through an independent electoral process, a candidate committed to social justice could take control of the increasingly neoliberal regime and return the country to the ideals of the 1910 Revolution. This construction was reinforced during and after the electoral process of 1988, when PRI-dissident and nationalist Cuauhtémoc Cárdenas lost to PRI candidate

Carlos Salinas (see the increasing importance of elections in the previous chapter). After this important event, the Mexican version of transition to democracy became exclusively focused on elections. It did consider social change and included, as it did in the Southern Cone, a demand for the rule of law, a strong party system, accountability of representatives, and the exercising of civil liberties. However, the emphasis was on a functional and autonomous electoral system that could guarantee clean electoral processes.[4]

The Mexican context of repression was for many considerably less serious than in Argentina, Chile, and Central America. Human rights activist Father Jesús Maldonado notes that on a trip to El Salvador he realized that:

> ...the Army was all over the place, there were tortured people in the public bins, not hidden in secret jails. There were dead, murdered people in the bins. It was something else altogether. Here in Mexico people didn't talk about a dirty war in Guerrero state...we did know about repression, but it was a lot more hidden. I mean, there were very serious things going on in Central and South America, surely very serious things here, too, but in a different way. Apart from the 1968 and June 10 (1971) massacres, apart from those very violent events, I believe the dimension of problems here was a lot less serious. I mean of a different dimension in relation to Central and South America (Maldonado 2004).

While repression in South and Central America was widespread, in Mexico this repression was related to opposition to neoliberal reforms and increased repression during and after the 1988 electoral fraud (Centro de Derechos Humanos "Miguel Agustín Pro Juárez" 1992b, Rodríguez Castañeda 1990). In contrast to Central and South America, repression in Mexico was applied "selectively." The first human rights report in Mexico showed that the use of executions, forced disappearances, and torture was not as generalized as in Argentina, El Salvador, and Guatemala. There, the victims could be anyone identified with opposition politics, whereas in Mexico these practices were systematic but not generalized as they were applied only to independent union leaders, student activists, farmers' leaders, and eventually to members of the newly formed Party of the Democratic Revolution (PRD, Spanish acronym for Partido de la Revolución Democrática) (Concha Malo and Centro de Derechos Humanos "Fray Francisco de Vitoria" 1989).

Consequently, in Mexico, human rights as a strategic objective in transition to democracy were not used so much for opposing authoritarianism, as in South America, but were used more as a sociopolitical discourse, as shall be discussed later.

Democracy Meets Liberation Theology: The Roots of Holism in Early Human Rights Discourse

Human rights discourse started to develop in Mexico in the intellectual and political context of transition to democracy and served the strategic purpose of defending social agents involved in the sociopolitical struggle for transition to democracy itself. It was only in this context that such development was possible, because until the 1980s, human rights discourse has been used exclusively in the diplomatic arena and had no relation to domestic politics. Put quite simply, in Mexico human rights were a discourse for diplomats not for activists.[5] Neither torture and illegal detentions, nor any other government abuses occurring in Mexico were related to the rights listed in the UDHR. These rights were related only to the broader and more general idea of political repression.

It was, in fact, the Mexican Left that first started to problematize human rights issues in the early 1980s. Leftist activists did not do this in relation to the Mexican situation but in relation to the armed conflict in Central America, especially in El Salvador and Nicaragua, where many local human rights groups were set up in order to denounce abuses. Mexican activists began to use human rights in order to deal with the governments' physical abuse of social and political leaders, abuse taking the form of torture, forced disappearances, executions, holding people incommunicado, arbitrary detentions, political assassinations, and the like. These were the established issues of human rights discourse as used in their most closely related models: the NGOs dealing with repression by national security regimes in the Southern Cone and guerrilla warfare in Central America. It was now that Mexican social movements began to challenge the status of the diplomatic field as the only institutional site where human rights could be discussed.

In El Salvador many human rights activists had been killed; others were persecuted, like Roberto Cuéllar and his brother Benjamín Cuéllar who founded the human rights committee "Socorro Jurídico Cristiano de El Salvador." They were forced to flee El Salvador and seek asylum in Mexico, a country with a long and rather contradictory tradition of offering asylum to political activists fleeing dictatorships, especially those of Latin America and Spain. The Cuéllar brothers had an important link with the Dominican Order in El Salvador, so when they arrived in Mexico they went directly to the headquarters of the Dominicans in Mexico City and requested they be provided with an office and the means to continue their human rights work for El Salvador. They launched a human rights solidarity campaign for El Salvador in Mexico, which was later joined by academics, popular education promoters, and priests sympathetic to liberation theology. These people went on to establish the first human rights organizations in Mexico in the mid-1980s as will be discussed later in the chapter.

Once the concept entered the country via the solidarity movement with Central America, it began to develop because of the conjunction of two different, but interlinked, theoretical conceptions of human rights at play in political struggles in other Latin American countries: transition to democracy and liberation theology. In transition theory democracy was defined in terms of the regional political and intellectual movement for democratization formulated by CLACSO, as explained in the previous section.

Academics, social-left activists, and party members informed their views of human rights based on transition to democracy. However, unlike much of the work on human rights in Southern Cone countries, where socioeconomic issues were completely obscured by the widespread repression of political activists, in Mexico academic human rights defenders could still maintain a holistic view of human rights as they could see the dangers of removing socioeconomic issues from the idea of democracy. They aimed to promote the human rights necessary to advance a form of democracy in which law was enforced in favor of individuals so that these individuals could choose their leaders and opt for a different economic future. Pablo González Casanova in fact stated that the struggle in defense of human rights in Mexico should be differentiated from the U.S. promotion of human rights inasmuch as it should be based on the Mexican Constitution and therefore include the issues concerning social rights recognized therein (González Casanova 1989:24).[6]

The second framework was based on the "pastoral practices" of the Catholic Church in the Southern Cone and Central America, and then on liberation theology ideas resulting from reflection on these practices and the political impact of transition to democracy thinking. Liberation theology was not a framework naturally linked to democracy and its principles as it was inspired by Latin American structural approaches such as dependency theory and its critique of development. In 1968, Father Gustavo Gutiérrez advanced the theoretical foundations for a new theology that would combine theory and practice (praxis); had its locus in the poor; was related to the Word of the Bible and intended to liberate the poor from oppression; and used the social sciences in order to analyze the causes of oppression—Marxist analysis of class struggle. These ideas were further developed by other theologians such as José Miguel Bonino and Hugo Assmann (Berryman 1987, Sigmund 1990). In their writings these theologians rejected democracy and human rights for the same reason social left activists did: for them, rights were linked to U.S. foreign policy. In the best case, some of them, like Assmann, called for the creation of an "alternative language" and proposed that instead of human rights they talked about the "rights of the majorities" or the "rights of the poor.[7]

The exception was José Comblin, who shared the view of his liberation theology colleagues that the Church should focus its efforts on criticizing development. However, he pointed out that, in practice and given the spread of the national security doctrine, human rights were becoming the key in a new pastoral approach to the problems posed by dictators. He noted that as ideas of national security had become widespread in Brazil, Paraguay, Uruguay, Argentina, Bolivia, and Chile, the churches in these countries had to produce public declarations "in defense of human rights," especially in Chile and Brazil. Challenging criticism of human rights within liberation theology, he claimed that:

> With such a historical background to the recent declarations of human rights by the Church... it hardly seems necessary to stress that they are not theoretical studies of an ethical doctrine conducted in a vacuum. They are public acts of confrontation with a political system. They define how the Church perceives its presence in the midst of a real world and its real position in relation to the state (Comblin 1979:105).

As democratization gained acceptance within the social left in the Southern Cone as a result of generalized repression and violence extended throughout Central America, Comblin's ideas started to make sense. Supporters of liberation theology used human rights discourse pragmatically in order to search for the disappeared and defend those tortured and arbitrarily detained by those governments supporting the doctrine of national security—Chile, Paraguay, Brazil, Uruguay, Argentina, and Bolivia.

Consequently, scholars became more receptive and those based in El Salvador started to theorize liberation theology in the language of rights (Sigmund 1990:77). Leonardo and Clodovis Boff, Ignacio

Ellacuría and Jon Sobrino, the latter two based at the Jesuit Central American University of El Salvador (UCA, the Spanish acronym for Universidad Centroamericana), advanced the idea of human rights as the "rights of the poor" following the liberation argument of "God's preferential option for the poor." The idea of rights of the poor contrasted with the individualism promoted by the liberal doctrine of rights since it proposed human rights to be those of a human *community* rather than the rights of the human *individual* (Czerny 1992).

A major influence on theorization of the rights of the poor was Ellacuría's idea of the historization of human rights, which emphasized a socioeconomic context for the construction of given understandings of human rights. He claimed that before analyzing "the human rights problem" it was necessary to discard any abstract notions and examine the context to see if the existing concept served to maintain the status quo and serve the interests of the rich minority at the expense of the impoverished majority (Ellacuría 1990). This view of contextually defined human rights rejected any separation between civil and political rights (CPRs) and ESCRs. It also proposed a necessary hierarchy based on people's struggles for liberation—with liberation this time understood as the struggle of people against oppression in order to achieve true liberty. This hierarchy had to be chronological and prioritize one right over all others: the right to life—note that by the time of these writings, thousands of people had been murdered, tortured, and had disappeared in Central America (Czerny 1992, Ellacuría 1990, Sigmund 1990).

In Mexico, liberation theology was never as important as it was in the rest of Latin America in the 1970s.[8] Nevertheless, due to the involvement of the Mexican left in the human rights campaign for El Salvador and the solidarity movement with Central American refugees in Mexico, the writings of liberation theology scholars advancing human rights ideas were widely read among activist priests, especially those of Boff, Ellacuría, and Sobrino. Consequently these ideas informed the human rights understanding of Jesuit and Dominican priests who founded the first human rights NGOs in Mexico.

The differing academic and religious views of rights generated different types of human rights NGOs: the religious NGOs—mostly Jesuit and Dominican—and the professional academic NGOs. Encouraged by the work of the Cuéllar brothers and responding to the problem of Central American refugees in Mexico, the Dominican Order-linked Fray Francisco de Vitoria Human Rights Center (Vitoria Center) was set up in April 1984; and the secular Mexican Academy of Human Rights (Academia, which stands for Academia Mexicana de Derechos

Humanos), formed by academics, politicians, and social-left activists, in October of the same year.[9] Four years later, the Jesus Society founded the "Miguel Agustín Pro Juárez" Human Rights Center (Prodh Center). By 1988 there were only six human rights NGOs in Mexico (Maldonado 1995), including these three that were the most important. The number increased the following year as these three started to produce further groups, although for very different reasons that will be discussed later.

However, before the Vitoria and the Academia could address these issues in the Mexican context,[10] they had to gain legitimacy through public support. First, they had to convince public opinion that human rights did not necessarily constitute a pro-U.S. and pro-government discourse. Human rights had acquired a negative image for the Mexican left because the Carter administration had demanded human rights compliance as a condition for its aid and democratization programs. The inclusion of human rights—defined as civil and political rights exclusively—allegedly served to give content to its demands for democracy, but it also served to prevent revolution and maintain asymmetrical relationships. In addition, the Mexican government defended human rights in its foreign policy by accepting political refugees. NGOs also had to gain social support because it was very dangerous to talk about repression or other anomalies under the PRI government. The Vitoria Center and the Academia shared the view that the best way to do this was to inform government officials, academics, and activists what human rights were, creating a mass and popular human rights culture by means of public discussion, thematic seminars, and more importantly popular education for the creation of grassroots human rights groups.

Second, they had to produce their own human rights information in order to show that human rights were being violated in Mexico. This was a very important factor because human rights research in Mexico would come to be constructed on figures and exemplary cases to be defended legally. A significant breakthrough in the production of human rights data was the publication of *Las violaciones a los derechos humanos individuales en Mexico* (Violations of Individual Human Rights in Mexico), a report tracing Mexican press coverage of violations of the right to life, personal freedom, and respect for personal integrity during the period 1971–1986 (Centro de Derechos Humanos "Fray Francisco de Vitoria" 1990c). Included in the *Primer Informe sobre la Democracia* (The First Report on Democracy 1988), edited by González Casanova, the Vitoria Center interpreted police news through the lens of human rights, finding that union, farmer, and student leaders had been selectively and systematically killed, arbitrarily detained, tortured, held incommunicado, and so on (Concha Malo and Centro de Derechos Humanos "Fray Francisco de Vitoria" 1989). The report was extremely important because it was the first document to enunciate issues of Mexican human rights discourse constructed in the terms mentioned above. It was the first human rights report in Mexico ever and encouraged the Vitoria Center to begin work in the Mexican context. In 1989, therefore, the Vitoria Center published its first report on human rights in Mexico in its own human rights quarterly bulletin using information included in the report published in the book referred to above. By 1990, information on Mexico as well as Central America was being published on a regular basis (Centro de Derechos Humanos "Fray Francisco de Vitoria" 1990d, 1990e) and their experiences in the analysis of human rights data and the formation of public opinion were finally shared with a wider public (Centro de Derechos Humanos "Fray Francisco de Vitoria" 1990e).

By this time, the two types of NGOs started to develop different forms of strategy for their struggles. Both shared the view that in general terms the underlying problem of political repression was "structural" and that addressing ESCRs was fundamental to any human rights struggle. However, their frameworks led to different strategies for tackling the problem. While religious organizations opted for organizing people at the grassroots level in defense of their rights, secular NGOs focused on conceptual construction and the rule of law.

The priests heading religious NGOs had first worked with grassroots groups organized by the Church (CEBs, the Spanish acronym for Comunidades Eclesiales de Base) and then with social movements, therefore they believed that grassroots organization in defense of human rights was the key issue in achieving the goal of democracy. Consequently, one of their fundamental objectives was "to support organizations persecuted by the Mexican State and only occasionally would it defend independent persons (the aim of this was defending popular organizations)" (Maldonado 1995:4). They concentrated on helping people set up their own human rights committees. The appeal for the setting up of human rights organizations was reinforced after the influential political weekly *Proceso* published an article on the Prodh Center's report. Father Maldonado, then the chairperson of the Center, received calls from dozens of people anxious to receive both human rights training and help in organizing their own human rights committees. He believed that the dramatic multiplication of groups that followed was attributable to the publicity provided by the *Proceso* article, which stated that the Prodh was helping people who wanted to form their own committees (Rodríguez Castañeda 1990:15).

In a wider sense, the multiplication of human rights NGOs is related to the intensification of repression and the popularity of transition to democracy discourse. As committees multiplied, Maldonado called on the over 40 existing groups—those inspired by religious interests and those inspired by secular interests—to form the Red TDT in 1989. Their objective was to carry out joint action related to the construction of a human rights agenda, which included impunity related to, and violations of, what they called "fundamental rights," that is, the liberal, natural rights to life, freedom, personal security, and physical and psychological integrity.

Second, the Academia, formed by academics and politicians, preferred to concentrate on education and research into theoretical human rights issues in order to contribute to the construction of a human rights culture on a national scale. They held seminars and forums for the discussion of such issues as the ombudsman and the rights of indigenous people. In 1989, however, the mainstream strategy of secular NGOs changed after a split within the Academia led to the setting up of the Mexican Commission for the Defense and Promotion of Human Rights (CMDPDH, the Spanish acronym for Comisión Mexicana de Defensa y Promoción de los Derechos Humanos). As violations of individual rights multiplied after the 1988 electoral fraud, some members of the Academia were not satisfied with simply organizing courses and seminars on general issues. As the Academia confirmed its commitment to "defending causes, not cases," associates headed by Academia founder and former director of Amnesty International Mexico, Mariclaire Acosta, set up their own group. This new NGO carried out similar tasks to those of the Vitoria and the Prodh centers but added legal defense, that is, case litigation (Academia Mexicana de Derechos Humanos 1990a). This would have an enormous impact on the development of future strategies and eventually eradicate holism from the discourse as will be discussed below.

In spite of the different strategies employed by the two frameworks, there was clarity about the importance of establishing the link between selective violations of CPRs and massive violations of ESCRs. In the documents of founder NGOs there is a very clear contextualization of such violations of CPRs as torture and extrajudicial executions. These were located within the context of massive violations of

ESCRs. In fact, when the Prodh produced its first report in 1990, it included human rights violations in the field of political repression, but also detailed union rights. It also offered a comprehensive analysis of the socioeconomic conditions leading to human rights violations. The report studied repression and the violation of individual rights in a socioeconomic context that clearly identified the massive violation of human rights in the areas of rural politics, urban movements, independent trade-unionism, elections, police investigations, and drug trafficking. It described each of these fields in great depth, especially in the context of the workers movement. It provided a context and a link to the greater struggle for transition to democracy and against neoliberal economics (Rodríguez Castañeda 1990).

This holism was confirmed in 1990 with the setting up of the first official human rights body, the National Human Rights Commission (CNDH, the Spanish acronym for Comisión Nacional de Derechos Humanos). The CNDH was created on June 6, 1990, a few weeks after the assassination of human rights lawyer Norma Corona Sapién in Sinaloa state on May 21 and a few weeks before then president Carlos Salinas traveled to Washington in order to participate in negotiations for the NAFTA with the United States and Canada. NGOs accused the government of setting up the CNDH in order to gain legitimacy in trade negotiations with the United States and Canada who were very sensitive about civil rights and electoral democracy (Acosta 1992, Alvarez Díaz 1996, Centro de Derechos Humanos "Fray Francisco de Vitoria" 1990b, Centro de Derechos Humanos "Miguel Agustín Pro Juárez" 1991, 1992b). Obviously the government denied the accusation but the political motives behind the setting up of the CNDH became clearer as the Mexican government argued that politics should be alien to human rights observance and that courts already existed to deal with labor issues. The government decided that the CNDH would not accept complaints about violations of political and labor rights, two of the most systematically violated rights in the country at the time and two of the priorities of the NGO agenda. Only by explicitly declaring their interest in promoting a holistic view of human rights that included both ESCRs and CPRs could NGOs establish a difference between their own discourse and the government's. This self-affirmation made the discourse very holistic. The Prodh Center wrote the following on this point:

> We can say that the State's concept of human rights, in addition to being partial—it reduces the concept of human rights to issues exclusively pertaining to civil and political rights—possesses a distinctively

pragmatic character; this has been seen in practice: the State becomes officially interested in human rights if through these it can establish a positive national and international image...but in reality the State is not interested in improving the material, political, cultural and spiritual conditions of the majority of the population, nor is it interested in transforming from the bottom-up those State authorities responsible for the most flagrant violations of citizens' individual guarantees (Centro de Derechos Humanos "Miguel Agustín Pro Juárez" 1992a:23).

NGOs explicitly declared their interest in the promotion and defense of both CPRs and ESCRs in order to challenge the government's attempt to restrict discourse to civil rights—torture, incommunicado and illegal detentions, executions, and so on. To sum up, the merging of democracy and liberation within the context of transition to democracy and neoliberal economics led to a holistic human rights discourse.

INTERPRETATION AND LEGALIZATION: THE LOSS OF HOLISM

Although in NGO rhetoric ESCRs were as important as liberty, in practice NGOs worked exclusively in the field of civil rights, for which they had developed a sophisticated approach by the early 1990s. In the late 1980s the scope of human rights was defined within the realm of political repression of activists, namely the violation of rights to physical integrity and security, life, justice, freedom of expression, association, and opinion, as the result of murder, torture, illegal and incommunicado detention, execution, and so on. By 1991 the discourse was extended to include non-political-related abuses of regular citizens. The historical analysis of violations and the increasing development of expertise in the field of law added structural issues to the agenda: impunity of police abuse, as well as violations perpetrated by the military in the fight against drug trafficking.[11]

This sophistication showed that it was necessary to include more issues and appropriate strategies. Democracy scholar and human rights activist Sergio Aguayo indicates: "When a governmental institution is set up, the agenda gets liberated...The 1990s is the decade of broadening the agenda. The term 'human rights' is no longer used solely for elementary abuses like torture and disappearance as those were very elementary, basic rights. The time comes to ask: what's next?" (Aguayo 2004). However, this move could not be made in the direction of ESCRs for two major reasons that not only made dealing with these rights virtually impossible but also directed the practice toward civil and political rights. The first is the adoption of the "three-generation approach to human rights" and the second the lack of expertise to deal with ESCRs.

First, the adoption of the three-generation approach to human rights was the interpretation of the two main frameworks informing human rights locally, namely transition to democracy and liberation theology. The centrality of transition to democracy led to a rather dogmatic interpretation of the historization effected by liberation theologians. Repression was so systematic, and NGOs' knowledge and resources so limited, that activists had to establish their own priorities. Liberation theologians recommended that hierarchization had to be chronological and therefore prioritized the right of life but also a sequential fulfillment of the different types of rights.

The expression of the prioritization of rights based on a chronological fulfillment was the adoption of the three-generation approach to human rights. Following the appearance of rights in industrial Europe, the approach sees concerns with individual protection as informing a first generation of rights (CPRs); concerns with social equality as informing a second generation of rights (ESCRs); and concerns with peace, the environment and world socioeconomic conditions as informing a third generation of rights (rights of peoples) (Davidson 1993). The Mexican view of human rights based on this approach established that violations of CPRs (torture, assassinations, arbitrary detentions, forced disappearances, electoral fraud) were the obvious expressions of widespread violations of ESCRs (the structural causes of repression). More importantly, this indicated that ESCRs could only be fulfilled once CPRs were fully respected, or, in the specific context of transition to democracy, once Mexicans could freely elect a president willing to advance social change.

The three-generation approach to human rights, which was also subordinated to the wider project of transition to democracy, favored the view that CPRs were to be fulfilled first and only then could ESCRs be considered. This situation blurred the original differences between the two different types of NGOs since both were pursuing more or less the same objectives focused on CPRs—defending individuals from state repression in the struggle for the transition to democracy. Differences between the two disappeared and legal defense became a widespread strategy. Consequently, given the issues of the common agenda (impunity and transition to democracy), the work of NGOs, which in the early days was fundamentally political, became increasingly legalistic.

The merging of liberation theology and transition to democracy in the three-generation approach can be observed in the strategic formulations constructed in the reports and bulletins of both secular and religious NGOs. In their writings, both types of NGOs advanced the idea that violations of CPRs were rooted in political, social, and economic causes, and that the defense of these rights should eventually lead to a democratic regime supporting social justice (the prioritization of CPRs could lead to the achievement of ESCRs). These priorities were partly marked by the circumstances—widespread repression of social leaders—but also by the increasing importance of transition to democracy itself, which prioritized CPRs in an effort to redirect social conflict to the institutional realm.

Second, apart from the adoption of the three-generation approach that prioritized CPRs, two issues made the tools for the defense of ESCRs scarce: the scope of international discourse and the lack of expertise within organizations. First, whereas the defense of CPRs was clearly carried out in courts by lawyers, ESCRs were not necessarily justiciable in the way the former were. The defense of ESCRs was neither as straightforward nor as clear as the defense of CPRs, not even in the international framework. In fact the International Bill of Rights—the UDHR (1948), and the International Covenants on Civil and Political Rights (ICCPRs) and Economic, Social and Cultural Rights (ICESCRs) (1966)—provided weaker tools for the defense of ESCRs than for CPRs. Implementation under the two covenants differed in at least two respects: language and machinery.

On the one hand, the contrast in language is clear in at least three features. One, the ICECSR was written in a language of "progressive realization" rather than one of "immediate realization" as was the case with the ICCPR. Two, the rights of the ICESCR were "recognized" as opposed to "declared"—with the exception of the right to unionize, which is based on the civil right to associate. Three, states were committed "to take steps" for the realization of, rather than to "immediately" enforce, those rights, using "available resources," the nature of which—national or international—was not specified (Trubek 2000). On the other hand, unlike the ICCPR supervisory mechanism, the ICESCR was designed to be extremely complicated and ineffective. States had to submit a report subject to noncompulsory revision involving the UN Secretary General, the Economic and Social Council (ECOSOC), specialized agencies, the Human Rights Commission, and interested state parties. A Committee on Economic, Social and Cultural Rights was set up in 1987 in order to facilitate the procedure and reinforce the supervision of these rights—before its creation the ICESCR existed as little more than "a textual reference" (Craven 1995:1).

Second, together with this technical restriction, local organizations did not have the expertise to develop approaches and methodologies to challenge the legal and international limitations of ESCR defense. This can be observed in their publications. For example, in its 1991 and 1992 annual reports, the Prodh Centre also included analyses of ESCRs such as the rights of workers and indigenous peoples to a clean environment, decent housing, food, and education. However, the approach either lacked references to actual human rights instruments (for instance, in the case of the right to food it focused on the national average calorie intake per capita) or focused on violations of CPRs in a socioeconomic context (for example, the analysis of indigenous people's rights highlighted repression in the context of land conflict) (Centro de Derechos Humanos "Miguel Agustín Pro Juárez" 1992a, 1993a, 1993b). A similar situation can be observed in the case of the Vitoria Centre, which registered labor and indigenous rights but from the perspective of repression of individuals (Centro de Derechos Humanos "Fray Francisco de Vitoria" 1991, 1992).

As tools for the defense of ESCRs were scarce and NGOs focused on developing legal expertise, most work on ESCRs became a matter of the individual conviction of activists. For instance, much of the work at this time was the initiative of Father Maldonado, then the chairperson of the Prodh Center. On May 28, 1991, he called on other organizations, independent unions, academics, lawyers, intellectuals, and so on to carry out observation of the union elections at the Ford Motor Company's Cuautitlán factory.[12] He formed an observation committee that reported intimidation and partiality on the part of authorities who allowed employer involvement, thereby violating the human rights of workers declared in international and inter-American human rights covenants (Comité de Observadores Independientes 1991, Fuentes 1991b).

The primacy of the three-generation approach that favored the development of CPRs, together with the limitations for addressing ESCRs, made the expansion of Mexican human rights discourse toward socioeconomic issues too difficult. Therefore, when there was a need to multiply issues and strategies, the move was toward political rights, in particular the rights to be elected for office and to vote in democratic elections, which further reinforced the subordination of human rights to democracy.[13] Some human rights NGOs had even been actively and consciously seeking extension of the human rights agenda toward the wider struggle for democracy, and elections were a key part of this agenda. One of these was the Academia, headed by Sergio Aguayo, who became chairperson of the Academia in December 1990 and was convinced that free elections were central to a human rights agenda.[14]

Two events provided the motif for the construction of electoral rights as issues of human rights discourse in Mexico as they transformed the typical electoral strategy of the PRI—fraud—into a violation of a universal entitlement and added mechanisms for argumentation concerning the larger democratic cause. The first was a resolution issued by the Inter-American Commission for Human Rights (ICHR), an organ of the Organization of American States (OAS), in 1990 and 1991 in response to complaints advanced by the rightist PAN with respect to electoral fraud in local electoral processes in Chihuahua, Durango, and Nuevo León states in the second half of the 1980s. The Commission's resolution stated that the federal government had violated articles 2, 23, and 25 of the American Convention of Human Rights as it had failed to respect Mexicans' right to participate in authentic democratic elections and had also failed to provide a legislative framework for people who wanted to lodge a complaint if they believed that their political rights had been violated (Concha Malo 1994a).

The second took place during the 1991 federal mid-term elections when over 40 NGO groups forming part of the Red TDT conducted electoral observations in Mexico City and those states where local elections were to take place—these included San Luis Potosí, Guanajuato, Jalisco, and Coahuila. Since the PRI once again committed electoral fraud, and there were human rights activists observing the process, on this occasion electoral fraud became the issue human rights discourse could latch on to: the manipulation and buying of votes, media partiality, and dishonest handling of the voter list. In this scenario the electoral rights recognized by the ICHR acquired meaning in the context of the Mexican transition to democracy. In addition, accusations of politically related abuses of civil rights such as murder and detention were also extended to include political party leaders.[15]

A strong citizen movement explicitly defending electoral rights sprang up all over the country, subordinated to the wider and stronger transition to democracy project, which articulated many struggles including the anti-free trade struggle. From 1991 to 1993 human rights remained in the field of elections as NGOs from all over the country carried out 15 electoral observations and four speed countings during this period (Aguayo Quezada and Parra Rosales 1997:39).

They also addressed the issue of electoral observation in their publications.[16] By 1994, some NGOs such as the Academia and the Potosino Center for Human Rights—which coordinated the 1991 electoral observation in San Luis Potosí—dedicated their time exclusively to electoral rights.

Together with 450 NGOs and independent citizens from all over the country, who gathered to carry out observation during the presidential elections, they formed Civic Alliance, a nationwide network that eventually became a civil organization. From January to August 1994 it assessed the reliability of the voting list and the objectivity of the media, analyzed electoral reforms, carried out three surveys, proved that governmental officials had bribed people for their votes, and finally carried out electoral observation. Civic Alliance concluded that the electoral process was plagued with irregularities, but recognized that these did not considerably affect the final outcome, that is, the PRI winning yet again. At the same time, they spread the idea that electoral rights were human rights (Aguayo Quezada and Parra Rosales 1997:39).

To sum up, the centrality of the three-generation approach to human rights, the lack of expertise perpetuated by the increasing need to have legal and political experts within organizations, and the lack of a more structural interest in socioeconomic issues finally led to the disappearance of the holistic features of human rights discourse for a time, even in religious NGOs where ESCRs together with the right to life formed the core of the "rights of the poor." This was further reinforced by the introduction of electoral issues to the human rights agenda and the subsequent subordination of human rights discourse to democracy. Elections in fact became so central to the human rights agenda that the entire discourse became subordinated to the objectives of transition to democracy, leaving ESCR neglected, as we shall see in the next chapter.

Conclusions

Human rights discourse in Mexico did not develop as an exclusively liberal discourse but emerged as a combination of liberal democracy and liberation philosophy-inspired human rights approaches that led to the inclusion of both ESCRs and CPRs. Furthermore, given the influence of structural approaches, the struggle for human rights was perceived as part of a process of liberation from structural violence in which the violation of CPRs was symptomatic of the state's authoritarian response when faced with resistance to massive violations of ESCRs. However, as human rights discourse developed in the political context of transition to democracy, it lost holism and became predominantly liberal.

Since political and methodological issues prevented the expansion of human rights discourse in Mexico in the direction of ESCRs, transition to democracy-related human rights issues were advanced and the latent holism of the early stages was eventually lost. Human rights discourse in Mexico therefore changed from a sociopolitical discourse to a heavily legalistic one.

Chapter 3

The Exhaustion of Transition to Democracy Discourse: Human Rights Discourse Enters Anti-free Trade Struggles

Human rights emerged in Mexico as a very holistic discourse comprising both socioeconomic rights and liberties due to its roots in liberal democracy and liberation theology (1980s). Nevertheless, this holistic discourse eventually lost its comprehensive character as it became subordinated to transition to democracy discourse (1990s). This scenario in fact marked the evolution of human rights as it prevented the early inclusion of socioeconomic issues, including free trade. It was only with the demise of transition to democracy as a hegemonic project that free trade entered human rights discourse, establishing the basis for human rights to become an empty signifier fixing meaning in the struggle against neoliberal trade (2000s).

This chapter examines how the exhaustion of transition to democracy as a political discourse articulating social agents allowed for free trade issues to be broached within a human rights framework in terms of both agenda and articulation. Accordingly, it first establishes how transition to democracy systematically prevented the inclusion of socioeconomic issues in the human rights agenda, especially the question of free trade. It then examines how social conflict moved from the electoral to the socioeconomic field as the transition to democracy agenda was accomplished. It goes on to discuss how this exhaustion was also reflected in the anti-free trade struggle thereby allowing human rights to become an empty signifier. It finally assesses the potentiality of human rights for addressing free trade, given the failure of human rights NGOs to change their strategies.

Transition to Democracy and the Systematic Neglect of Socioeconomic Rights

Throughout the 1990s NGOs defined the core of their strategies within the parameters of the discourse of transition to democracy. For example, much of the NGO agenda consisted of the construction of "paradigmatic" legal cases that were "adopted" by legal defense teams due to their being considered archetypical of state abuse in terms of rights violations, the circumstances in which they occurred, and the authorities involved. In addition, some NGOs specialized in electoral issues making elections an issue for human rights discourse for the first time.

The focus on CPRs related to electoral processes and repression related in the sphere of party politics prevented activists from developing approaches to socioeconomic and cultural rights even though socioeconomic problems were prominent. It is true that there were some attempts to address ESCRs but these failed for the same reason they had failed previously: organizations had little human rights expertise in socioeconomic issues. However, this time the lack of expertise resulted from a focus on the legal defense of individual cases, a trend established by the CMDPDH.

The lack of expertise perpetuated by the increasing need to have law and politics experts within organizations, and the lack of a more structural interest in socioeconomic issues finally led to a systematic neglect of socioeconomic rights in their work, even in religious NGOs where ESCRs together with the right to life formed the core of the "rights of the poor." Therefore, when free trade appeared on the NGO horizon with the negotiation of the NAFTA, free trade could not become a human rights issue even though it was a major issue for independent unions and farmer organizations. Instead, free trade became, for the few NGOs interested in the issue, a site for the promotion of human rights as a strategic objective of transition to democracy. However, even in this context a mere handful of national human rights NGOs joined the struggle launched in 1991 with the setting up of the RMALC.

Former chairperson of the CMDPDH, Mariclaire Acosta, organized a trinational conference dealing exclusively with trade and human rights. Only two Mexican NGOs, the CMDPDH, and the Centre for

Border Studies and Human Rights Promotion AC (Cefrodhac, the Spanish acronym for Centro de Estudios Fronterizos y Promoción de Derechos Humanos AC), attended the conference, Tri-national Exchange: International Perspectives on Human Rights, held in Reynosa, Tamaulipas, Mexico, from September 11–13, 1992. At this conference organizations from the three countries tried to establish the issues to be addressed in the field of trade and discussed whether a trinational strategy was viable. The conference was a complete failure because organizations found it difficult to see the relationship between their local problems and the trade agenda; sponsors did not like the conference because it was too critical of the integration agenda; and the three countries had different views of what constituted human rights (American NGOs considered only civil and political rights) (Comisión Mexicana de Defensa y Promoción de los Derechos Humanos 1992).

However, human rights issues explicitly remained part of their "democratic demands" rather than a concern generated by the potentially negative impact of the terms of NAFTA. From this perspective, the major human rights goals within the free trade agenda were: influencing other governments and organizations to put pressure on the Mexican government to liberalize politics, end impunity, stop police and military abuse of social leaders and poor people and recognize the autonomy of indigenous peoples. Therefore, the more general link between free trade and human rights violations became a simple matter of indicating that democratic countries should not engage in business with an undemocratic government that systematically violated human rights—in particular political rights—as was the case with the Mexican government. If such violations were committed, democratic countries were obliged to force violators to improve their human rights performance.

In keeping with this view, during the international forum, Public Opinion and Negotiation of the Free Trade Agreement: Citizen Alternatives, held in Zacatecas, Mexico, October 25–27, 1991, a human rights agenda for the anti-free trade struggle was drawn up and this included two types of demands. First, the signature of all UN human rights instruments by the parties involved. This was the beginning of a trend developed over the following years to incorporate international human rights discourse in the local construction of rights.[1] Second, there were the so-called traditional abuses, which were linked to the political repression of social and political leaders, police abuse in civil contexts, and military abuse in antidrug trafficking operations. No free trade-related abuses of economic and social rights were included in the agenda (Red Mexicana de Acción Frente al Libre Comercio 1991c).

Some human rights NGOs did try to establish a link between free trade and such human rights violations as the repression of strikes organized by independent unions and the exploitation of workers in sweatshops by preparing socioeconomic analyses of employment, agriculture, the environment, and the situation of indigenous people. However, once again this was a matter of personal initiative. In more general terms Mexican NGOs only supported the predominantly U.S. and Canadian demands for the inclusion of labor rights and environmental protection, demands that resulted in parallel labor and environment agreements totally lacking a human rights perspective (Red Mexicana de Acción Frente al Libre Comercio 1991c).

The focus on CPRs to the detriment to socioeconomic issues, especially free trade, did not change, not even after the uprising of the Zapatista Army for National Liberation (EZLN) on January 1, 1994, the very day NAFTA came into effect. The Zapatistas demanded the dismissal of President Carlos Salinas, democratic elections, and the fulfillment of a series of basic social needs (work, land, housing, food, health, and education) denied to indigenous people due to the discriminatory policies of successive governments in power since after the 1910 Revolution.[2] These were clearly issues related to a socioeconomic rights agenda, but neither these issues nor human rights NGOs were taken seriously by the government as its response simply made violations of CPRs more evident.

The Zapatistas identified a lack of democracy as the root cause of their problems and those of the country in general, making it clear they were immersed in the hegemonic project for transition to democracy. Similarly, human rights NGOs considered the Zapatista demands to be legitimate and related to massive violations of ESCRs. However, they focused their efforts on simultaneously trying to prevent further repression and investigating violations against Zapatistas.[3] During the first months of the conflict, human rights NGOs denounced issues coherent with the civil rights agenda supported thus far: arbitrary detentions, house break-ins, intimidations and threats, torture, forced disappearances, killings of civilians in unclear circumstances, extra-judicial executions, and the de facto suspension of civil liberties in the conflict zone. Over the next few years, militarization and the governmental sponsorship of paramilitary forces increased as did violations of the CPRs of people living in the conflict zone and of human rights defenders themselves (Centro de Derechos Humanos "Fray Francisco de Vitoria" 1994).[4]

Although the focus was on civil and political rights, the Zapatista uprising drew attention to the terrible living conditions of indigenous people and their exclusion from NAFTA, thereby forcing human rights activists to take socioeconomic issues into account, albeit indirectly. The Zapatista uprising obviously reminded activists of the need to take action concerning economic and social rights because this action served as a constant reminder of the circumstances leading up to the uprising itself, including the issue of free trade. Nevertheless, no subsequent action was taken, apart from the appearance of articles in certain magazines published by these human rights organizations (Cruz Ramón 1994). Since NGOs had addressed indigenous peoples' cultural rights and the problem of structural discrimination from the late 1980s, they therefore addressed the socioeconomic issues related to indigenous peoples from a cultural rather than a socioeconomic perspective.[5] This was evident in their lobbying of the International Labor Organization's (ILO) Covenant 169 on Indigenous Rights for the San Andrés Accords.[6] The cultural approach to indigenous people's economic rights meant once again taking up an old interest that NGOs had in culture and indigenous people. This interest in indigenous peoples' rights declined in the period 1991 to 1993, although there was a brief revival in 1992 as events were organized throughout the hemisphere to commemorate 500 years of resistance to Spanish colonization. However, this revival of interest did not lead to the long-term inclusion of ESCRs.

The link between socioeconomic issues and free trade was also absent from subsequent articulations against free trade. Such was the case with a group established for the promotion of citizen participation in the negotiations of the Agreement on Economic Partnership, Political Co-ordination and Co-operation between the Mexican Government and the European Union (Global Agreement), headed by RMALC. This articulation was set up shortly after negotiations for the agreement started in May 1996. This group advanced political-democratic objectives rather than ESCR issues related to free trade due to the general political environment and the specific circumstances encouraging activists to articulate. During a round of negotiations in October, the Mexican government staged a walkout as the EU insisted on the inclusion of a democratic clause establishing respect for the principles of the UDHR and the unilateral termination of the commercial agreement if the EU considered that its counterpart was involved in the massive violation of human rights. At that time the government's civil rights record was extremely poor due to the militarization of Chiapas and because it had tried to prevent EU sponsorship of NGOs for peace activities and electoral observation. To justify its opposition to the democratic clause, the Mexican government argued that such a clause was not directed toward the mutual commitment to democracy and human rights, and to the principle of nonintervention and respect for self-determination, but to unilateral measures (Margier 1997).

By mid-1997 the government's virulent opposition to the democratic clause, which in fact was included in all the EU's commercial agreements concerning political coordination and cooperation, had developed into a scandal (Margier 1997). Human rights NGOs then saw an opportunity to pressure the government into withdrawing the Army from Chiapas and ending the persecution of human rights defenders. Activists concluded that, given the fact that the most heated point of negotiations was the democratic clause, "we must center our strategy around it" (Casasbuenas 1997). Therefore they agreed to apply pressure to make it a condition for signing the accord, thereby pushing the government to advance the civil and political rights agenda of the time. Because of this strategy, only general references were made to economic and social rights. However, pressure based on political democratic demands was no longer possible after 2000 when the first clean elections were held. The direct result of this electoral process was a prolonged delay on the part of NGOs to relaunch the campaign, as will be examined in chapter six.

To sum up, during the first half of the 1990s, human rights were subordinated to transition to democracy and neither the Zapatista uprising nor advocacy activities against free trade managed to draw attention to ESCRs. However, democracy ceased to articulate social agents as its narrow national definition—clean elections—was accomplished, as discussed in the next section.

The Relaxation of the Democratic Agenda: From Crisis to the Inevitability of Socioeconomic Rights

Democracy no longer formed the axis of human rights discourse when democracy, defined merely as clean elections, was accomplished as a goal. Relaxation of the electoral agenda began in 1997 when the leftist PRD won the first mayoral election held in Mexico City. Before this the president had assumed responsibility for appointing the mayor, a practice that had lasted for 50 years. In 1997, there was no electoral fraud in the country's capital and leftist leader Cuauhtémoc Cárdenas was recognized as the city's new mayor. This convinced NGOs that in the year 2000 electoral history would be made. And it certainly was: the candidate of the PAN, Vicente Fox, became the first president from a party other than the PRI since the foundation of the PRI in 1929. With the victory of Fox in 2000, the electoral agenda became almost irrelevant. For human rights NGOs the change of party in the presidential office not only made the hegemonic project of transition to democracy an outdated cause but also changed the rules of the game in the NGO-government relationship.

This was because Vicente Fox established a deceptive human rights policy. While Fox responded positively to the demands informing the 1990s human rights agenda, at the same time he enforced policies that worsened socioeconomic conditions. On the one hand, he began an aggressive international campaign to improve the Mexican state's record on human rights by naming CMDPDH founder Mariclaire Acosta as Mexico's "human rights ambassador" (a position that he was never able to justify and eventually had to abolish). He then signed UN human rights conventions, admitted the jurisdiction of Inter-American human rights bodies, invited UN special rapporteurs[7] and released the so-called prisoners of conscience whose "paradigmatic cases" had been litigated by national NGOs for years.[8] As for the human rights record itself, NGOs gave him a chance to show political will to improve it and the situation did improve slightly: "violations continued to occur, but not with the intensity and magnitude that we registered between 1994 and 1998" (García Alba et al. 2004). On the other hand, the new rightist government showed no signs of changing neoliberal policies. In fact, Fox reinforced them by placing businessmen and businesswomen in such posts as the Labor Secretariat, refusing to renegotiate the terms of free trade agreements and favoring corporations and major national businesses.

This contradictory situation was an indicator that the power struggle had moved from the political to the socioeconomic field and further delay in dealing with economic and social rights was no longer viable. NGOs knew that they had to start treating socioeconomic issues as human rights issues rather than as symptoms of a failure to respect CPRs. However, they did not have a clear idea of how to do this, lacking sufficient expertise in economics, political economy, and social policy to construct an agenda based on the new issues. In addition, they also found it difficult to establish priorities as they followed traditional patterns marked by the objectives of transition to democracy—the "first generation" of rights had to be fulfilled first. The scope of socioeconomic issues was very broad and it was difficult to tell which issues were "urgent" for the protection of physical integrity since the observation of elections was fundamental to the project of transition to democracy.

As a consequence, human rights NGOs entered into crisis. Since they could not find their place in the political panorama of post-2000-election Mexico, between 2000 and 2002 they reached an impasse. During this time they concentrated on familiar terrain, that is, on CPRs. A number of them concentrated all their efforts on discussion of the indigenous rights bill[9] and on taking advantage of the new president's attitude toward international human rights policy, such as shaping the agenda of the technical cooperation agreement signed between the UN and Mexico in 2000.[10] Electoral rights were completely abandoned and this was a bad move, according to Edgar Cortez, who believes that transition to democracy has yet to be achieved.

The NGOs needed time to find their niche and develop expertise within the vast area of social and economic policy. Therefore it was not until 2002–2003 that human rights NGOs began to find their place in post-2000 Mexico, addressing "traditional" issues from a more structural perspective, for example, reform of the judicial system and law and order policy. They also tried to tackle poverty and neoliberal economic policy. Some organizations took advantage of the opportunities presented by international human rights discourse and expanded their work in the field of minority rights, especially in the field of discrimination.[11]

Others found their niche in the area of social policy, which became an issue of human rights discourse because of two factors. First, NGOs dedicated to electoral rights in the 1990s wanted to broaden democracy discourse. The NGO networks that fought for electoral democracy, particularly the Convergencia and the MCD changed their strategy after the 1997 elections when they realized that electoral democracy was becoming a reality. They began to advance the idea that the political-electoral dimension was necessary, but not sufficient in itself, to achieve democracy and needed to be complemented with economic and social democracy. Therefore they decided on a human rights approach to social policy as a way of moving the democracy project toward "consolidation."

Convergencia stated that "[while] In Mexico there has been a movement toward electoral democracy, the policies that continue to be applied in the economic and social spheres have excluded broad sectors of the population from the social benefits, this has affected women and infants in particular, making the progress of Human Rights, among other things, impossible and increasing the number of people in situations of poverty and extreme poverty" (Convergencia de Organismos Civiles por la Democracia 2005). It also claimed that: "... diverse Mexican non-governmental organizations committed to the promotion of development and democracy have been incorporating a Human Rights focus in their efforts, as we are convinced that Human Rights conceived integrally constitute an axiological framework of specific norms for the construction, on the one hand, of policies to combat poverty, and on the other, of processes of social participation and accountability that guarantee democratic advances (Convergencia de Organismos Civiles por la Democracia 2005). Therefore they launched an ESCR program in 2001 (Canto 2004). In addition, the Academia had claimed in 1997 that "a country's degree of democratic development can be measured by the degree of human rights observance exercised by the government as well as society" (González 1997:5).

Consequently, the Mexican Academy of Human Rights (popularly known as Academia) started to expand its work in this area, creating in 1998 a department dealing with social rights aimed at encouraging the promotion of these rights, especially the rights of indigenous peoples, women and migrants, labor and union rights, and the right to a clean environment. Second, there was a trend toward including the social development agenda as a consequence of international summits such as the International Conference on Population and Development, held in Cairo, 1994; the World Summit on Social Development, Copenhagen, 1995; and the Fourth World Summit on Women, Beijing, 1995.

Finally, a limited number of human rights NGOs moved into a completely new field of human rights activity that was eventually linked to the socioeconomic aspects of free trade: international economic policy. Two issues demonstrated the need to become involved in this area. First, the financial crises occurring between 1994 and 1997 in Asia and Latin America—including Mexico—which revealed the vulnerability of individuals and human groups vis-à-vis unregulated trade and direct and portfolio foreign investment. Second, the consequences of the unfair terms of NAFTA during the first three years of enforcement were systematized by the RMALC. These included increasingly lower wages; bankruptcies of small and medium companies because corporations were not required to buy from Mexican producers; and the crisis of Mexican agriculture due to a lack of support from the government and direct competition with agricultural corporations (Red Mexicana de Acción Frente al Libre Comercio 1997). These events brought changes to the way free trade had been dealt with, because up to that point free trade had mainly been seen as an opportunity to address the transition to democracy agenda. This time, in the light of the influence of the global political economy at the local level, free trade was to become a direct issue of human rights discourse, but not without a struggle.

The "Miguel Agustín Pro Juárez" Human Rights Center (Prodh Center) followed up its experience lobbying negotiations for a free trade agreement with the EU in order to assess the impact of free trade and the global political economy on economic rights. The Prodh rejoined a small working team—formed by the RMALC and Equipo Pueblo—lobbying the inclusion of the "democratic clause," which this time was aimed at lobbying the EU and the Mexican government for the inclusion of legal mechanisms for making it "effective." Making it effective now meant changing traditional interpretations. For a long time NGO interpretations of the democratic clause mimicked governmental interpretations that saw the clause in a negative way, that is, as the need to terminate an agreement or to impose sanctions on the party that seriously violates human rights—usually the third party. This interpretation served the broader objectives of the democracy project that were to pressure the Mexican government into tackling massive rights violations in Chiapas and to create more spaces for citizen participation and government accountability.

This time, however, the group of NGOs advanced the idea that human rights were a fundamental aspect of trade and investment relations themselves. They argued that free trade relations must promote and respect human rights, including state and corporate respect for, and protection of, economic and social rights, as well as state respect for the right to participate in trade policy and decision-making processes. In other words, they were making free trade and free trade negotiations central issues of human rights discourse, not only in terms of ESCRs but also in terms of CPRs serving the cause of participation in economic decision-making.

The new interpretation, however, was not entirely welcomed either by the human rights NGO community in Mexico or its counterpart in Europe where international NGOs such as the Brussels-based International Federation of Human Rights (IFHR) wanted the Global Agreement to legally enforce the full range of rights, whether they were related to trade practices or not—from torture in local prisons to education budget shortages. The Prodh accused its European colleagues of advancing an old-fashioned human rights strategy that, despite having worked throughout the 1990s in the struggle for democracy, was now outdated for the purposes of constructing a new agenda more suited to tackling globalization-related issues—including power relations between states. The Prodh had to seek wider support from Mexican human rights NGOs but found resistance there as well. While the new view was supported by organizations of the Red TDT, some organizations affiliated to the IFHR supported the old view.[12] In the end, the Prodh had to compromise and accept observation of civil and political rights but did manage to include free trade practices—investment, privatization, corporate activity, and so on—as central objects of their economic and social rights demands. While the Prodh managed to make free trade an issue of human rights discourse, resistance to change continued to be a problem, as will be discussed in chapter six.

To sum up, the exhaustion of democratic discourse forced human rights NGOs to broaden the scope of human rights discourse allowing in turn for the inclusion of human rights issues linked to free trade policy.

Articulation against Free Trade: From Democratic to Human Rights Struggles

The widening of the scope of human rights discourse as a consequence of the exhaustion of transition to democracy discourse within the human rights movement was not the only issue allowing human rights to become hegemonic in anti-free trade struggles. Transition to democracy became exhausted within this latter movement too, allowing for new discourses to develop and articulate.

The link between free trade and transition to democracy began in the late 1980s. In 1988, in the introduction to the classic book *Primer Informe sobre la Democracia* (First Report on Democracy), Pablo González Casanova stated that the increasing deterioration of the population's living standards was caused by neoliberalism. This, he said, would only change if a government controlled by the people replaced the PRI, a rather difficult objective in his opinion due to the lack of democratic conditions in the country at the time (González Casanova 1989).

The idea of procedural democracy as the only possible solution to increasing economic liberalization and the loss of economic sovereignty became central to the struggle against free trade in its initial stages, which commenced more formally in 1991 with the setting up of the RMALC on April 11 of that year. This network brought together organizations that had started to discuss economic integration in 1990, shortly after the Mexican government launched negotiations with its Canadian and American counterparts for the establishment of NAFTA. However, at that moment, Mexico's foreign debt, rather than its lack of democracy, was the major concern for activists analyzing the country's economic policy (Arroyo interview 2004). This is evident in documents from the first binational meeting between Mexico and Canada that was held from October 5–7, 1990, in Mexico City. However, the use of democracy in terms of transition to democracy was almost immediate and lasted throughout the NAFTA negotiation period. This situation is described in the following way by Arroyo: "The axis established by the RMALC during the initial stages, while negotiations were under way, was heavily economic. It was a critique of the economic model, the critique of free trade theory. The proposals of the initial stage were framed in a very economic discourse and in a political discourse of sovereignty and democracy" (Arroyo 2004). Furthermore, the RMALC was not set up "in opposition to the idea of negotiating a free trade agreement with the United States and Canada, but in the search and struggle for an alternative development project to neoliberalism and within the struggle for transition to democracy" (Arroyo and Monroy 1996:11).

The project to create the network established that the affiliates of RMALC were those willing to take joint action against the government's free trade agenda and who shared common objectives and a common platform. The founding members were mostly trade unions, together with a handful of civil and social organizations, research centers, and universities. Much of the platform referred to Mexico's need for transition to democracy and demanded "wide and democratic" participation by citizens and Congress in discussions related to the negotiations and respect for human rights, including the right to strike and the right to association. It openly stipulated the "modification of electoral legislation and the adoption of a political agreement guaranteeing respect for voting and the true autonomy of federal powers" (Red Mexicana de Acción Frente al Libre Comercio 1991a).

The RMALC also pursued the democratic objective of citizen participation in decision-making related to the signature of NAFTA, in which they wanted to include compensatory policies aimed at tackling the possible consequences of the progressive elimination of tariffs between countries displaying significant economic asymmetries (Red Mexicana de Acción Frente al Libre Comercio 1991a, 1994b). Carlos Heredia stated in May 1991 that: "The relationship between the struggle for democratization and the debate about free trade is direct and very important: what used to be a space reserved for political parties and organizations has been transformed into a space where proposals generated by society are also discussed" (Heredia 1991). Respect for human rights was also central in order to define the terms of the right to association and unionism.

However, citizen participation together with human rights became secondary objectives when the struggle against free trade became articulated with the discourse of transition to democracy interpreted by activists simply as clean and free elections. This occurred during the San Luis Potosi state elections and expressed itself during the meeting, Public Opinion and Free Trade Agreement Negotiations: Citizen Alternatives, a forum bringing together organizations and unions from the three countries in Zacatecas, Mexico, from October 25–27, 1991.

During the San Luis state elections, held on August 18, 1991, and simultaneous to a federal by-election, political activist Salvador Nava was the joint candidate of all local opposition parties for state governor—notably the leftist PRD and the rightist PAN. Observers documented manipulation not only of the voting list and votes, but also of the use of public funds and the mass media in support of the PRI. Hundreds of local people, not only party members, demonstrated in the streets "in defense of the vote." Women were particularly active in the process that culminated in the governor's resignation and the appointment of a new governor by the local Congress.[13] The demand for free and clean elections in order to achieve transition to democracy became generalized throughout the country after this and as a result, transition to democracy—defined simply in terms of free and clean elections—became an empty signifier, articulating a wide variety of social agents gathered at the Zacatecas Forum who did not necessarily design a trade agenda but did see free trade as a threat to their own interests. In their opinion, this threat could only be defused through the holding of clean and free elections.

The stated objective of the Zacatecas Forum was the discussion of issues that should be included in a social agenda vis-à-vis free trade: development; sovereignty and debt; labor rights, social rights, and health; the environment, urban development, and agriculture; democracy, human rights, and women; and education, culture, and ethnicity. Unlike previous meetings, where most participants were union members, the Zacatecas meeting included not only union members but also representatives of the mass media, NGO activists, research centers, universities, and opposition political parties, all of which managed to advance their own agendas in the promotion of transition to democracy and opposition to the unfair terms of trade

(Red Mexicana de Acción Frente al Libre Comercio 1991c). The fact that the RMALC had constructed the struggle for fair trade within the struggle for transition to democracy led to great diversity within the Mexican delegation at the Zacatecas meeting. This was because the democracy project—clean elections, respect for human rights, and the construction of civic awareness—managed to bring together people who otherwise found trade a strictly economic issue, notably human rights NGOs and women's groups who were very active in observing the electoral process and denouncing fraud.

The August 18 elections served as a systematic reference for the Mexican delegation to the Zacatecas meeting and it constructed transition to democracy as a condition for the signing of NAFTA. This was based on two arguments. First, that the Canadian and U.S. governments should not sign trade agreements with an undemocratic country, that is, a government that lacks the support of its own people and fails to provide information and consult social sectors. Second, that the Mexican government was liberalizing economics while refusing to liberalize politics.[14] This twofold argument was identified by Mexican intellectual Jorge Castañeda, who became one of the major exponents of transition to democracy theory in the Mexican case. In Zacatecas he posed the question as to whether there should in fact exist political and human rights conditionality for the signature of NAFTA. His own answer was positive and was based on three interrelated factors: the Mexican transition to democracy was "stagnant"; external factors in democratic transitions were "decisive"; and free trade did not automatically lead to democracy (Red Mexicana de Acción Frente al Libre Comercio 1991b). He said:

> [W]e have a blocked transition to democracy in Mexico. It does not advance. Few people believe that elections have represented a step forward. Results in at least half of the three hundred electoral districts have been challenged, which demonstrates that the current electoral system is not working (Red Mexicana de Acción Frente al Libre Comercio 1991b).[15]

However, by the time NAFTA negotiations came to a close in August 1992, emphasis had shifted from transition to democracy to citizen participation. This was because transition to democracy had been built on a minimum basis (clean elections), and the political moment was no longer defined by this. Once NAFTA was signed and approved by the Congresses of the three countries, the idea that the Mexican government had failed to consult citizens and provide information in the discussions of the finally approved draft of NAFTA meant that the emphasis on "transition" moved to citizen participation and consultation. This shift can be observed in the following quote taken from a speech made by union activist Manuel García Urrutia, from Authentic Labor Front (FAT, the Spanish acronym for Frente Auténtico del Trabajo):

> ...from the beginning of free trade agreement negotiations, in Mexico the social movement grouped around the RMALC has questioned the arbitrary origin of the government's decision by virtue of the fact that this strategy does not form part of any plan and that in the months previous to the announcement concerning the intention to sign a free trade agreement with the United States and Canada this possibility was denied. Recently, the communication of appropriate information to the public concerning the free trade agreement, the goals of the negotiation and their scope, has been proposed. Similarly, the lack of any real participation by the productive sectors has been noted along with the need to change the dynamics of negotiations so that sectors can directly accede in the defense of their interests (Red Mexicana de Acción Frente al Libre Comercio 1992).

Citizen participation and consultation had always interested the RMALC, but as part of transition to democracy. However, since transition to democracy became synonymous with clean elections, it had ceased to be central. After the agreement was approved, participation and consultation became central ideas separated from democracy, which was then seen as a separate goal and conceived exclusively in terms of free and clean elections. In discussion of the parallel accords, the right to consultation and the right to information became the focus. In March 1993, the RMALC presented negotiators with a proposal for approaching labor, environmental, and human rights (which in fact dealt with the civil rights of Mexican migrants to the United States); in each of the three cases the common claim was the establishment of mechanisms for citizen participation (Red Mexicana de Acción Frente al Libre Comercio 1993a, 1993b).

In July 1994, environmentalists discussing a proposal for a parallel citizen commission to the environmental committee of the NAFTA environment accord stated in a meeting that citizen participation:

> ...has perhaps been the most important aspect of agreement and action for environmentalists linked to the free trade agreement. Insistence on the right to information, the participation of social groups and organizations in both the negotiation process and decision making has been a central aspect of our proposals (Red Mexicana de Acción Frente al Libre Comercio 1994a).

These ideas were, however, less connected to transition to democracy and more related to the idea of sustainable development as constructed in the Rio Declaration, the product of discussions at the Earth Summit of June 1992.[16] Nevertheless, the link between democracy and free trade was again reinforced in 1994 with the Zapatista uprising. With this event there was a revindication of indigenous identity in opposition to NAFTA and a call for democracy, but understood in a broader sense than that previously advanced with its focus on procedural democracy. Zapatista leader *Subcomandante* Marcos argued that "NAFTA is a death sentence for the indigenous people of Mexico who are considered superfluous by the administration of Carlos Salinas."[17] The Zapatistas had a major impact on the understanding of democracy, which to that point had been defined in terms of transition to democracy theory. They redefined the concept of democracy as the participation of citizens in a project of nation building rather than that of voting and nothing more (Stephen 1995).

For the EZLN's spokesperson and military commander *Subcomandante* Marcos, the Zapatista's struggle for democracy could not be limited to the achievement of clean, transparent, and fair elections. The Zapatistas proposed a democracy based on the idea of "command-obedience," that is, a relationship between those who govern and those who are governed in which people participate as political actors, making proposals and ensuring that those who govern fulfill the needs of citizens: "In the new relationship that we are proposing, representative democracy would be more balanced. It would enrich itself with direct democracy, with the continual participation of citizens, not only as electors or as consumers of electoral proposals, but also as political actors" (Durán de Huerta 1999).[18]

However, while the Zapatistas became protagonists of the anti-free trade struggle and opened up the limited democratic discourse constructed by Mexican civil society, democracy ceased to articulate social gents opposing free trade for two reasons. First, the Zapatistas, who received support from all over the world, became the catalyst for national and international dissent not only against free trade, but also against economic globalization in general and in favor of the promotion of democracy, justice, and freedom. In January 1996, they called the First Inter-Continental Meeting for Humanity and against Neoliberalism, which took place from July 27–August 3, 1996 in La Realidad, Chiapas (Ejército Zapatista de Liberación Nacional 1996). Three thousand people from over 43 countries attended the meeting and discussed alternatives to neoliberal economics. The meeting had a sequel in the summer of 1997 in Germany. These meetings served as the precursor and inspiration for subsequent meetings of global movements.[19]

Second, democracy discourse had been narrowed to such an extent that it was comprised of little more than electoral issues and citizen participation in the national context. In 1994 the PRI again won federal elections and the democratic cause remained at the top of the social agenda, including that of the movement for fair trade. However, after 1997, when the leftist PRD won local elections in Mexico City, the democratic cause lost hegemony in the anti-free trade struggle. This was reinforced in 2000 when Fox won the presidential election. Whether this represented the cherished transition to democracy is the subject of debate, because while some believe there was no transition but simply a change of party in the presidential office, others argue that transition was completed and what we are now seeing is the consolidation of democracy. The important issue here, however, is that once transition to democracy, understood as clean elections, was completed in 2000, electoral fraud ceased to form part of social agendas and consequently democracy ceased to articulate social agents. This does not mean that democracy disappeared from their agendas, but it does mean that democracy has finally become a more complex concept and forms part of broader articulations using other discourses, such as human rights.

One such articulation is the Mexican branch of the Hemispheric Social Alliance (HAS), which lobbies an alternative trade model to that of the FTAA, which will be discussed in detail in chapter six. Social agents are articulating using human rights discourse, as the following quote from the Second Declaration of the People's Summit shows:

> ...The FTAA project is a statute of laws and liberties for investors that establishes the supremacy of capital over labor, transforming life and the world into commodities, denying human rights, sabotaging democracy and undermining State sovereignty.
>
> We reject this project of trade and investment liberalization, of deregulation and privatization. We oppose a racist, sexist, unjust and environmentally destructive neoliberal project.
>
> We propose the construction of new means of continental integration based on democracy, equality, solidarity, respect for the environment and human rights.
>
> We want to prioritize human rights and collectives as they are defined in international treaties governing trade agreements. These rights should be respected without distinction or exclusion based on gender, sexual

orientation, age, ethnicity, nationality, religion, political convictions or economic conditions.[20]

This quote reveals that while democracy informs the agenda, it is human rights discourse that articulates agents. Democracy is therefore no longer seen as a means to achieve social justice and economic sovereignty because human rights principles, such as the absence of discrimination and human dignity, now form the core of any trade agreement.

The Limitations of the Human Rights Approach to Socioeconomic Issues: Assessing the Implications for Free Trade

The exhaustion of transition to democracy discourse in both the human rights and the anti-free trade movements, together with the inclusion of socioeconomic issues in human rights discourse, suggest increasing potentiality for human rights discourse to articulate social organizations and human rights NGOs in a single movement against free trade. Nevertheless, the limitations of the approach to ESCRs adopted by human rights NGOs puts shift into perspective.

One recent case helped to impress upon NGOs the shortcomings of their approach and the strategies designed to deal with socioeconomic issues: the preparation of a UN diagnosis of the human rights situation in Mexico, which included CPRs and ESCRs; the rights of women, indigenous peoples, and vulnerable groups; discrimination; and general aspects of all types of rights. The diagnostic process, which lasted a year, highlighted the limitations of NGOs in terms of methodology, expertise, and knowledge in the field of economic and social rights. During the presentation of the Vitoria Center's own report on ESCRs, father Miguel Concha stated that the idea of preparing their report came in response to the poor quality of some of the information provided in the UN diagnosis. In the opinion of activists, the human rights approach to economic and social issues still does not function properly, or at least falls short of the standards employed in their approach to more legalistic rights like CPRs.

Reflecting on the history of human rights in Mexico, the problem seems to be that NGOs assume that social and economic problems can become issues of human rights discourse through the application of traditional practices: the construction of legally defendable cases and the systematization of information, a strategy that separates them from other agents, as I shall demonstrate in the following chapter. Because ESCRs are not rights that protect people from the state but from the terms of socioeconomic arrangements, they cannot be dealt with in the same way as CPRs—preparing figures, lobbying reports at the international level, constructing paradigmatic cases. This is especially true in the case of economic rights related to free trade because shifting the human rights struggle to the field of the global political economy means renegotiating the terms of free trade. In turn, this means joining other subjects already disputing power in other discourses. Free trade is already an issue in other discourses that the social agents directly involved—farmers, workers, indigenous people, women, and so on—identify with in order to carry out collective action. What this indicates is that human rights NGOs have only recently joined a discursive struggle that has been underway for some time.

Human rights NGOs have adopted a heavily legalistic approach to human rights that excludes other type of organizations handling ESCRs, organizations that come from a different array of disciplines and possess expert knowledge concerning the discourses dealing with violations. While human rights could serve as a discourse that articulates a broader struggle against free trade, human rights NGOs seem unwilling to abandon legal approaches even though, as this genealogy shows, human rights work in Mexico was possible in the early years without legal defense—it was argued in chapter two that in the late 1980s, human rights NGOs encouraged organization at the grassroots levels as a principal strategy because socioeconomic conflict provided the context for major violations.

With this failure to try other strategies, human rights NGOs are effectively placing obstacles in the path of the political potentiality of human rights discourse in the free trade struggle because they are failing to form alliances with other social actors already working in other discourses. While forming alliances with development NGOs in their approach to social and economic rights linked to welfare services proved easy because development NGOs are still NGOs and employ similar practices (lobbying, preparation of reports), forming alliances with grassroots activists is not so easy because their strategies are neither legalistic nor based on case-litigation and do not necessarily include lobbying. Their strategies are mainly political.

Human rights NGOs have yet to realize that human rights discourse has a political dimension and that this dimension has not been recognized due to their continuing focus on addressing specific cases of violations of individual rights. They realize that social agents see human rights as a strong political tool because it can help them construct legitimate arguments vis-à-vis the state—demanding entitlements rather than privileges or favors—and could mark a new direction for policymaking. This becomes evident given the waning of other political discourses used for mobilization, especially transition to democracy. Some activists realize the need to work with these organizations and to transfer tools to them. Most national NGOs are aware of the increasing need to address these issues and they have attempted to encourage hegemonic relationships with social movements and organizations.

Nevertheless, recent attempts are simply not working. One example is the Advocacy Group for the National Unity against Neoliberlism (Popularly known as Promotora, which stands for Promotora de la Unidad Nacional contra el Neoliberalismo), an NGO articulation that has produced a series of public statements referring to globalization and human rights (Promotora de la Unidad Nacional contra el Neoliberalismo 2002). Although social agents and unions have subscribed to them, their impact on discourse is debatable. For instance, no human rights reference whatsoever was made during the March against Structural Reforms (electricity privatization and value-added tax on medicines and foodstuffs), called by independent unions, farmer organizations, and the Promotora on November 27, 2003. In addition, while the farmers network Agriculture established some contact with the CMDPDH and the Prodh Center when it was first launched, the relationship remained superficial and could not develop.

Hegemonic relationships between human rights and social movements and organizations are neither deep nor common, and human rights NGOs are aware of this. They know that movements need to have a deeper understanding of human rights discourse. Some of them believe that in order to establish successful relationships, mutual understanding of their strategies is necessary. More importantly, it is necessary to respect their political identities, that is, to realize that they are social movements modifying their identities in the wider articulation but without abandoning such identities in order to become "human rights defenders." However, acknowledgment is not followed by action, which reduces the potentiality of human rights discourse in the struggle against free trade because it is evident that while human rights NGOs focus on justiciability, other agents focus on the political impact of the idea of state duty.

Given the differences between social agents, human rights possess an uneven potentiality for collective action. The extent to which this occurs and the forms it takes will be the subject of the following chapters.

Conclusion

While transition to democracy opened the doors for human rights struggles on various fronts, it limited its scope to civil and political rights as it was serving general objectives. Because of this, free trade offered an opportunity to forward democratic demands. This can be demonstrated by the fact that once clean elections had been held electoral fraud ceased to form part of the social agenda and therefore failed to articulate them. Consequently, human rights finally expanded into socioeconomic fields and made free trade a human rights issue. The potentiality of human rights discourse is, however, uneven, as NGOs are unwilling to question their own strategies. Nevertheless, democracy did manage to establish the basis for the development of human rights as such.

Part II

Introduction

Subjective as well as structural issues have allowed for human rights to constitute a discourse dealing not only with issues of civil and political rights, but also with problems related to economic, social, and cultural rights. However, this human rights discourse has its limits. Part II of this book aims to establish how human rights discourse is employed and how limitations are discursively constructed. It accordingly establishes how articulation, subject positions, and hegemonic projects are constructed using human rights as an empty signifier.

As mentioned in the Introduction, this will be achieved using insights from Laclau's discourse theoretical framework (Laclau 1990, 1994, 2005, 2006, Laclau and Mouffe 2001), and Wetherell and Potter's notion of interpretative repertoires (Wetherell and Potter 1992). In the following three chapters I shall examine the kinds of human rights interpretative repertoires social agents use to construct their views of free trade, subject positions, and common agendas when they articulate using human rights as an empty signifier. Interpretative repertoires are the lexicons of terms that have been provided by history and brought into discursive practices; they assume the status of facts and are taken for granted as true or accurate descriptions of the world (Neigel Edley, in Wetherell and Taylor, 2001:190).

When fixing meaning in hegemonic articulation, human rights values, principles, themes, instruments, and language assign a human rights interpretation to the different views and activities that construct alliances and common agendas. In the hegemonic articulation framework these views and activities are to be found in such categories as hegemonic projects, subject positions, and hegemonic articulation. For this reason, in discursive practices, these categories could be examined through the analysis of three issues: construction of free trade according to human rights standards (hegemonic projects); terms in which social agents construct their identities according to human rights values and practices (subject positions); and construction of particularities and specific interests within a human rights agenda (i.e., how particularity expresses itself in a human rights hegemonic articulation).

In addition to analyzing interpretative repertoires, I shall also look at nodal points, which refer to the specific rights that agents use when employing human rights as an empty signifier.[1] For example, a nodal point derived from using human rights as an empty signifier against free trade could be the "right to food." This right defines such concepts as "security," "land," and "sustainability" in terms of human rights treaties, jurisprudence, and rhetoric, which are based on ideas of human dignity, decent living standards, and cultural adequacy rather than on ideas of capital, efficiency, and profit, which are notions linked to the discourse of economic enactment. I shall analyze this by looking at how activists use human rights in conjunction with other discourses. I examine how different identities manage to identify with human rights and use them to articulate with others while also using different discourses such as environmentalism, food sovereignty, development, gender, unionism, and the like. For a summary of the above, refer table 1.

With the intention of establishing the factors that contribute, or do not contribute, to the political potential of human rights discourse, the analysis conducted in the following three chapters will rely on the empirical differences established between two types of social agents: social movement organizations (SMOs) and nongovernmental organizations (NGOs). The terms SMO and NGO are used here as descriptive denominations for organizations that represent

Table 1 Categories derived from the theory of hegemonic articulation used in the analysis of discursive practices

Category	Applied to
Empty signifier	A discourse articulating social subjects in the struggle against free trade.
Fixing meaning	The meaning that a particular nodal point or empty signifier gives to specific agendas or mobilization strategies.
Hegemonic articulation	The joint political activity of social subjects against free trade.
Hegemonic project	A view of social, economic, political, and cultural life that is defined by a particular empty signifier fixing meaning in hegemonic articulation
Nodal points	Specific human rights, the content of which fix meaning in the shared agendas and mobilization of subjects.
Subject positions	The position that a subject assumes vis-à-vis a given phenomenon according to the discourse they identify with.

Part II Introduction

overlapping phenomena in collective action against free trade. They serve the particular purposes of this analysis and should not be seen as an attempt to suggest yet another definition of civil society organizations since such differentiation is largely based on the general definitions found in the relevant literature and the specificities of Mexican organizations.

Generally, SMOs are seen as groups with a permanent organizational structure established by activists in order to sustain collective action. According to McAdam, they are at the heart of social movements: "Following the emergent phase of the movement, then, it is these SMOs and their efforts to shape the broader political environment which influence the overall pace and outcome of the struggle" (McAdam, McCarthy, and Zald 1996:13). Some scholars differentiate between NGOs and social movements on the specific grounds of their organizational characteristics, indicating that NGOs are more formal and institutional (Eschle and Stammers 2004, Kaldor 2003), or simply that social movements are wider in scope (Cohen and Arato 1992). Eschle and Stammers also argue that on occasions NGOs are not linked to social movements at all. In most cases, though, SMO is a term that has been widely adopted for use in empirical and theoretical studies of domestic and transnational social movements and some scholars use it interchangeably with the term NGO. For their part, NGOs are described in general terms as formal organizations either linked to, or independent from, SMOs. They are nonprofit, value-concern organizations focused on particular issues and are generally institutional and professional in nature. While some of them function as service providers, all of them are focused on advocacy and lobbying.[2]

In the specific case of the Mexican organizations studied here, SMOs and NGOs are therefore differentiated at the empirical level. First, NGOs are formed by value-concerned individuals and tend to carry out advocacy and lobbying work, whereas the SMOs analyzed here tend to use a mix of lobbying and mass mobilization strategies. Unless they maintain a close relationship with SMOs, the tendency of NGOs is neither to organize nor join mass mobilizations. Most of the time this does not occur, as shown by the work of Peter Houtzager in his comparative analysis of Mexico and Brazil. He claims that Mexican and Brazilian NGOs have developed very differently: while in Brazil "middle class organizations" (understood as NGOs in Mexico) work closely with "grassroots organizations" (SMOs), in Mexico middle class organizations do not work with grassroots organizations (Houtzager 2006).

Second, SMOs are organizations of people working to improve their own social, political, economic, or cultural conditions as a community vis-à-vis free trade, rather than working toward the promotion of a model governed by certain values or ideals, which is the main concern of NGO activists. SMO action is designed to achieve goals for their own members, while NGO action is intended to achieve certain values that would bring benefits for the SMOs they

Table 2 Differences between NGOs and SMOs

	NGOs		SMOs
Concerns	Interests: Issues, values		Interests: Group agenda
	Identity: Citizenship		Identity: Group identity
Strategies	**Human Rights NGOs:** Legal lobbying and advocacy	**NGOs:** Political lobbying and advocacy	Political lobbying and advocacy
	Case litigation	Mass mobilization only when required, established through links with SMOs	Mass mobilization
		Service provision (to SMOs)	
Links	Do not emerge directly from social movements	Do not emerge directly from social movements	Emerge directly from social movements
			SMOs
	NGOs	NGOs	NGOs
	SMOs (rarely)	SMOs (but not always)	Human rights NGOs (rarely)
Examples	• Prodh Centre • CMDPDH • Mexican League • Vitoria Centre	• RMALC[a] • FIAN-Mexico • Equipo Pueblo • MCD • AMAP	• GyE • MF • FAT • SME • FDC • ANEC

Note:
[a] RMALC is a *sui generis* case. It could be said to be an articulation itself as individual NGO and SMO members articulate with "free trade action." However, RMALC's coordinating committee possesses the characteristics of an NGO as it is constituted by middle-class and professional members (NGO and SMO members are not represented on the committee; staff are appointed in terms of their expertise), is concerned with issues and values and forges links with SMOs only when necessary. RMALC's activities never include mass mobilization, except in specific cases, such as demonstrations held in the context of the social forum or similar gatherings.

work with or for society in general. In this sense interests and identities are constructed differently. While SMO activists are concerned with their own interests and a reaffirmation of their specific group identity, NGOs are concerned with values and the reaffirmation of an identity that allows them to promote this principled agenda, that is, citizenship. The term SMO is consequently used to differentiate these organizations from NGOs, based on the use of mass mobilization and members' pursuit of their own interests. This difference defines the human rights discourse they mobilize and the strategies they use to forward their demands. For a summary of the differences between NGOs and SMOs, refer table 2.

Chapter 4

Constructing Free Trade Worldviews with Human Rights Discourse

Introduction

Although neoliberalism was the dominant discourse during the first stages of economic liberalization, more recently the stress has shifted to "free trade," which has become a discourse in its own right. The terms of free trade as established by neoliberals are based on a series of theories and principles that systematically erode state control over economic policy, social welfare, and the enforcement of labor and environmental law. Given that the core of human rights discourse is precisely state duty, and since this core has been modified in response to global issues, it provides SMOs and NGOs with a discursive platform they can use differently to construct a normative horizon of trade and therefore define their agendas. This chapter addresses how activists employ human rights in such a way, presenting first an overview of free trade theories and principles and how they establish the limits of state duty. Next, it shows how international human rights discourse has changed in order to address such issues. Finally, in the light of free trade impact on the state and the expansion of international human rights discourse, the chapter offers a discourse analysis of how Mexican activists construct worldviews using a human rights framework against free trade and how this view can impose limits on their strategies.

The Terms of Neoliberal Free Trade

Neoliberal free trade policy has been built on three mainstream free trade theories. First, the Theory of Absolute Advantage advanced by Adam Smith in his book *The Wealth of Nations* (1776). This theory strongly attacked mercantilist ideas of restrictions on imports and protection of domestic production, saying that countries must produce and export what they are best at producing cheaply and import what they cannot produce so efficiently. If other countries do the same, they all obtain gains. Second, the Theory of Comparative Advantage, published in 1817 by David Ricardo in *The Principles of Political Economy*, which according to Trebilcock and Howse established that "a country should specialize in producing and exporting goods in which its comparative advantage is greatest, or comparative advantage is smallest, and should import goods in which its comparative advantage is greatest" (Trebilcock and Howse 1999).

Third, the Factor Proportions Hypothesis, or Heckscher-Olin Theorem, which was named after the two Swedish economists who formulated it in the 1920s. This theory argues that "countries will tend to enjoy comparative advantages in producing goods that use their more abundant factors more intensively, and each country will end up exporting its abundant factor goods in exchange for imported goods that use its scarce factors more intensively" (Trebilcock and Howse 1999:5). According to these theories free trade is the best choice for nations, because it allows for specialization, efficient trade patterns, and increased welfare and consumer choice. Any barrier or restriction to trade is thus a distortion of markets because they create monopolies (Gilpin 2001, Román Morales 1992, Trebilcock and Howse 1999).

According to M. Friedman, free trade is important for both economic and political reasons. In the economic sphere, he claims, restrictions to trade (tariffs as protectionist measures) exploit the consumer: "The gains to some producers from tariffs and other restrictions are more offset by the loss to other producers and especially consumers in general. Free trade would not only promote our material welfare, it would also foster peace and harmony among nations and spur domestic competition" (Friedman and Friedman 1981:60). Politically, he says, liberalization promotes the cause of freedom while tariffs are a cause of friction among nations. Furthermore, through the principle of comparative advantage, every country wins and thus harmony is advanced (Friedman and Friedman 1981:61–76). In this analysis, however, differences of power arising from economic inequality between countries are not addressed or even questioned.

Based on these assumptions and building on the classical theories described above, neoliberal free trade today is characterized by three factors. First, it is characterized by blindness to national and exporter inequalities through the imposition of nondiscrimination and expropriation principles, and nonprotection of national economies through the prohibition of rules of origin and performance requirements. Second, simultaneous trade liberalization at the regional and the multilateral levels with WTO and free trade agreements such as the NAFTA. Finally, the centrality of corporations in trade policymaking that favors them through the principles and provisions referred to above, and which is enshrined in multilateral and regional agreements. These features are at the core of major social problems and therefore have become the target of social movements dedicated to influencing trade policy change. It is therefore important to study them closely.

Blindness to Inequality

Building on mainstream free trade theories, more contemporary theories were first established in the General Agreement on Tariffs and Trade (GATT) and later strengthened in the WTO and NAFTA. These include the so-called nondiscrimination principle, indirect expropriation practice, and the prohibition of measures for the protection of national economies. First, nondiscrimination, which is a central target in articulations such as those addressed in chapter six, is enhanced by the implementation of two provisions: the Most Favored Nation principle and the National Treatment principle. The first establishes that all advantages and benefits given to a trade partner should be extended to all other members of the agreement or union. The second establishes that foreign producers should have the same advantages as domestic producers, and that no prohibitions or special taxes or regulations should be imposed on them (Trebilcock and Howse 1999:27–29).

There are two temporal exceptions to the application of the nondiscrimination principle: the safeguard provision and the infant industries provision. On the one hand, the safeguard provision establishes that if any product is being imported into the territory of that member in such increased quantities or under such conditions as to cause or threaten serious injury to domestic producers, that country is entitled to suspend or modify obligations or concessions on a temporary basis (Trebilcock and Howse 1999:30). On the other hand, the protection of infant industries are those that, if protected from international competition, will become sufficiently strong and competitive to ensure survival when protection is eventually removed (Gilpin 2001:200).

Second, indirect expropriation, which is defined in broad terms and therefore allows corporations to claim compensation on the grounds of expropriation when governments prevent them from doing business according to regulatory frameworks established for the protection of health, the environment, labor, and so on. This precept radicalizes the traditional concept of "expropriation," in which one state may demand compensation from another for the expropriation of property for the public's benefit. Expropriation may take the form of government action, be it an environmental law or health measure, which prevents a corporation from obtaining earnings it would otherwise generate (Oloka-Onyango and Udagama 1999:15–16). This provision was taken from NAFTA, where it has led local governments to pay corporations sums of money in excess of their own budgetary resources (Bejarano González 2003).

Third, in addition to those principles disputed in commercial courts, investment agreements impose on states—states either accept them or they are imposed—two prohibitions that prevent them from regulating their economy: prohibitions on setting rules of origin and on demanding performance requirements. On the one hand, rules of origin are standards that require that imported and exported products in the region covered by the agreement be made with inputs produced there or in the signatory countries. On the other hand, performance requirements for foreign direct investment set forth a minimum level of cooperation with the host country. They include, among other things: giving preference to the contracting of local workers, guaranteeing a minimum level of domestic partnership, complying with the highest international standards regarding the environment and work, and ensuring the transfer of technology (Trebilcock and Howse 1999). Although this direct intervention for the protection of national interests is banned, recent trade theories are refuting the assumptions of the nondiscrimination principle in order to protect certain sectors outside the scope of the application of the safeguard provision and the protection of infant industries. For instance, the strategic trade theory establishes investment in human capital and technology in order to promote efficiency in trade (Gilpin 2001:200).

These principles and provisions are key to formulations of articulations against free trade because it is precisely the lack of state control that makes such discourses as human rights suitable for addressing these issues, as will be discussed later in the chapter.

Multilateral and Regional Liberalization

Trade liberalization includes the progressive elimination of tariff barriers on imports as well as direct and indirect non-tariff barriers (any government measure for the regulation—even for social and environmental purposes—of the volume, composition, or direction of trade). Direct restrictions include quotas on imports, restrictions on import quantities, support for exporters, customs delays, and the policies of governments buying from domestic producers. Indirect restrictions include health and safety measures, and labor and environmental regulations (Held et al. 1999:165). Both multilateral and regional legal protection for traders is marked by differences in the new international division of labor—poor countries manufacture cheap goods and the transnational corporations of rich countries run the businesses.

On the one hand, multilateral liberalization of trade could be seen as comprising two stages. The first starts in 1944 with the creation of the Bretton Woods Institutions, including the IMF and the WB. Although the international community could not reach an agreement for the setting up of an International Trade Organization, they established GATT, a multilateral forum for tariff negotiations. It included a secretariat providing technical services for multilateral trade liberalization (Held et al. 1999:164). The second stage is characterized by the setting up of the WTO in 1995, an organization that replaced GATT. The WTO was the outcome of talks held during the Uruguay Round (1986–1993). The round launched negotiations for liberalization on such polemical issues as the elimination of protective measures in agriculture and textiles; limitations to safeguards; and trade-related intellectual property rights and investment. Although the agriculture issue was not resolved, agreement was reached in 1993 when the Uruguay Round established agreements on property rights, and the WTO was created (Held et al. 1999:165, Tussie and Woods 2000:64).

The WTO is a stronger institution than the GATT given the fact that it is aimed at removing non-tariff barriers and has a powerful dispute mechanism. There have been negotiations for the establishment of protection measures for the environment and labor, as well as negotiations for greater liberalization in investment and agriculture (Held et al. 1999:165, Trebilcock and Howse 1999:37, Tussie and Woods 2000:62–67). Reaching agreement, however, has proved impossible for many reasons and can be linked to the opposition of social movements, the refusal of the EU and the United States to abandon protectionism, the resistance of developing countries to the indiscriminate exploitation of their resources by corporations and the use by governments of cheap labor, and loose environmental regulations as "comparative advantages."

On the other hand, regionalization, "as opposed to globalization, implies that trade flows are clustered between similar countries which tend to be geographically continuous, and that markets within a region are (at least) partially insulated from the rest of the world" (Held et al. 1999:168). Three major geographical networks have been established simultaneously to multilateral institutions: the NAFTA, the EU, and Asia-Pacific Economic Cooperation, which includes most of the rich economies (Held et al. 1999:167, Trebilcock and Howse 1999:23). There are also other networks, such as the Common Market of the South (Mercosur) in South America, and the Common Market for Eastern and Southern Africa (Trebilcock and Howse 1999). There is debate about the compatibility of multilateral institutions and blocks in the sense that regions could tend to exclude other regions and countries through protectionist measures, such as the EU in agriculture (see for instance Trebilcock and Howse [1999] and Held et al. [1999]).

Both regional and multilateral trade liberalization are the focus of human rights articulations against free trade because it is at these levels that agreements and policies are made, and therefore they are the sites where state and private responsibility are located.

Foreign Direct Investment and Transnational Corporations

Foreign Direct Investment (FDI) is defined as ownership and control of business or part of a business in another country and takes the form of new equity capital, reinvested corporate earnings, and net borrowing through the parent company or affiliates (Trebilcock and Howse 1999:335). It is important for two reasons: free trade agreements are signed between countries, but the bulk of international trade is conducted between transnational corporations; and countries, especially those with low and medium incomes, strive to attract investment however they can, even if this means eliminating environmental and labor protection.

Given the assumptions and principles of underlying free trade, FDI is seen as one of the major means of achieving economic growth while fully integrating into global markets. It is therefore the subject of major protection under free trade agreements and multilateral and bilateral investment agreements whereby corporations are protected from state regulation for the protection of economic self-determination, the environment, health, and labor.

Corporate activities are a major concern in collective action, and therefore constitute a focus in the construction of strategies. However, social movements are sometimes overwhelmed by the power of corporations and try to force the state to control them. This is a limited view, as I shall argue later in this chapter.

To sum up, neoliberal free trade builds on mainstream liberal trade theories and has three key features that systematically erode state control over economic policy: 1) the imposition of nondiscrimination and expropriation principles; 2) multilateral and bilateral trade and investment agreements that guarantee the primacy of these principles over human welfare and the environment; and 3) the centrality of corporations are enormously benefited by the principles enshrined in multilateral and bilateral agreements.

International Human Rights Discourse vis-à-vis the Social Consequences of Free Trade

While neoliberal free trade discourse has become dominant, human rights discourse has also changed in response. The International Bill of Rights—the UDHR (1948), and the ICCPRs and ICESCRs (1966)—were the outcome of international negotiations held at the time. However, the issues negotiated were defined by the dominant Keynesian agreement among Europe's social democracies, which managed to set the agenda through their overwhelming majority—it should be noted that there were few socialist and developing countries at the time (their numbers would increase only with the decolonization of Asia and Africa in the 1970s). These rights did not reflect the political needs or aspirations of societies around the world, but rather the historical achievements of the European workers' movement, and these were recognized in the exercising of social citizenship. The implementation of such rights was therefore a political matter rather than an economic one until the 1970s, when the Keynesian covenant collapsed in Europe, and the 1980s when it was dismantled in Latin America as ordered by international financial institutions.

By this time, problems with ESCRs in globalization were no longer exclusively based on politics (rights associated with corporatism) but on economics (the rolling back of the state and the centrality of private actors) and implementation (practical justiciability and exigibility).

Consequently, academics and researchers of the UN started to examine the nature of state obligation throughout the world, and new human rights principles and texts emerged (International Commission of Jurists, Faculty of Law of the University of Limburg and Urban Morgan Institute for Human Rights, 1986, 1997). Simultaneous to these changes, human rights discourse became increasingly internationalized and therefore a legitimate tool for social movements to address global issues. These movements have been concerned with free trade issues from the mid-1990s.[1]

Even though the study of the relationship between economic globalization and human rights dates from at least the beginning of the 1990s,[2] a specific focus on the relationship between free trade and human rights is very recent. The more or less systematic study of the relation between the two begins in 1999, possibly because of three events occurring chronologically from 1994 onward and which revealed human and environmental vulnerability vis-à-vis free trade. First were the various financial crises occurring between 1994 and 1997 in Latin America and Asia. These crises clearly indicated the vulnerability of individuals and social groups faced with the nonexistent regulation of trade and foreign investment, in particular, portfolio investment.

Second was the notorious failure of negotiations to set up the Multilateral Agreement on Investment (MAI) by the Organization for Economic Cooperation and Development (OECD) in 1998. The OECD aimed to establish a judicial backup for the protection of foreign investment, mainly based in developing countries. Negotiations were carried out in secret from 1995, but the leaking of a draft alerted social movements and poor countries to its existence. They immediately challenged and eventually overturned negotiations and the agreement itself in 1998. The problem with the MAI was that it included the principles and provisions discussed in the first part of the chapter, plus a dispute regulation mechanism. This mechanism would allow corporations to sue governments and seek monetary compensation in the event of a governmental policy violating their rights as established in the agreement (Mabey 1999).

Third was the ILO's Declaration of Rights and Fundamental Principles in the Workplace of 1998. This document was a response to the WTO declaration issued during its Inaugural Ministerial Meeting (Singapore, 1996) to the effect that it was the ILO and not the WTO that should assume responsibility for matters related to employment and trade, as certain trade unions and rich governments demanded. The ILO accepted the challenge and not only managed to curb demands for a "social clause" but also succeeded in substituting the term "labor standards" with the term "labor rights" for the first time in the sphere of free trade (Pangalangan 2002).[3]

In addition to these events, a major concern in political globalization is the consequences of global processes for the nation-state, particularly in relation to whether state power has diminished or not as a result of globalization. Authors from different schools do not agree on whether globalization heralds the demise, or weakening, of the state or rather its transformation. The transformationalist account of globalization asserts that the state has not become powerless, but rather it is transforming itself "in response to the growing complexity of processes of governance in a more connected world" (Rosenau in Held et al. 1999:9). In globalization, the link between territory and political power, and thus of the sovereignty of the Westphalian state, has been broken for three interrelated reasons: 1) multiplication of sites of power; 2) increasing internationalization and institutionalization of policymaking; and 3) a rising number of international regimes for addressing issues that not only cut across national boundaries but also concern individuals and human collectives, such as human rights (Held 2000, Held and McGrew 2003, Scholte 2001). Coordination, regulation, and cooperation among states via this multilayered institutional setting challenges sovereignty and threatens state legitimacy because the state can no longer make decisions autonomously and because it is systematically challenged by international and national state and non-state actors.

In addition to this, the increasing importance of human rights discourse for addressing free trade is linked to the fact that globalization is placing not only states but also individuals and private actors at the center of regulation. The human rights regime establishes the primacy of the individual over state sovereignty, which used to be safeguarded irrespective of its consequences for individuals, groups, and organizations. This challenge to sovereignty is reinforced by the notion that a legitimate state must respect democratic values and human rights: "Legitimate political power must be, on the one hand, a form of political power that is accountable to the members of the political community in which it is embedded and, on the other, a promoter of fundamental human rights" (Held et al. 1999:69).

Summarizing, although international human rights started as a rather limited discourse, this discourse has undergone changes over the last 20 years in response to global change and collective action. More specifically, human rights discourse has expanded its rubric toward state and corporate responsibility in free trade-related issues. The inclusion of free trade matters in international human rights is related to its character as a sociopolitical construction in the way explained in the Introduction—that of linguistic legal-political constructions immersed in processes of intertextuality that consistently widen their scope. Consequently, international human rights discourse today includes two features that appeal to social movements: a focus on the state, and more recently, a focus on the almost legally binding responsibility of corporations. While the state becomes the center of the main "interpretative repertoires" mobilized by organizations to formulate anti-free trade agendas, corporate responsibility tends to be neglected. This, I argue, is a limitation in their human rights approach to free trade.

Focus on the State

According to NGOs and SMOs, in free trade there is an incidence of cases where the negative impact of such trade on the agricultural sector, labor, access to markets, the living standards of women, and the survival of small and medium businesses is directly related to the lack of state involvement. This occurs in two areas: first, in economic planning and the formulation of policies to boost the internal market. Here, if the state was involved, the transfer of technology and the contribution of corporations to national development corporations would include national chains of production in the export sector. In addition, with state involvement, industries threatened by imports would not vanish with the subsequent violation of the right to work and a dignified life. Second, in the regulation and accountability of transnational corporations, which enjoy legal privileges that undermine state sovereignty for compliance with human rights obligations.

While state nonintervention has become dominant in numerous free trade agreements, in human rights discourse it has been central for a long time—from the International Bill of Rights to the American Declaration of the Rights and Duties of Man. Recently, as the state weakened social spending and economic control, a better understanding of the nature of state responsibility has been developed in the Limburg Principles for the Implementation of the International Covenant on Economic, Social and Cultural Rights, and the Maastricht Guidelines on Violations of Economic, Social and Cultural Rights. Both establish the extent and nature of the state's obligations concerning the violation and protection of ESCRs. In 1986, in response to a call from the International Commission of Jurists, the Faculty of Law at the University of Limburg and the Morgan Urban Institute for Human Rights at the University of Cincinnati organized in Maastricht a meeting of experts in law to discuss the scope and nature of UN state parties' duties regarding human rights. Ten years later, these institutions again called on experts to elaborate on the Limburg principles, the result being the Maastricht Guidelines. These documents deal with moral and ethical issues concerning state duty toward people. For activists, these four obligations form the core of their approach to ESCRs (1986, 1997a). According to these international instruments, the state has four basic obligations regarding human rights: to respect them (not take any actions adversely affecting human rights); to protect them (prevent others from violating human rights); to fulfill them (take legislative, administrative, budgetary, and legal measures so that human rights may be fully applied); and to ensure there is no discrimination (abstain from excluding individuals or groups based on their sexual orientation, gender, race, ethnicity, language, marital status, etc.).

In free trade, the failure of the state to comply with these duties can be observed at the structural level and at the level of commercial activities in specific sectors. At the structural level, this is seen when the state cannot—or will not—act to protect domestic production and thereby allow for the generation of the necessary wealth to satisfy human rights as set out in international law. The formulation of domestic policies establishing the structural conditions for complying with human rights, in other words, the satisfaction of the right to development, is also linked to international cooperation in the creation of a fair and just international order. This means that states, especially wealthier states, are obliged to do two things in order to guarantee sustainable development for all countries, especially the poorer ones: first, to donate 0.7 percent of their gross domestic product to the development of very low revenue countries, second, to ensure that international organizations—namely the WTO and NAFTA, and eventually the FTAA—set rules to guarantee that states will be able to carry out plans for national development in which the rights of corporations are restricted by a set of explicit commitments to the development of the host country, such as rules of origin and performance requirements.

Corporate Responsibility

The problems related to investment leave no doubt that responsibility for development does not correspond exclusively to the state, but also directly to corporations. The direct responsibility of corporations is related to FDI and portfolio investment since these have clear implications for human rights. However, the debate is currently centered on the first, due to the transnationalization of the mode of capitalist production as well as the growing impact of corporations on the environment and the lives of millions of people in countries of low and medium income. Impact is related to their commercial and productive operations and alliances with repressive governments or promoters of social or environmental dumping.[4] FDI is of paramount importance because free trade agreements are signed between countries, but the bulk of international trade is conducted between transnational corporations. Countries, especially those with low and medium incomes, strive to attract it however they can, even if this means violating human rights.

Beginning in the mid-1990s, much of the debate has centered on how to regulate corporations in terms of their socioeconomic and environmental impact. In this sense debate has focused on defining whether this regulation should be voluntary and based on the ethical principles of social responsibility, or should rather be made binding through human rights legislation that establishes more or less universal standards through a series of covenants and treaties to be signed by the majority of world governments (Skogly 1999).[5] This is due to the new rules of international political economy, in particular the protection of investment (national treatment, indirect expropriation, no performance requirements, and suits brought by corporations against nation states).

The debate is essentially theoretical and is related to the fact that in liberal philosophy, theory and legislation of human rights, private entities have no responsibilities with respect to human rights and for this reason are under no obligation to present reports pertaining to them. From this perspective, only the state has moral and legal obligations, and hence it is the state that is ultimately responsible for the protection of human rights from the activities of third parties, including transnational corporations, that may violate said rights (Addo 1999b, Jochnick 1999, Muchlinski 2001). Nevertheless, empirical evidence accumulated through the documentation of cases shows that transnational corporations are directly involved in the violation of human rights. In addition, there is a challenge to the ontological status of the division between the public and private spheres, and the allegedly irrefutable power of corporations in the world today. This is tipping the balance toward those who favor imposing obligations on corporations with respect to human rights Clapham 1993 (Monshipouri, Welch, and Kennedy 2003).

This perspective has been suggested in academic work (Addo 1999b, Meyer 1998, Monshipouri, Welch, and Kennedy 2003, Muchlinski 2001, Skogly 1999, Woodroffe 1999). In addition, it has informed diplomatic activities. On August 13, 2003 the UN approved the *Norms Governing the Responsibilities of Transnational Corporations and Other Commercial Companies in the Area of Human Rights* (United Nations Commission of Human Rights 2003).[6] It takes as its point of departure the UDHR and extensive work in the elaboration of mostly voluntary codes of conduct. It goes on to establish that although the primordial responsibility concerning human rights falls essentially on states, corporations—and the people working for them—also have the responsibility to promote and protect human rights, given that their actions and operations have a negative impact on people and the environment.[7] This includes environmental policy and relations with consumers and governments.

These standards set forth that corporations must comply with the following points: not discriminate; not benefit from or take part in war crimes or crimes against humanity; not use forced, slave, or child labor; offer a fair wage, provide a sanitary environment for work, and respect union membership; respect the objectives of national development; not bribe government employees, candidates for elected posts, or members of the armed forces; above all contribute to the rights to development, food, water, health, housing, privacy, education, freedom of thought, conscience, belief, and opinion; respect consumer rights in compliance with principles such as prevention; and respect national and international environmental laws and regulations.

As far as the mechanisms for implementation are concerned, the standards specify that corporations must include these standards in their internal legal regime, and also apply them to their suppliers and subcontractors. The document then points out that "Transnational and other commercial companies shall be subject to periodic monitoring and inspection using national mechanisms and international mechanisms of the United Nations that either already exist or are yet to be created, with regard to the application of the Standards" (United Nations Commission of Human Rights 2003:prgh 16). The document adds that compliance with the standards will be monitored by examining the information of the companies themselves and of NGOs, as well as any alleged violations. It also states that governments must create legal and administrative monitoring mechanisms and that corporations must compensate any person affected by the violation of these standards.

Although the standards were still under discussion at the time of writing this chapter,[8] they constitute a major breakthrough in the formulation of mechanisms designed to make corporations accountable as they are binding. However, it is also necessary to point out that, as is the case with other UN documents examining the relationship between human rights and free trade, there is no systematic questioning of the existing economic order that affords companies so much power. At the same time, the instruments for implementing these standards are still not clearly defined—there is no mention of which international organizations will monitor compliance, what the prosecution procedure will consist of, how often monitoring is to take place, which penalties will be applied, and the form of compensation. For such reasons, social movements are not working actively in the field of constructing direct responsibility of corporations; they prefer to focus on state responsibility that, while constituting a useful approach, can also be a limitation given the dynamics of globalization, as will be argued in the next section of this chapter.

In summary, the expansion of human rights discourse into the economic field is making this discourse suitable for addressing free trade related problems as it allows for an analysis of state as well as corporate duties. In addition, since political globalization encourages the internationalization of policymaking and legal regimes, as a discourse it is acquiring the characteristics necessary to address the problems presented by global trade, and is therefore used by social movements.

THE HUMAN RIGHTS HEGEMONIC PROJECT

For the purpose of this study, a hegemonic project is understood as a particular articulation's view of social, economic, cultural, and political life, which is defined by the use of a particular empty signifier. In the framework used here, empty signifier is the name given to the system of identities partially fixed by a particular word in a particular context (see Introduction). A hegemonic project provides subjects with specific interpretations of the structural problems they face along with possible solutions. However, and although there could be similarities, interpretations are not the same for all kinds of subjects; it depends upon whether they are SMOs or NGOs.

NGOs and SMOs see human rights as a hegemonic project in economic globalization since human rights, specifically ESCRs, place people rather than markets at the center of the GPE. For both SMOs and NGOs, human rights is an identifiable hegemonic project in the transformation of the free trade system since human rights are used as an empty signifier to fix meaning in their agendas and mass mobilization. For example, in the case of the HSA, which articulates both NGOs and SMOs (this case will be discussed in detail in chapter six), the axis is human rights as they serve to fix meaning in free trade by establishing that commercial exchange must take into consideration human dignity (Alianza Social Continental 2003). The following quote offers a good example of how human rights are used as an empty signifier since the Gender and Economy (GyE, the Spanish acronym for Género y Economía) contrasts the discourse of economic efficiency with that of human rights in order to discursively construct an understanding of free trade in which human rights, rather than economic gain, represent the main objective. In the terms of the framework used here, we see that human rights fix meaning by making "people" rather than capital the priority of trade:

> ...For women, strengthening the development of human rights in the economy is key. As Elson and Gideon point out, on this topic there are two separate approaches, one is the discourse of human rights and the other is the discourse of the efficient economy. "The first deals with people as ends in themselves, the second treats people as resources subject to financial calculations. The efficient economy supposes that it will widely promote the fulfillment of economic and social rights specified in the International Economic, Social and Cultural Rights pact via economic growth and an increase in the availability of goods and services. But greater availability of goods and services will only allow a progressive fulfillment of those rights, provided that the rights of the poor and other excluded groups are strengthened. What is needed is for economic policies to not only increase the availability of goods and services in a sustainable way (without destroying the social and natural environments), but also to strengthen the rights of excluded groups so they are able to enjoy the fruits of increased productivity" (Red Mexicana de Acción Frente al Libre Comercio 1993a:14).

Farmer SMOs, for example, see international human rights law, especially ESCRs, as an important tool for the legitimacy of subsistence agriculture at the national level in an increasingly efficiency and productivity-led global economy that excludes people who produce solely for community consumption. They mobilize human rights and food sovereignty discourses in order to effect a more structural analysis of the issues concerning agriculture and thus farmers' interests. This construction can be seen in the following fragment of an interview with Victor Suarez, who claims that:

> In that area we have used human rights discourse in the defense of the rural economy, and to assert our country's right to food sovereignty. Food sovereignty is understood as the sovereign right of farmers and their communities to continue living on what they produce from their land, at both an individual and community level. And also the right of the country, of the nation, to produce its own food (Suarez 2004).

While the primacy of people and human life over trade is central to both NGO and SMO work, there are certain differences in their understandings of human rights as a hegemonic project. These differences are marked by the type of human rights discourse they mobilize to fix meaning in their concepts of free trade. These discourses are *state duty* and *law enforcement* and are both based on the state-centered focus privileged by human rights discourse.

In the first place, state duty represents an appeal to policy design according to the legal obligations of the state established in international human rights law. More specifically, it is a question of how activists understand human rights—mostly based on the work of the UN. State duty refers to recent developments concerning the nature of state responsibility in human rights as discussed in the previous sections. State duty discourses are mobilized to construct and lobby arguments in favor of state intervention, the control of economic policy, and the promotion of group demands within a framework that establishes these demands as entitlements. Although legitimacy is a more complex concept than state duty—it includes issues of justice, public interest, and welfare, among many others—, in the discursive practices of activists, state duty is constructed as the basis of political legitimacy in the exercising of state power at both national and international levels. For instance, state duty discourses are employed to establish the obligations of the state with regard to people when designing economic policy. This is evidenced in the following quote from an interview with food rights NGO activist Carriquiriborde:

> …in an idea of human rights where everyone has the right to food, and that it is therefore necessary to design policies, there is a need to promote policies that guarantee people enjoy greater development in terms of access to food, whether as producers or as salaried consumers. Or via public policies that can only be demanded in cases of hardship. That is to say, the government is under no obligation to feed anybody.

> The government needs to respect and protect access to food, and safeguard that the country produces sufficient food for its people and, in times of hardship, cover people's basic needs...
>
> The responsibility of the state is to make viable, within the Development Plan, economic policy in general, from the production of food for the feeding of people in prison or in public hospitals, that is to say exceptional cases... Therefore the right ensures that the feeding of children is the responsibility of the family, or in exceptional cases the responsibility of the state. We are not saying that parents aren't responsible for the feeding of their children (Carriquiriborde 2004).

In the second place, law enforcement refers to state application of relevant laws such as labor, environmental, constitutional, human rights, and so on. These are applied to civil servants and private agents involved in activities that violate human rights in accordance with the state's duty to protect those human rights. Activists mobilize repertoires of law enforcement to construct legal responsibility in situations where civil servants favor trade activities rather than community welfare. To illustrate this, we can consider the case of the expropriation of indigenous people's lands for transport infrastructure in Puebla State referred to by activist Rangel. In this example, people mobilize a discourse of law enforcement to construct responsibility in specific cases in which indigenous families have been threatened with eviction if they refuse to sell their land. They demand the law be applied to local authorities violating the right of indigenous people to land and natural resources as stipulated in ILO Convention 169 concerning Indigenous and Tribal Peoples in Independent Countries (Rangel 2004).[9]

They do not, however, take the cases to court, and simply use them to support their demands. Case litigation is more linked to human rights NGOs, which usually take law enforcement discourse a step further by claiming the justiciability of human rights cases. Justiciability refers to the possibility of constructing human rights cases by taking them to a national court or an international human rights tribunal, and claiming indemnity and punishment for those committing violations.

SMOs and NGOs mobilize both discourses in the construction of their agendas and joint action. As long as they use laws conceived in terms of, and supported by, a legal system, activists construct both state duty and law enforcement as "nonideological" forms that can be used to challenge global economics via state intervention. In their view, human rights arguments go "beyond rhetoric," unlike simple political demands addressed to the state that have either a class or other "ideological" basis. They usually see law enforcement and state duty as complementary and necessary.

In the terms of the framework used here, for both NGOs and SMOs human rights represent a discourse, fixing meaning in terms of the combined interpretative repertoires of state duty and law enforcement, which are means to regulate trade in favor of people. First, a focus on state duty constitutes a more political form of fixing meaning with human rights because it is conceived in terms of a relationship with the state. Second, a focus on law enforcement, particularly justiciability, represents a more legalistic approach as it involves application of the law either in terms of demands or case litigation. Emphasis on one or the other determines whether an organization is an SMO, an NGO, or human rights NGO: SMOs emphasize state duty and therefore adopt a more political approach, while the latter two emphasize law enforcement and consequently adopt a more legalistic approach.

The Political Approach of SMOs

SMOs use a more political approach because the fixing of meaning with state duty is more coherent with their strategies, which are usually intended to establish some form of negotiation with the state. They use human rights as a political strategy that helps them to legitimate their demands and to adopt a shared subject position that locates them in the hegemonic articulation based on the equality of human dignity. For SMO activists, human rights represent group and individual entitlements protecting people from the abuses of capital and symbolizing state duty in the provision of services and subsidies that guarantee the existence of farmers, workers, and women. In their view, global trade privileges capital and productivity, so fixing meaning with human rights allows them to place human life at the center of arguments used to oppose free trade and demand its regulation. They mobilize a state duty discourse to construct the argument that human rights law could lead to a reversal of the global trend toward weakened state responsibility in social welfare and the state's failure to assume control of national economic development.

For example, GyE mobilizes a discourse of privatization in order to construct the concept of violations of women's right to health. Such an argument, based on ideas of the state's duty in assuming control of health programs, offers the only means to reverse the current scenario of human rights abuse. They claim: "Reduction of the role of the state as a consequence of free trade agreements and the privatization of services means that women lose their rights pertaining to health, education and food, among others. The creation of the State Health Insurance (*Seguro Popular*) is an example of the loss of rights already gained" (Red Género y Economía et al. 2003:39).

For their part, Suárez (2004) and Aceves (2003) are convinced that state obligation is the most important human rights argument because it gives legitimacy to their own claims: if the state has a duty toward human rights, and their demands are human rights, the state has to negotiate these demands. This type of argumentation can be used for negotiations at both national and international levels. While they do believe that law enforcement is important, they tend to discard such an approach for three reasons: it is time consuming, it has practical limitations, and it requires lawyers. For instance, Victor Suárez of ANEC mobilizes a state duty-based legitimacy discourse to construct the advantages of using human rights discourse in negotiations:

> The topic is not in the statutes and cannot be appealed to with respect to ESCRs. It can be appealed to in part with respect to individual rights, in particular that pertaining to individual guarantees and the flagrant and evident violation of those rights, that you are killed or jailed without trial, and you can appeal to certain human rights or government authorities, for example the justice system. But the broadest aspect of human rights covered by ESCRs cannot be appealed to before any authority, whether it be the government of the Federal District or human rights commissions...I believe the greatest discovery on our part as a farmers' movement has been to put aside our own economic claims regarding prices, costs and financing to present our claim fundamentally based on the question of rights, the right to a dignified existence for the rural population, rights to a full life, a dignified life and a break with these paradigms or prejudices regarding people who live from the land, that simply because they are farmers they do not enjoy rights and much less have the right to a dignified life...
>
> I believe the discourse of human rights has helped to construct a more integrated proposal that has had an impact on the urban population. We have constructed a discourse that has received support from the media...People react more positively to an argument based on rights than an economic argument about unfair competition from the United States. Therefore, the discourse of rights for people is much clearer because it is something you cannot deny, whether rationally, politically or ethically. It is a powerful weapon, both for building and development (Suárez 2004).

As for workers, they mobilize state duty-based human rights discourses when negotiating minimum standards in trade agreements. They mobilize discourses of state duty in order to construct the government's responsibility in guaranteeing that corporations respect minimum labor standards. Aceves mobilizes a discourse of human rights duties to establish the limits of corporations in globalization:

> ...We do not reject their plans to come here and provide work. We do not refuse to offer opportunities for them to come here, but what we do refuse is to send them the message that the activities they wish to engage in here will be arranged without regulation and that we will not question their activities...This is a problem of the role of the State. I think that for this reason, with respect to human rights, the central element, or subject, to be watched is the State as it is the authority, it is the body charged with guaranteeing that a balance is established in the relationships between private parties, between publics, between publics and private parties, and even within the government itself (Aceves interview 2003).

For their part, women contrast a discourse of state duty in welfare with one of privatization in order to highlight the fact that they are usually the most affected by the privatization of education, health, and water services, and consequently have to take unskilled jobs in sweatshops that offer low wages and poor working conditions. The following quote from GyE offers a good example of how women mobilize state duty-based human rights discourses to forward the argument that the state has to take control of social services if human rights are to be respected:

> For women, a direct result of the abandonment of state responsibility and the privatization of services is an increase in their workload, given that it is women who assume responsibility for the care of children, the elderly and the sick.
>
> In the labor field, the disappearance of small companies, and to a lesser extent medium sized companies, has led to a loss of employment sources for women. Increasing poverty has contributed to an increase in domestic violence and the principal victims are women. Laws to protect women from such violence are either insufficient or are not applied. Non-governmental institutions do not have the capacity to respond to this situation without greater intervention from the State (Red Género y Economía et al. 2003:39).

NGOs: Between Legalistic and Political Approaches

While SMOs are clear in their preference for political approaches to human rights, NGOs have assumed a more ambivalent position. For NGO activists, a political human rights approach is key when working with grassroots organizations, but at the same time law enforcement is "necessary." For them, state duty-based human rights discourses provide an important tool in their efforts to create awareness in grassroots movements and for lobbying policy proposals and assessments. In this sense they tend to mobilize state duty discourses because they are more political than legal and therefore better translate into the language and strategies of social movements. Framing public policy design and lobbying in terms of state duty with respect to ESCRs is more appealing than law enforcement as legalistic human rights approaches tend to require longer timeframes for the resolution of specific problems or concerns.

Activist Alberto Arroyo, from the RMALC contrasts a discourse of "existing reality" with one of "law enforcement" in order to advance his argument that political approaches to human rights are more useful than legalistic ones:

> ...In general movements demand results, and many of these rights can be assumed as discourse, but they know that will not resolve anything. You can make food a constitutional right, that's fine, but in this economic model such a right remains on paper, it is limited solely to writing like so many other rights. If they remain in the letter of the law they will not solve anything because having food depends on having a job and a well-paid job at that. And another thing is a guarantee from the State. If you are unemployed and without an income (in certain countries), there is free, public food...in our countries (Latin America) the State does not have the economic capacity to do that. When more than half the population is in poverty there is no public budget available for you to guarantee that 40 million people eat. It is impossible. Therefore people are more practical in this sense too...they will translate this into the need for good, well-paid jobs, or the need for unemployment benefits. This is also a means to guarantee the question of food when you are unemployed, or a means to guarantee the need for social policy. Therefore it is translated into a more operational discourse (Arroyo interview 2004).

Arroyo (2004) claims that awareness of the importance of human rights discourse for trade, in terms of state duty, is extremely important because it means that basic services such as education, housing, and health cannot be left to market forces. Like Canto (interview 2004), he argues that references to state duty and law enforcement in the human rights framework neutralize refutation of, and opposition to, activists' arguments. This is because its grounding in law makes it an authoritative framework that could be used for argumentation in policy proposals, as well as for lobbying at the national level and in international arenas.

For NGOs, human rights are a powerful tool for exerting pressure on local authorities intimidated by the ideas of international bodies such as the UN. For instance, ideas of state duty help them to challenge the issue of infrastructure projects and the design of public policy, which necessarily imply the participation of the state, even in globalization. In addition, they allow NGOs to articulate with grassroots organizations, as in the case of the construction of a motorway in Puebla State as part of the Puebla-Panama Plan. Sandoval, for example, mobilizes a repertoire of state duty and one of local development to advance the argument that NGOs like hers do not require legalistic approaches to human rights:

> ...in this NGO we do not have a legal area and neither do we take on cases such as occurs in human rights centers. We do not appeal to national or international systems for the protection of human rights because we are not involved in litigation, but we are conducting work that is almost inevitably recognized as human rights work. Our human rights work comes more from the perspective of promotion, it is as much about sensitizing the public as becoming involved in discussions with the government, in generating proposals, in public denunciation if not the documenting of cases, and in this sense ESCRs [economic, social and cultural rights]—which we eventually incorporate as ESCRs to include environmental rights—above all in the work we do for social development (Sandoval interview 2003).

The mobilization of state duty discourses in the construction of human rights views of free trade allows NGOs to work more closely with grassroots organizations and forward arguments for both national and transnational negotiations. However, NGOs continue to emphasize the advantages of law enforcement while recognizing the limits of such a legalistic approach. Unlike SMOs, NGOs do like legalistic approaches, but do not see them as feasible in the present context since most free trade related cases are violations of ESCRs, the legal defense of which is limited. They do mobilize law enforcement discourses in order to build cases used to reinforce arguments concerning state duty with respect to human rights, but they do not take these to court. For these NGOs, the legal enforcement of ESCRs offers a very limited approach, whereas human rights legitimacy for lobbying and policy is a more useful tool. Canto contrasts repertoires of ideals and realities to explain why legal approaches to ESCRs are still ineffective:

> For it to become actionable is a shared aspiration. For it to become effective in the present to resolve situations is where it is questionable as

many of the instruments for action with respect to ESCRs have yet to be developed, therefore the path to make them actionable, in part due to the number of reforms, requires many state reforms...So it is not a case of preferring one to the other, but recognition that in political terms one has to choose the path that exists. If what you have is a positively established obligation, even though no instruments exist to make it actionable, you can demand it via the political route. I think that is where we find the difference and that effectively it is here, at the level of action, that we discover the shared aspiration...(Canto 2004).

Environmental NGO activist Villamar, however, claims that while state duty is the most appealing aspect of human rights law, the possibility of enforcing law through the courts is also very important, although human rights instruments that offer no practical use are of little help, instruments such as the democratic clause in the Global Agreement. For Canto, this means the construction of a completely new methodology that serves both law enforcement and state duty for the articulation of both social movements and NGOs. He mobilizes discourses of legality and politics to construct the notion of a "human rights methodology" that employs aspects of both:

...(first) the long-term vision that a legal trial implies in response to an immediate claim, that in effect is more a political demand, and the second is that which appears more frequently for organizations, whether social or civil. Of course this is not to say that the law should be put to one side, but that they are distinct resources that can be used according to the case...Therefore, I think that when we speak of ESCRs we are speaking of a *sui generis* situation in the human rights field, as this implies productivity, public policies, and of course it would be necessary to create a specific methodology with the participation of organizations specializing in human rights and those that have focused more on development...(Canto 2004).

In short, NGOs unlike SMOs see a need to mobilize law enforcement repertoires together with those of state duty. However, they claim to be realistic and do not expect much from a legal approach. The exception here are the human rights NGOs, which focus on justiciability when fixing meaning in all cases, including those involving ESCRs, despite the shortcomings evident when attempting to implement them legally. They insist on law enforcement and justiciability in their approach to ESCRs even though there is evidence that such an approach is not necessarily working. For instance, human rights lawyer and activist Herrera mobilizes discourses of both state duty and justiciability in order to discursively describe the articulation of actors that have dealt with ESCR issues for a significant period of time, and possess the knowledge and expertise lacking in human rights NGOs:

> ...in human rights work it is important that these be taken into account and valued in the social movement, particularly in the face of economic integration. For example, the use of participative mechanisms for proposals or accusations or the search for justice in cases of human rights violations. This is where we can identify a comprehensively studied area, consistently worked by the human rights movement, which cannot fail to be recognized by the other branch of the social movement. In the other area I think we need to recover a common language and a broad international consensus that has also been achieved by governments in terms of human rights discourse. Governments have themselves exploited this discourse (Herrera interview 2004).

Limitations of Political and Legal Approaches

The fixing of meaning with both state duty and law enforcement discourses is strongly linked to a state-centric view of human rights implementation that seems somewhat constrictive in a field such as free trade where non-state actors play a key role. There are advantages in the focus of human rights discourse on the state but not taking on board new developments in the field of corporate responsibility has limitations. This focus of SMOs and NGOs on the role of the state can be attributed to two specific circumstances. The first of these is the nature of the relationship between social movements and the state in Mexico, and Latin America in general. Latin American social movement scholars have pointed out that the cultural specificities of the region have necessarily led to the historical establishment of socioeconomic demands directed toward the state, such as the crisis of development and the lack of a universal welfare system (housing, health services, unemployment benefits, etc.) (Calderón, Piscitelli, and Reyna 1992, Escobar 1992).

This relationship makes power issues such as Mexico's reduced bargaining power in globalization the main problem in free trade policy and therefore the center of the political potentiality of human rights discourse. In this view, the terms of the global political economy do not allow the government—or on occasion, it is the government itself that refuses— to take action with respect to the regulation of capital, investment in social welfare and agriculture, and protection of small Mexican enterprises, workers, women, and the environment. Consequently, human rights bring state duty and regulation to the fore, reinforcing demands for a stronger state in supranational and intergovernmental institutions such as the WTO, and bilateral or regional free trade agreements such as NAFTA.

Second, in Mexico, understandings of human rights in both NGOs (including human rights NGOs) and SMOs are based on either the three-generations approach to human rights, natural rights approaches, or a combination of the two. These remain unchallenged in both the field of activism and academia. Human rights are generally seen as emerging from either positive law or political philosophy (natural rights), therefore law enforcement and state duty are the "natural" parameters of discourse.

Having said this, activists do acknowledge the limitations of their legal and political approaches. For example, a feminist activist mobilizes discourses of globalization in order to construct the limitations of law enforcement and state duty as a consequence of the state's loss of power vis-à-vis major political and economic actors such as international financial institutions (IFIs) and corporations. Therefore in order to be an efficient empty signifier, human rights also have to "go global."[10] She mobilizes discourses of economic and political globalization to point out the need to widen the field of human rights beyond the "human rights methodology" that remains fixed within state boundaries:

> …At the conceptual level, and this applies to everyone, not only women, the human rights movement must demand that the State perform certain functions that the economic model does not allow it to perform. However, it is not allowed to because the economic model establishes that it can't. It's that simple. The economic model reduces the functions of the state. In this respect, four areas are explicitly identified: 1) offering services to the poor, 2) administration of the environment, 3) the judicial system and 4) the military, and this is still subject to debate. Outside of these areas it has few functions. Therefore, when the time comes to act, the rights represented by ESCRs enter the equation. So the question is how you can demand them of the State if the State does not make such decisions, at the theoretical level, and we are talking about the most basic level. It is a question of understanding…In truth I agree that the framework of human rights is the one we should be working with, but within a framework of global rights. The framework needs to be expanded (Anonymous interviewee).

Arroyo (2004) also mobilizes discourses of globalization to argue that the state cannot ensure law enforcement and control over policy because of the complexities of global economics and politics whereby the state is no longer autonomous but has to make decisions in compliance with international commitments. For these reasons, rather than trying to make human rights enforcement international, the correct argumentation in free trade should be one of radical structural changes in free trade agreements so that human rights can be fulfilled according to existing law. These changes should not only emphasize the significance of state control of economic and social policy, but also the need to expand human rights discourse to establish the human rights duties of private actors, especially businesses and corporations.

In spite of this acknowledgment, in their discursive practices, NGOs and SMOs emphasize state duty and the role of the state in law enforcement. The extension of human rights discourse toward private and international responsibility is not a goal that most NGOs and SMOs actively work toward. However, in their agendas many do expand the discourse beyond state responsibility when mobilizing discourses of corporate responsibility in the regulation of economic globalization. Their view of human rights as a hegemonic project is mostly limited to relations with the state and its role in globalization, although new approaches have emerged.

Conclusion

Summarizing, activists mobilize two types of human rights repertoires when constructing their view of free trade: law enforcement and state duty, but emphasis on one or the other depends on whether activists belong to SMOs or to NGOs. While the former are more politically oriented and prefer to focus on state duty, NGOs (especially human rights NGOs) are more inclined toward legal or law-based strategies. Both types of organizations fail to realize that human rights discourse can be effective beyond state boundaries. This failure is linked to the historical relationship of Mexican social movements with the state, and the uncritical adoption of human rights discourses that view rights as either natural or necessarily positive in law.

In addition, for the construction of agendas, both SMOs and NGOs generally use ESCRs, as opposed to civil and political rights or human rights in general because they see these offering a more specific reference to the problems presented by free trade. More specifically, SMO activists mobilize a variety of discourses with which they identify, together with the group rights of activists. NGOs, for their part, mobilize such ESCRs as the right to development and the right to food, together with other nodal points formed by food sovereignty.

Nevertheless, while organizations do question the limitations of state-centered approaches to human rights, in their discursive practices they continue to identify state duty as one of the central features of human rights discourse. This is explained, and justified, by the cultural specificities of the region and Mexico's reduced power bargaining in the global political economy. Nevertheless, such emphasis should not become an obstacle to the political potential of human rights beyond national frontiers.

CHAPTER 5

THE CONSTRUCTION OF IDENTITIES AND SPECIFIC AGENDAS WITH HUMAN RIGHTS DISCOURSE

INTRODUCTION

The previous chapters showed how human rights provide activists with the means to construct fairer terms of trade in a legitimate framework. At the same time, it showed that human rights discourse can be a source of identification encouraging them to act politically and organize collective action against free trade. Bearing in mind the differences between agents, this chapter discusses how activists identify with human rights and how this identification is reflected in the construction of agendas and mobilization.

IDENTIFYING WITH HUMAN RIGHTS: BECOMING CITIZENS, BECOMING AGENTS

In the construction of human rights-related subject positions vis-à-vis free trade, differences between social NGOs and SMOs are fundamental. This is explained by the tendency of NGO activists to see themselves as something other than subjects of rights; they see human rights as an ideal to be promoted while participating as citizens in decision-making processes joining other citizens also interested in the same issues. For their part, SMO activists are more subjective: they identify with humanity (human dignity) or citizenship (equality in the enjoyment of rights), establishing a sense of sameness with other social groups that in other respects are different.

The Subject Positions of NGO Activists

NGO activists do not claim to represent any particular group or individual because their job is to lobby their own policy proposals and assessments, which are designed to benefit the SMOs they work with. Therefore, rather than using human rights as the reflection of a particular subject position—for instance, women claiming women's rights—they mobilize legal and political repertoires in order to make the state accountable for its human rights obligations in the context of free trade. They mobilize a citizenship discourse in order to forward a wider goal, which is establishing a fairer trade by defining it in human rights terms. They see themselves as citizens exercising their right to participate in economic decision-making processes in order to demand policy change for the benefit of the "majority" rather than for their own benefit. The mobilization of a citizenship discourse can be observed in this quote from an interview with Areli Sandoval, who states that: "We (in Equipo Pueblo) feel we are defenders of human rights as well as promoters of development, and we feel we are simply members of an organization seeking better standards of living in this country, we clearly feel we are human rights defenders without being lawyers" (Sandoval 2004).

When mobilizing discourses of "human dignity" they refer not to their own human condition, but to the condition of those subjects for whom they work. They want people to realize they are holders of rights because of their human dignity, so policy has to change in order for that dignity to be respected and protected. The reference to human dignity as a social value and not as a personal dimension is clear in this statement of food rights activist Alicia Carriquiriborde: "…in a conception of human rights within which everyone enjoys the human right to eat, it would therefore be necessary to resolve existing policies and promote new policies to guarantee that people enjoy greater development in terms of access to food, whether as rural producers or salaried consumers" (Carriquiriborde 2004).

The mobilization of citizenship discourses for the construction of a human rights subject position is rather new in some fields of NGO work, such as the environment or indigenous people's land rights—barely five years according to the archives consulted. However, in some NGOs, for example, those involved in food rights or development, identification with citizenship has been part of NGO discursive practices for a relatively longer period. For instance, Areli Sandoval from Equipo Pueblo claims that development NGOs started to mobilize discourses of democracy and ESCRs in the early 1990s as a means to influence policy at the national level because of the emphasis on human rights on state duty. Human rights helped them to pass from project implementation to the reincorporation of state participation in social welfare, that is, from fighting poverty to the fulfillment of human rights through national social policy, which radically changed as a result of the implementation of structural adjustment programs in the 1980s.

To sum up, NGO activists construct their human rights subject positions making human dignity a value and adopting citizenship as the identity that allows them to make that value part of economic policy. Citizen participation allows for the promotion of human rights values in free trade policy.

The Subject Positions of Women, Workers, and Farmers

While NGOs establish human dignity as a value, SMO activists identify with it as "humans": since everyone is human, everyone has dignity and is therefore entitled to the rights attached to that dignity, which is protected by international human rights law. As Douzinas argues, this construction is possible because the "man" of human rights is a signifier with several matching signifiers thanks to the metaphorical transfer of meaning of "human dignity." He claims that: "The rhetorical operation of metonymy allows the transfer of the presumed dignity of human nature to entities that are by no means similar or analogous to 'man' or to human subjects but which are contiguous with them, like the unborn, the environment or animals" (Douzinas 1996:124). At the same time, he says, human rights carry surplus meaning that is partially arrested when the signifier human rights is attached to a particular signified, such as "the rights of women." Following Douzinas, the subjects of rights have no essential identities outside this symbolic construction, a construction that is different for women, workers, and farmers. It is therefore necessary at this point to consider when each of these specific groups began to construct human rights-related subject positions, and which discourses they mobilize in order to construct their own identity and join the hegemonic articulation created by human dignity.

Women
Women began to construct human rights subject positions in 1987, when feminists from all over the globe met at a summit held in Mexico. There, they discussed the potential and limitations of human rights in advancing their gender demands. The feminist summit pointed

out that human rights could offer a very useful framework but it was a male-centered discourse: while most of the abuse women faced took place in their own homes, human rights only considered abuses occurring in the public sphere. Consequently, in theory women were not humans. In their view, in order to be truly *human* and not just *men's* rights, human rights had to include women's rights too, rights that were specifically relevant to the particular interests of women, interests that had not been given a specific focus in the rights incorporated into declarations existing at that time.

In 1991, under the banner "women's rights are human rights," international feminists launched the World Campaign for the Rights of Women, shortly before the Vienna World Human Rights Conference (1993). They drafted a petition demanding that sexual violence and discrimination be recognized as violations of the human rights of women. They did consider other issues to be violations of women's rights, but the Campaign was based on the strategic decision of highlighting the issues of sexual violence and discrimination since they were clear illustrations of how traditional human rights concepts and practices were gender-blind and excluded most violations suffered by women (Facio 2000). The recognition of gender violence and discrimination was seen as a starting point in the construction of women's rights. After Vienna, campaigners decided to promote the indivisibility of ESCRs and CPRs. Therefore, during the International Conference on Population and Development held in Cairo, 1994, the Campaign shifted to highlight reproductive rights and the right to health; at the World Summit on Social Development, Copenhagen, 1995, the emphasis was on socioeconomic rights related to trade policy and financial institutions; and at the Fourth World Summit on Women, Beijing, 1995, a human rights-based plan of action was put into effect (De la Cruz, Tamayo, Antolín 2001, Facio 2000, Organización de las Naciones Unidas 1995).

Leonor Aída Concha (2003) claims that the defense of women's ESCRs in Mexico started after Beijing with the setting up of international women's networks such as GyE, which dealt with the impact of structural adjustment programs on women's welfare and sought to establish alliances with organizations, both mixed and women's. Another important network was the Women's World March set up by the Federation of Women in Quebec in 1995 and launched in Mexico in 2000. Its first action was to conduct a national survey on women's ESCRs that included questions concerning the rights to food, work, and decent wages, wage equality, and improvements in working conditions, education, domestic violence, physical, sexual and psychological integrity, fair distribution of domestic work, and full citizenship (Concha 2003).

Concha claims that the experience of using human rights discourses to advance gender issues, and particularly free trade related issues, is increasing awareness among women with respect to the importance of human rights; consequently, they organize workshops and seminars for discussion of whether they consider their struggle a human rights struggle. For instance, during the International Forum, Women's Rights in Free Trade Agreements and the World Trade Organization, held in Mexico City, February 27–28, 2003, women and men discussed the economic and social implications of free trade, the implementation of economic, social, and cultural rights in this context, and the formation of a multisector force contributing to the drawing up of proposals for the modification of neoliberal policy.

Women activists in the anti-free trade struggle mobilize a human dignity discourse together with various types of feminist discourses in order to construct the human rights subject positions of women. They claim that because they are human, they are entitled to the human rights to health, food, education, welfare, and so on, which they cannot access if they are discriminated against and their specific conditions are not recognized—women's rights are human rights. This banner fixes meaning in terms of equality: women struggle for human rights in free trade because they are humans and consequently their rights are human rights. This construction is coherent with their struggle against discrimination: discrimination violates human dignity and prevents women from exercising their economic, political, social, and cultural rights in the same way as men. In the following quote, for example, GyE mobilizes a discourse of human dignity in order to construct women's rights as human rights: "the change still to come is an understanding that when it comes to human rights, women are also human, that we have the right to dignity, health, food, a life without violence, education, voluntary maternity, work, land, housing, basic services, leisure time, and political and social participation" (Red Género y Economía et al. 2003).

Workers

Labor rights have been recognized for a very long time, but workers themselves did not necessarily consider their rights to be human rights in the sense of their identification with human dignity. In the case of Mexico, this was mainly due to the focus of human rights discourse on CPRs during the initial years of discourse construction. Workers themselves, however, have been the subjects of human rights discourse in Mexico since the 1980s, when the first human rights NGOs became concerned with the increasing repression of union leaders. The consideration of specific workers' rights as human rights—the rights to a decent wage, to strike, to a healthy working environment based on human dignity rather than class—are a more recent local construction. Labor rights as human rights are related to the increasing power of corporations and the state's failure to mediate between employers and employees in the context of globalization. The human rights approach to labor rights is a conceptual effort to make labor, and thus humans, rather than production, the central focus of a system characterized by increasing technological innovation and the global division of labor (Paredes Olguín 2004:104). It applies to global trade because human rights form the international legal framework guaranteeing dignity for everyone. Union activist Ramon Aceves, for example, mobilizes a discourse of human rights in order to identify limits with regard to the exploitation of labor by capital in economic globalization:

> ...the processes of change force workers to enter a dynamic in which labor productivity is the necessary condition for economic development, and this, with its capacity for capital reproduction, cannot offer a notion of work as a means to completely satisfy human needs...Without forgetting, of course, that according to the logic of the market the worker should continue to produce without concern for earnings, as these are subject to the capacity for production...In this way, globalization in its current form has sidestepped the issue of human rights (Aceves 2000:5).

For workers, humanity is at the heart of their concerns when speaking of labor rights in human rights frameworks. Observe how Ramón Aceves (2003) also mobilizes a discourse of human dignity to construct workers' rights as human rights:

> ...any struggle developed by workers for the defense of labor rights is based precisely on human rights...because human rights are the basis for everything. That is to say that together human rights place the human at the centre and at that level we are all human. The human factor is related to how we go about recovering that idea, how we go about introducing it into discourse, how we go about orienting action towards human rights, therefore it is a process of construction we want to conduct successfully (Aceves, 2003).

Workers identify with the idea of humanity underpinning human rights discourse and through identifying themselves as human subjects they construct their human rights subjects position and build solidarity with other groups who, beyond their status as "humans," would otherwise be considered "different," that is, women, farmers, indigenous peoples. It is possible to see this construction of solidarity on the basis of identification with humanity in the following quote from an interview with Antonio Villalba (2004), who mobilizes a discourse of human dignity to construct workers' support of women's rights: "…we are developing the theory that the struggle for labor rights is the struggle for the human rights of workers, that the struggle to ensure that women are not subject to pregnancy tests is the struggle for the most basic rights of women, and struggling for all of these is to struggle for human rights" (Villalba 2004).

Farmers
Farmers, like workers, have been subjects of human rights for over 20 years, mainly due to their suffering governmental repression over a significant period of time. However, a more strategic view of human rights in which farmers become more than mere subjects of repression is rather new—some five years, according to archives consulted. This strategic view is related to new discourses and does not yet represent a broad mobilization for the purpose of constructing subject positions. At present it is mostly used by farmers' leaders, as the majority of farmers understand human rights in the traditional sense whereby they are a tool for the identification of CPR violations. Farmers therefore see human rights as a means to defend themselves from governmental repression, which is still widespread (Oficina del Alto Comisionado de las Naciones Unidas para los Derechos Humanos en México 2003). NGOs working with farmers, like Food First and Informational and Action Network (FIAN International), share this view. They note that farmers do not see their demands in terms of rights; human rights constructions of farmers' rights are an NGO strategy, FIAN International activist Alicia Carriquiriborde claims. She argues that if leaders mobilize human rights discourses, it is because the government accepts them as legitimate framework for negotiation, but that does not mean that most farmers mobilize human rights discourses in the construction of subject positions or even agendas (Carriquiriborde 2004).

The mobilization of human rights repertoires by farmers' leaders for the construction of subject positions expresses itself in a slightly different way to the cases of women and workers. This can be considered a consequence of the specific circumstances of the discrimination suffered by farmers and indigenous people in Mexico. They use discourses of human dignity to advance the idea that "people" should be located at the center of free trade. However, human dignity does not account for their subject position; they identify with the idea of "citizens" in the sense that all citizens enjoy equal rights. However, the identification of farmers with citizenship is not of the same order as that of NGO activists, because while the source of identification for farmers is equality of rights on the basis of human dignity, the source of identification for NGO activists is the right to participate per se.

Citizenship is a powerful subject position for farmers—who are largely indigenous people—as they are frequently discursively constructed as "poor," "illiterate," and the recipients of government privileges and favors (Suárez 2004). Suárez mobilizes a citizen rights discourse to claim that farmers are equal to urban populations and in this way they have legitimate entitlements to services offered to the rest of the population, such as education, housing, and health. This is important in terms of specific farmers' needs, because their demands have traditionally been constructed in terms of subsidies or credits and rarely in terms of services directed to the fulfillment of the rights of a particular social group. This discursive construction effectively means that if they are equal to urban populations and have equal rights, then their particular rights as a group are legitimate rights.

As Victor Quintana explains, only on rare occasions have farmers been considered citizens. He contrasts a discourse of citizenship with farmers' experience in order to highlight the importance of their construction as citizens. While civil society is characterized by the entitlement to rights and the existence of social movements, he noted, farmers are one of the most active movements so they are members of civil society but have no rights. Their demands are not usually seen as rights, but as grants. Human rights can be used to counterattack this argument because every human and citizen has rights. In addition, the possession of rights empowers farmers in negotiations with the government because such rights make them citizens in these constructions. As citizens, farmers have the right to do the job they see as culturally acceptable—the majority of farmers are indigenous people who have a close cultural and spiritual relationship with the land, so working as farmers is the most culturally acceptable job for them.[1] If they have to migrate to the cities or the United States due to a lack of support for agricultural activities, they are prevented from being farmers and thus from exercising their labor and cultural rights. The state therefore has to guarantee that farmers can fully exercise their rights as citizens.

Construction of the human rights subject position of farmers as citizens can be observed in the following quote from Suárez:

> And the other fundamental point is the question of the treatment of citizens and of equals, because farmers are seen as farmers and not as citizens. There is a problem here with respect to farmers assuming citizenship.... I would see it as a struggle, of a transition from the absence of citizenship in rural areas to a process of citizenship construction in these areas by farmers. It is also a question of constructing autonomous subjects of rights in rural areas that includes individuals, citizens, collectives, communities, peoples and organizations in relation to the State and institutions. I think this is a central issue of what we are currently facing with respect to the denial of their rights and the failure to recognize them as citizens. Historically they have always been identified, at best, as agricultural and farm producers and eventually as a population subject to the political control of groups outside their sphere such as political parties, in particular the PRI, the federal government, state government or local party bosses. They represent a population that has been denied rights throughout history. Therefore, in the country's transition to democracy we see, with great force and inequality, the rise of citizen movements for the defense and recognition of citizenship rights and human rights in rural areas (Suárez 2004).

Farmer identification with citizenship in terms of equality in the enjoyment of rights can also be observed, in the case of Mexico, in the construction of the "right to be a farmer," which is the result of an argument based on the intertextuality of two rights: the right to work and the right to culture, which was suggested by the human rights NGO "Miguel Agustín Pro Juárez" Human Rights Center (Prodh Center) in 2003 (Centro de Derechos Humanos "Miguel Agustín Pro Juárez" 2003).[2] Farmers' leaders have now adopted this construction, the legitimacy of which rests on the recognition of the two legally recognized rights underlying it. In the following quotes, Suárez and Quintana use "the right to be a farmer" as a discourse that helps to identify the different ways that free trade prevents them from being farmers and forces them to leave their land and emigrate to the United States:

> The right to be a farmer on one's own land. That is to say, that while the land is no longer profitable and there is a reduction in government subsidies, farmers are forced to migrate and cease to be farmers against their wishes...Yes, (it is a question) of identity, as they are forced to work outside the country. In the case of Chihuahua a

minority works the land, while others work in the cities, in the service industry, therefore what we see is a loss of farmer identity. But there is also a disruption of families and a tearing of the social fabric of communities, so the right to maintain communities and the right to sustain an integrated family are also affected (Quintana 2003).

...a central proposal of the farmers' movement, and a central part of its claims, is respect for the right to continue being farmers, to pursue this activity and not have this right violated. The right to continue being farmers and the right not to have to migrate is used in opposition to a policy that forces them to abandon their productive activities and expels them from their communities, not allowing them to respect their decision to be farmers. Therefore, we have strongly argued this point, the right to continue being farmers and the right to not have to migrate (Suárez 2004).

Summing up, identification with human rights discourse is different in SMOs and NGOs, therefore subject positions are different in each case. On the one hand, NGO activists do not claim to represent anyone in particular because their job is to lobby their own policy proposals and assessments. They therefore construct subject positions in terms of citizens demanding participation in policymaking, the meaning of which they fix with human rights. On the other hand, SMO activists identify with the idea of equality based on human dignity: since everyone is human, everyone has dignity and is therefore entitled to the rights attached to such a concept. Because there is no fundamental identity beyond the symbolic construction achieved by identification, in each case (women, workers, and farmers) this construction is different.

CONSTRUCTION OF AGENDAS AND MASS MOBILIZATION WITH HUMAN RIGHTS

SMOs and NGOs use particular rights that are issue-specific when employed in the mobilization of human rights discourses for the purposes of fixing meaning. For example, activists may use the right to food as a nodal point fixing meaning in terms of state control in agricultural policy. This right defines such issues as security, land, and sustainability in terms of human rights treaties, jurisprudence, and rhetoric, all of which are based on ideas of human dignity, decent living standards, and cultural adequacy, rather than those of capital, efficiency, and profit, which are notions linked to the discourse of economic enactment. However human rights cannot fix meaning in absolute terms since SMOs and NGOs mobilize other discourses with which they identify, such as development, food sovereignty, and gender, and fix meaning in terms of human rights using specific nodal points such as group rights or the rights to life, to food, to work, and to development, as well as the broader idea of ESCRs in order to produce different effects of meaning. They use either ESCRs or group rights as nodal points according to whether they are SMOs or NGOs.

The Agendas of SMOs: Constructing Agents' Interests

In the first place, SMOs appeal to their human rights subject positions, that is, their particular group rights (i.e., women's rights). For instance, women fix meaning in their human rights agendas using gender and ESCR discourses. In the following quote we can see how Concha constructs violations of women's right to decent living standards by mobilizing a discourse of women's interests (services, health, and labor) and a discourse of ESCR:

> …the question of services affects us greatly because it is a question of medicines, of the withdrawal of the state from health care, which has to cover women, and which complicates their work and increases costs. The question is therefore important because due to investment the sources of work are disappearing, people are being fired, so these are some of the aspects and some of the consequences (for women's rights)…(Concha 2003).

A similar construction is to be found in the following quote from Quintana, who mobilizes a discourse of farmers' demands together with one of ESCRs in order to determine how free trade exercises a negative impact on farmers' lives:

> In the first place it affects their right to work by damaging the profitability of many crops, and they really have to work but they do not make a living, therefore the right to live with dignity from their work is affected. The right to food is affected because by receiving less for their products their diet is negatively affected. The right to live from the land is affected for they have to move with their families to seek employment elsewhere. These rights are seriously affected by the Agreement and in the case of Chihuahua the value of basic crops has tumbled, the prices for crops such as beans, corn and oats have collapsed and it is increasingly difficult to survive as farmers, to live off the land and not abandon it (Quintana 2003).

The Agendas of NGOs: The Rights to Development, to Food and ESCR as Nodal Points

NGOs do not use human rights-related subject positions (citizenship) to claim their own rights as we see in the case of SMOs. However, they frequently mobilize demands for the rights to participation and information when access to organizations is denied, as is the case with policymaking at the WTO. As I pointed out earlier in this chapter, NGOs are concerned with human rights as a series of values that in their view should underpin trade policy. Consequently, in their agendas they mobilize nodal points related to the issues falling within their specific field of concern. In the case of the NGOs studied here, they mobilize a series of nodal points dealing with various dimensions of the problems they are interested in addressing.

More specifically, they address structural issues concerning trade policy using two rights as nodal points: 1) the right to development, which refers to the entitlement of each state to control its economy and defend its economic self-determination[3] and 2) the right to food, which refers to the various stages of the agricultural process: production, storage, commercialization, and nutrition.[4] In order to establish issue-specificity in their broader economic arguments, together with the right to development and the right to food, which can be used either independently or in conjunction, they mobilize nodal points that are narrower in scope, particularly the cultural rights of indigenous peoples in terms of their access to natural resources, and the rights to water and to a clean environment. Finally, in order to address the individual or community, dimension of the impact of trade policy, they mobilize ESCRs and the right to life.

When the right to development is mobilized together with any of the other nodal points, it fixes meaning in three specific agendas related to free trade: social development, the economy, and the environment. First, the right to development when used in conjunction with ESCRs and the rights to participation and information fix meaning in social policy for the provision of welfare services. The following quote illustrates how Sandoval mobilizes a state duty discourse of human rights and the idea of ESCR to challenge the idea that the state is powerless and can do nothing to provide welfare. In this construction, the mobilization of the right to development shifts the discussion from ability to obligation:

> We are more involved in handling the range of economic, social and cultural rights, specifically within the conceptual framework of an

adequate standard of living, and we see very few civil and political rights except in connection with the right to information and the right to association, in terms of citizen participation. But we do manage a concept of how to ensure that our conceptual framework of social development gains greater force and effectiveness. Therefore we have reinforced our concept of development, of social development, with a human rights perspective in such a way that we now believe our concept of development incorporates elements of equity, justice and sustainability based on an ESCR perspective...

For the type of work we do, which is specifically focused on social development, we have discovered in ESCR the arguments and criteria that allow us to perform more effectively. We have privileged ESCR because they are more closely related to our work, but we also employ the concept of the right to development which basically brings together all rights, not only ESCRs but also civil and political rights, as well as the right to a healthy environment. On a daily basis we are probably more involved in the research, promotion and denunciation of ESCR violations, but in the broader view of the right to development we are aware of the integral nature of rights, and when I say that we focus more on ESCR...(Sandoval 2003).

Second, activists also use the right to development in combination with economic discourses so that meaning is fixed in development strategies and economic policy with ideas of state sovereignty and self-determination. In the following quote, Villamar contrasts a discourse of economic globalization with a discourse incorporating the right to development in order to construct a nodal point that makes policy diversity possible in a political economy marked by homogeneity:

...the right to development, which continues to be a very diffuse and abstract right, is nevertheless very useful to us as a means of support in the sense that it establishes obligations for the State to guarantee autonomy on the path to development. And if globalization offers anything it is the recipe, that is to say a process of uniformity in practice, a single globalization, a brutal process that attempts to hide the major interests that promote it and consequently reduces the diversity of paths to development...Therefore the first tool that the right to development provided us with is the government's commitment to respect the diverse paths to development and not just one. This was the first thing we discovered and it was very important for us...(Villamar 2004).

Third, the right to development is also used in the environmentalist agenda in conjunction with the rights to water, a clean environment, and the cultural rights of indigenous peoples to have access to natural resources. Together, these nodal points fix meaning in the environmental agenda around ideas of state responsibility in the enforcement of domestic environmental law in order to comply with human rights obligations. In the following quote, Villamar uses the right to development and the rights to information and consultation/participation as nodal points to fix meaning in terms of citizen participation in decision-making processes affecting the environment, as stipulated in the sustainable development discourse of Rio Summit documents.

> ...In practical terms it has come as a surprise, for the vast majority working on the problem of water, to demonstrate how Commentary 15 stipulates that access to water for all is a human right. Therefore, when you propose this and point out that it exists, that it was enacted just a year and a half ago...it is refreshing, because it offers you a very clear instrument for linkage and helps avoid a reductionist plan of action based on a constitutional framework...
>
> ...(Regarding ILO Covenant 169 concerning indigenous rights) I can offer an example of fellow workers involved in the struggle concerning a dam project in La Parota, Guerrero. They now use it. But the indigenous struggle, the discourse of all indigenous struggles right now in many parts of the world is Covenant 169...its origin is more from the perspective of multiculturalism, of respect for multiculturalism. The *ejidatarios* (holders of a share in communal lands) of Petén, Guerrero, are saying to their fellow indigenous peoples: the State has an obligation to respect this. Therefore, there is no reason why they should force the construction of a large dam upon us, a dam that will eliminate our culture in the name of modernization, or the governmental discourse that says they are against modernization...(Villamar 2004).

As for the right to food, it fixes meaning in the agricultural trade agenda at both structural and individual levels. While the issue of food sovereignty established in the right to food helps to tackle structural issues of agricultural trade, the individual and group impact of free trade is assessed by mobilizing a law enforcement discourse of human rights for the construction of individual cases. For instance, Carriquiriborde and Rangel mobilize the right to food to discursively construct the need to change structural issues that lead to individual violations of the right to food.

> Parents have a right to earn a dignified salary that allows them to feed their children. The problem is one of access to food. That is to say, how much access to food do you enjoy if minimum salaries are derisory and

do not cover (the basics)…in fact the concept of basic foodstuffs was withdrawn, because these basic foodstuffs cannot be purchased with a family income of 1400 pesos a month, and we are not talking about a large Mexican family here but a family of four: father, mother and two children. It is almost impossible on an individual level. So the proposals made are always articulated along with other rights because we maintain that human rights are not divisible…(Carriquiriborde 2004).

…the issue of land is the most important one to have arisen. Any affect on land means you are denying them the right to produce and also the right to development. Now we want to link this to the right to food…that is to say, the topic they wish to expropriate is the violation of the right to food. For example, in Tepeaca…we staged an action last October (2003) against the WDB where we stated: "we do not agree with your plan for the following reasons, for us development is something else" and we explained the type of development we wanted to see and how the PPP is an attack on this. We made it clear we did not want the PPP and needed them to provide us with detailed information concerning what they supported in Mexico, whether they were in fact meeting the World Development Bank's own environmental, informational and participative norms. In addition they were informed that we did not recognize the consultations they had held. The director of the World Development Bank here in Mexico informed us that they did not support the PPP (Puebla-Panama Plan, an infrastructure mega-project in Mexico and Central America) (Rangel 2004).

Regarding the environment, human rights cannot articulate the wider environmental agenda because it is not human-centered and environmentalists employ a variety of discourses that privilege nature and animal life over the life of humans. They use domestic law for the protection of nature, but have little knowledge of international human rights law. However, as environmentalist Alejandro Villamar indicates, since the lack of rules is what environmentalists share with everybody else in the anti-free trade struggle, environmental NGOs are finding the state duty and law enforcement discourses of human rights useful in their work with ecologist groups and for their own political work (lobbying, policy proposal). To this effect, Villamar mobilizes a discourse of legitimacy based on law enforcement and state duty to justify the use of a human-centered discourse for issues that require a shift from a focus on the human to a focus on the environment: "It is more a question of legitimacy than legality and that is the area for many of these struggles, where international instruments provide more legitimacy for struggles, resistance or proposals than a truly strong instrument, a binding instrument, with mechanisms for compliance such as sanctions" (Villamar 2004).

The Joint Agendas of SMO and NGO

When articulating these different agendas in joint political action against free trade, specificity is useful, especially for the articulation of SMOs with NGOs, and NGOs with NGOs, as opposed to the articulation of SMOs with SMOs—except in the case of articulating women's SMOs with mixed SMOs. Using ESCRs as a nodal point is particularly helpful as SMOs see these rights more in relation to the formulation of socioeconomic demands than CPRs, which are usually linked to instances of physical threat to activists (state repression). For SMOs, ESCRs are different from CPRs: ESCRs refer to the globalization agenda while CPRs are more related to the "traditional" field of expertise of human rights NGOs. At the same time, the use of specific nodal points, such as the right to food or the right to development allows SMOs to address structural issues while focusing on the individual and social groups. These rights allow for a hegemonic articulation of SMOs and NGOs. This can be seen in the following quote from Sandoval who explains the importance of a human rights political approach for articulation:

> For the work we do, which is specifically focused on social development, we have discovered in ESCR the arguments and criteria that allow us to perform more effectively. We have privileged ESCR because they are more closely related to what we do.... The question of human rights sometimes meets with resistance because people want immediate solutions to their problems, above all in the organizations we work with and on the subject of poverty... but once this community begins to see the importance of organization, the discourse of human rights helps them to strengthen their own organizations and achieve more, to improve other things (Sandoval 2003).

ESCRs are particularly useful for women. While farmers do manage to join other social actors, especially workers, through the use of food sovereignty discourses, women cannot articulate with mixed groups using gender discourses. Consequently, they join others in the broader struggle for free trade by identifying with the matter of human dignity. Concha constructs the role of human rights in articulating organizations in this way:

> ...(human rights discourse) has allowed them to achieve public awareness, to stimulate social awareness of the problematic of women and the need to find an answer and offer a solution to this problematic. The human rights perspective has therefore facilitated their entry into

the humanistic current that struggles for these rights throughout the world. They have therefore become established at the national and international levels...(Concha 2003).

Women are aware of the importance of joint action incorporating both women and men in the broader struggle against free trade if political pressure is to meet with success. They see human rights—particularly ESCRs—as the most effective way of achieving this success, as the following quote from a conference paper indicates:

> Influential work is also required to nourish our networks and coordinate common topics, maintaining close relations with the workers' and environmental movements, both North and South, as well as with international cooperation organisms proposing practical changes and policy changes at the global level as they have the advantage of gaining easier access to the international financial institutions and the WTO...It is recommended that the Latin American Women Transforming the Economy Network, together with social organizations, unions and human rights organizations, promote the formation of working groups to foster an effort to demand respect for people's rights in globalization (Red Nacional Género Comercio y Derechos Humanos et al. 2002:14).

Labor SMOs also seek articulation with social movements, understood in their broader sense, as they believe that uniting forces with NGOs in the struggle against free trade is key. Workers no longer believe that they have a privileged status in collective action, and argue that human rights—specifically rights such as the right to food—mobilized with other discourses—such as food sovereignty—could advance articulation with NGOs and other SMOs, such as women's SMOs. Equality in terms of human dignity allows for identification with others for, as union activist Villalba notes, the struggle for one's rights is also the struggle for others' rights: "...we are developing the theory that the struggle for labor rights is the struggle for the human rights of workers, that the struggle for women not to be subject to pregnancy tests is the struggle for the most basic women's rights, that the struggle for all of these is a question of human rights" (Villalba 2004).

Although workers, women, and NGOs seek human rights articulation based on human dignity, farmers do not. Farmers do not consider themselves part of the wider movement against free trade; they are only interested in their own agendas, and any articulation with other sectors is intended to bring solidarity to their own causes rather than entry into a hegemonic articulation based on the mutual solidarity created by identification with equality on the grounds of human dignity—human rights makes them equal to others but they do not identify with others. Although they use human rights in combination with food sovereignty in order to bring a more structural meaning to the issues concerning the agricultural economy, they do not see this as a means to articulate with others. However, when necessary, human rights allow them to receive the support of human rights or migration NGOs. When seeking alliances, they are interested in the solidarity of others with their own causes and not reciprocal support. Their human rights-related subject position as citizens, as opposed to humans, reinforces this argument as can be seen in the following quote from Suárez:

> These events (systematic killings, rights violations) attract the solidarity and support of human rights networks. But what is most interesting for us, at the heart of the most recent movement we have begun, is that this leads to a coalition of networks and unions, in particular the Mexican Unions Front, with the National Union of Workers, with the farmers' movement and also with human rights networks, in support of the farmers' movement. Consequently the human rights tendency articulates itself with the farmers' struggle for the right to existence and the right to food sovereignty. I believe that this human rights tendency is very important because it is also connected to the building of networks and alliances around the subject of rural migration. This covers migration networks from their points of origin and destinations in Mexico and The United States. Therefore, it is question of the rights of the rural population and the rights of migrants and this in turn is a vehicle for the articulation of extremely powerful networks and alliances (Suárez 2004).

Mass Mobilization

While the construction of joint agendas is possible through the identification of specificity, fixing meaning with human rights in mass mobilization proves to be much more problematic. This has specific implications for SMO's use of human rights discourse since mass mobilization is one of their main strategies (demonstrations, marches, sit-ins, etc.). This failure to articulate mass mobilization could be linked to the fact that the use of human rights discourse by SMOs is usually handled by the leaders of such organizations who use this discourse for articulation with NGOs in joint actions such as lobbying and public policy design.

At the grassroots level, workers and farmers do not mobilize human rights discourses—workers occasionally refer to workers' or labor rights, but these are not necessarily linked to the larger international framework of human rights, while farmers do not mention human rights at all. This was evident during the march against "neoliberal structural reforms" (electricity privatization, VAT on medicines and food stuffs) called by independent unions and farmers organizations such as El Barzón and Agriculture Can Take No More, together with the NGO network Advocate for the National Unity against Neoliberlism, on November 27, 2003. Although the latter's manifesto fixed meaning with human rights, it had no impact on the march whatsoever and human rights discourse was conspicuous by its absence in the mobilization. What united farmers and workers was opposition to their common foes: privatization, neoliberalism, and foreign investment. Farmers and workers believe, in effect, that articulation is better achieved by identifying a common enemy or problem, such as neoliberal structural reforms, the common enemy in the multisector march of November 27, 2003.

The absence of human rights articulation at the grassroots level is related, among other things, to the failure of human rights NGOs to work with SMOs in pursuing specific SMO strategies and goals; other issues influencing this are subject position constructions, but the absence of human rights NGO work is very important. Human rights NGOs play a key role in the hegemonization of human rights discourse because they are privileged subjects in the construction and intertextuality of that discourse. The problem is that human rights NGOs have failed to change their traditional, CPR-target strategies when dealing with ESCRs. Changing their strategies to make SMOs an important subject of ESCRs should include working with SMOs at the grassroots level since the subjects involved in mass mobilizations need to understand human rights discourse if they are to recognize its potential as an empty signifier, that is, as a discourse capable of providing the necessary means of identification on the grounds of equality with respect to human dignity, and of fixing meaning in terms of what most SMOs and NGOs seek in relation to free trade: rules for capital. This can be seen in the opinion of NGO activist Rangel who asserts that mobilization is generally a matter of identification:

> I believe it is fundamental that everyone is clear that what identifies us is the fact that our rights are being violated, some in one way, others in another way, but that they are being violated. And perhaps we should not even use the adjective human but refer to them simply as rights...but that this does bring us together. This unites us. And if

people do identify with this, if they say they are violating my rights too, I am the same as them. The problem is therefore a question of mobilization. For mobilization to exist, or for a more precise defence of your problem, that is where more specialization is needed regarding what each person is feeling (Rangel 2004).

To sum up, in the construction of joint agendas and mass mobilization, activists use human rights nodal points, as "human rights" represents too general a "name." For the construction of agendas, both SMOs and NGOs generally use ESCRs as opposed to CPRs or human rights in general, because they see these offering a more specific

Table 3 Subject positions and agendas with human rights articulation

Subject position	NGO			SMO		
	Citizen (participation)			Human (dignity) Citizen (equality in rights)		
Fixing meaning in joint agendas	Nodal point (principal right fixing meaning)	Mobilized with	Field where meaning is fixed	Nodal point	Mobilized with	Field
	Right to development	ESCRs	Social policy	ESCR	Gender	All fields
		The economy	Economic policy		Development	
		Indigenous rights/ natural resources	The environment		Food sovereignty	
	Right to food	Food sovereignty	Agricultural trade	Group rights (women, farmers, workers)	Gender Development Food sovereignty	All fields
		ESCR	Farmers' welfare			
Fixing meaning in joint action	NGO/NGO NGO/SMO			SMO/NGO Never occurs: • SMO/SMO • mass mobilization of SMOs/SMOs, SMOs/NGOs		

reference to the problems presented by free trade. More specifically, SMO activists mobilize a variety of discourses with which they identify together with the group rights of activists. NGOs, for their part, mobilize such ESCRs as the right to development and the right to food, together with other nodal points formed by food sovereignty. For the organization of mass mobilizations, human rights are not efficient enough in themselves because they represent a strategy most commonly employed by SMOs, and only SMO leaders are familiar with the discourse. To a great extent, this situation can be explained by the failure of human rights NGOs to change their ESCR strategy to include SMOs as subjects. For a summary of how subject positions and agendas are constructed in human rights articulations, refer to table 3.

Conclusions

As an empty signifier, human rights articulate different social agents with the underlying value of equality established on the grounds of human dignity and citizenship. However, human rights are not the only nodal points fixing meaning. Activists use a variety of discourses such as gender equality, food sovereignty, and sustainable development in addition to human rights in order to identify nodal points, fix meaning, and articulate themselves within the larger movement against free trade.

Chapter 6

Articulating Anti-free Trade Struggles with Human Rights Discourse

Introduction

The first part of the book offered a genealogical examination of the structural and subjective issues favoring the emergence of human rights as an insurrectionary practice in the field of free trade. In the second part of the book, so far the analysis of discursive practices has demonstrated how social gents construct hegemonic projects (worldviews), subject positions (identities), and articulation (mass mobilization and agendas) using human rights discourse. All that remains to be done now is to describe how subject positions, agendas, and trade views are handled in specific cases of articulation in the anti-free trade struggle. Therefore this last chapter assesses articulation through the study of the construction of agendas in two cases. First, the Mexican branch and general secretariat of the Hemispheric Social Alliance (HSA). This is an intersector and region-wide SMOs and NGOs articulation opposing the forthcoming FTAA, a hemispheric extension of the NAFTA, which is planned to come into force during the second half of the first decade of the twenty-first century. The focus is on the Mexican branch, RMALC, based in Mexico City.

Second, the articulation contesting the Agreement on Economic Partnership, Political Co-ordination and Co-operation between the Mexican Government and the European Union (Global Agreement). This articulation, which is referred to as the Democratic Clause Project (DCP), is an NGO-led articulation bringing together anti-free trade, development, and human rights NGOs. It is designed to articulate NGOs, and eventually SMOs, with the human rights principles underlying the so-called democratic clause in order to demand the formal recognition of a citizen committee and a social observatory as the means to comply with the government's human rights commitments. While articulation cannot be reduced to text construction, it does express itself in declarations and statements made at summits, meetings, and other NGO and SMO gatherings.

THE HEMISPHERIC SOCIAL ALLIANCE

Former U.S. president Bill Clinton first called for the FTAA during the Americas Summit, held in Miami, United States, in December 1994. While he called for the reinforcement of democracy and sustainable development in the region, as well as for regional economic integration, it was clear that the FTAA was planned as an expansion of NAFTA throughout the hemisphere, the preparation of which had seen low wages and loose labor protection used as "comparative advantages" in Mexico, and the closing of factories in the United States that were preparing to move to their poorer, less labor-regulated, new trade partner.

Organized workers throughout the country—including those from corporatist and independent unions—were aware of this situation. Consequently, the Workers' Inter-American Organization (ORIT—the Spanish acronym for Organización Regional Interamericana de Trabajadores) organized the First and Second Labor Forums, Workers and Integration. These took place simultaneously to the trade ministers' summits in Denver, United States, in 1995; and Cartagena, Colombia, in 1996. Workers discussed action plans and proposals to influence FTAA negotiations in favor of implementing labor standards (Osorio 1998). The discourses mobilized at these meetings to discursively construct the implications of free trade for workers were a series of labor-related repertoires, especially union rights. The discursive construction of rights here, though, was not based on the underlying assumption of human dignity in human rights discourses. Labor rights were constructed strictly on the basis of worker identity.

More specifically, in Denver, workers mobilized discourses of workers' rights without relating them to human rights in terms of the chain of equivalence created by human dignity. The declaration stated that: "A future FTAA should guarantee, at the very least, freedom of association and the right to collective bargaining, the prohibition of forced labor and discrimination in the workplace, and the promotion of higher standards with respect to health and safety, the working week and child labor."[1] In Cartagena, unions mobilized typically tripartite negotiation style discourses to demand consultation. They also requested that economic integration be coherent with the "universally recognized" rights to free trade unionism, collective bargaining, security, and industrial safety. Gendered labor discourses were also mobilized together with demands for the prohibition of forced and child labor and all forms of discrimination, including unequal payment based on gender.[2]

In both declarations workers mobilized rights discourses, but these were not connected to the idea of human dignity activists identify with when mobilizing human rights discourses. This demonstrates that although they were using "rights" discourses they were not framing their demands in human rights discourses but in more class-related notions of "workers' rights." The lack of a reference to workers' rights as human rights had to do with the fact that at the time human rights discourse was mostly referred to in issues related to transition to democracy. In addition, the role of rights repertoires in workers' construction of the impact of free trade was not that of articulating them with other subjects. Rights repertoires were used then to advance group interests, partly because they had not joined other subjects, or asked others to join them yet.

Diversifying the Struggle against Free Trade: NGO Involvement and the Incorporation of Human Rights Discourses

It was not until the Third Labor Forum, Workers and Integration, held in May 1997 during the Third Trade Ministerial Summit in Belo Horizonte, Brazil, that workers called for articulation with other sectors and types of organizations. This multiplied the discourses mobilized and consequently the subject positions included in their statements and declarations. The ORIT finally opened the free trade discussion to other sectors and the declaration itself was based on a document presented by SMOs and NGOs. This time a myriad of social agents, which included the ORIT, farmers and indigenous SMOs from Mexico, and NGOs from Brazil, Canada, Chile, the United States, and Mexico, ratified the final declaration. The inclusion of these sectors incorporated discourses that other SMOs and NGOs mobilized in their own agendas vis-à-vis the FTAA. Therefore, in addition to labor rights they began to use discourses of sustainable and fair development to construct notions of a desirable environment, economic policy, and food sovereignty. More importantly, they started to use human rights discourses to advance ideas of negative impact on specific social groups.[3]

The incorporation of gender and migration NGOs added human rights discourses in the ongoing construction of the socioeconomic agenda and incipient NGO-SMO articulation against the FTAA. For the first time, in opposition to the FTAA, activists started to mobilize "rights" discourses beyond workers' specific class interests in order to construct their view of the impact of FTAA enforcement. However, workers' rights were still the major nodal point fixing meaning in the agenda. The following quote, taken from the Final Declaration, shows how discourses usually mobilized by NGOs, such as democracy, together with discourses SMOs mobilize, such as food sovereignty, were used to construct meaning, but with a focus on workers' rights:

> We need an agreement that promotes development for peoples throughout the continent, that recognizes and strives to reduce inequalities, and that permits and promotes the integration of our economies, but based on democratically defined national development projects designed to complement each other. The FTAA should guarantee the protection and improvement of the environment, respect for the rights of migrants, promote food sovereignty and boost small and medium sized companies. With respect to foreign investment, performance requisites should be negotiated along with regulation that protects labor rights.
>
> So called "free trade" is in fact trade regulation that increases the advantages of international capital, whether speculative or not, with respect to productive investment and the rights and well-being of workers.
>
> ...There can be no FTAA if it does not include a social agenda covering at least the following fundamental elements:
>
> I) Broad and plural participation of peoples in the negotiations via truly democratic mechanisms.
>
> II) Respect for, and improvement of, all economic and social rights of workers.[4]

The coincidence of NGO participation and mobilization of human rights discourses in the anti-free trade agenda was more evident during the seminar, The Americas Solidarity Forum, held in Montreal, Canada, in September 1997. NGOs from Canada, Mexico, Guatemala, Uruguay, Colombia, Argentina, and Chile; workers (including women) from El Salvador, Haiti, Peru, Brazil; and environmentalists from throughout the region signed the final declaration, "Building

Sustainable and Democratic Americas, with Solidarity and without Poverty." They mobilized discourses of labor, the environment, migration, and gender, together with state duty-human rights repertoires in order to construct the need for state regulation of corporate activity for the protection of people and the environment.[5]

In this declaration, SMOs and NGOs used such discourses as gender and development, and a focus on the state's duty to protect women's and workers' rights and the environment from corporate abuse, while guaranteeing social welfare for the poor—as opposed to law enforcement discourses. This revealed that activists had adopted a more political, as opposed to legal, human rights approach to free trade. Rules for trade were constructed in a very holistic way that comprehended many of the subject positions involved in the struggle against free trade, although they did not explicitly refer to the human dignity underpinning human rights discourse. This meant that although subject positions had multiplied, human rights discourses were not necessarily mobilized as empty signifiers articulating subjects, but rather as nodal points fixing meaning in the agenda according to state duty with respect to the protection of rights and in conjunction with other discourses. According to Osorio, the demands were:

> To adopt a Social, Labor and Environmental Rights Charter for the Americas that includes: measures destined to arrest the negative impacts of economic liberalization; norms for the respect of human and democratic rights (in particular those of women and children); labor norms and sanction mechanisms for cases of violations of the same; mechanisms for the protection of migrant workers; mechanisms that guarantee the provision of public education and health services; harmonization of environmental norms; mechanisms for the protection of national cultures (in particular those of indigenous peoples); measures to guarantee food sovereignty.[6]

The creation of a joint SMO and NGO campaign against the FTAA was formalized one year later during the First People's Summit held simultaneous to the Second Americas Summit, in Santiago de Chile, April 15–18, 1998. This was because of the official setting up of the HSA, which was established in the First Declaration of the People's Summit. In the Proposal for the Action Plan, "Towards a Hemispheric Social Alliance, for Democratic, Fair and Sustainable Development," activists simultaneously mobilized discourses of participative democracy, sustainable development, social justice, cultural/ethnic diversity, and human rights. They demanded the fulfillment of group rights—women, workers, environmentalists, and citizens—vis-à-vis free trade. However, these rights were referred to in relation to each of these groups but not linked to ideas of human dignity. This again reveals that although a diversity of actors were using human rights discourses to fix meaning, human rights discourse was not yet articulating them. The following quote demonstrates how no reference is made to common ground in the mobilization of rights discourses:

> ...We are convinced that America does not need free trade: it needs fair trade, regulated investment and responsible consumption to privilege our national development projects.
>
> ...We call on governments to give priority to our peoples on topics not considered in official conferences. In particular we highlight all of those topics discussed at the Peoples' Summit: the human, social and labor rights of women, environmentalists and citizens; originating peoples and black communities; sustainable development; alternatives to socio-economic integration; rural workers and Agricultural reform, and ethics in political processes. With a cross-sector criterion, the forums also analyzed the following topics: globalization and integration; development and sustainability; investment; work and quality of life as well as a follow-up to the Summit.[7]

Incorporation of Human Rights NGOs: Negotiating Articulation

Up to this point, NGOs joining the anti-FTAA campaign had addressed a variety of issues (i.e., democracy, development, gender, the environment, and even human rights). However, human rights NGOs did not join until the First Peoples' Summit of 1998 when human rights discourse had already been introduced by such NGOs as the RMALC, which was familiar with human rights as a result of its inclusion in the democracy hegemonic project of the 1990s. Their participation in the First People's Summit of 1998 was modest in terms of attendance—a handful of organizations. A human rights forum was then held, simultaneous to other subject-specific forums such as those dealing with environmental issues, trade alternatives, education, ethics, indigenous peoples, women, parliamentary issues, and trade unions.

This forum addressed issues that were not directly linked to the social impact of trade but to the strengthening of a general human rights framework (the training of human rights activists and demands for state signature of human rights instruments), and accountability of financial and trade institutions via citizen surveillance. Human rights NGOs did not handle discourses usually mobilized to construct free trade issues, such as economic and development policy.

The only trade-related demand was that the WTO makes its normativity compatible with human rights covenants. Human rights NGOs were trying, however, to introduce a legalistic view of human rights that was not yet dominant in the agenda (1998).

The increasing participation of human rights NGOs did not guarantee a better human rights understanding of free trade in the declarations, as they did not address trade-related issues themselves (i.e., investment, tariffs, rules of origin, etc.). This has to do with the fact that international human rights discourses had not yet addressed trade-related problems as such. However, it also had to do with the fact that although the declaration includes other discourses that SMOs usually identify with, such as development and gender, these were mobilized with a law enforcement discourse. Observe this heavily legalistic approach in the following quotes from the declaration:

> (17) Emphasize transparency in public administration, and in particular, the creation of specific mechanisms that guarantee citizen participation in the design, supervision and introduction of public policy at the national and international levels. Similarly, ensure the creation of mechanisms for citizen participation and control of international financial institutions, the WTO, the Summit Implementation Review Group (SIRG) and the OAS.
>
> (18) The protection of the environment as an indivisible and interdependent right along with others. It is only through development policies that guarantee a safe, clean and ecologically rational environment that the right to a dignified life for present generations can be equitably satisfied, without affecting the right of future generations to equitatively satisfy their own needs. The irreversible nature of environmental damage demands that States prioritize abstention from activities that have a negative environmental impact despite the immediate benefits these activities may generate. Mechanisms should be established that guarantee developed countries assume responsibility for the environmental costs of those activities carried out in developing countries, by either the public sector or private sector, together with controls that minimize said costs and duly respond to the damage caused (1998).

In fact, the Human Rights Forum Declaration principally mobilized the discourses of citizen participation and law enforcement, which are discourses usually appealing to NGO activist identification but not to SMO activist identification. Human rights NGO participation was marginal, so this simplified view of human rights-related discourses did not manage to dominate the Final Declaration of the summit, which was constructed with a more political human rights approach based on state duty toward many types of social gents.[8]

This citizen rights-oriented human rights agenda was again taken to the HSA's first hemispheric coordination meeting held in San Jose, Costa Rica, March 12–14, 1999. This time, attendance at the human rights forum was broader and of a higher profile, which meant that free trade was starting to influence the agendas of human rights NGOs as democratic projects were on the wane. The most important international and regional human rights NGO articulations were present, such as Amnesty International, the Center for Justice and International Law—United States, the Latin American and Caribbean Committee for the Defense of Women's Rights, the Corporation for the Promotion and Defense of Peoples' Rights—Chile, Rights and Democracy—Canada, the International Federation of Human Rights (IFHR), the National Network of Civil Organizations—Mexico (RedTDT), and the Inter-American Platform for Human Rights, Democracy and Development. These organizations mobilized a more legalistic approach focusing on law-making for the protection of human rights in free trade and law enforcement in accordance with the Inter-American Convention and Court. It focused on citizen subject positions and proposed a participative democracy with a social dimension throughout the region together with the general encouragement of sustainable development alternatives with social justice. The means to achieve this was the design of an alternative social agenda and the promotion of human rights, among other strategies. The following quote shows how political and legal human rights approaches were mobilized simultaneously:

> ...the primary obligation of States is to respect, protect and favor the exercising of all universal and indivisible human rights. All other social and economic actors should also respect human rights. This obligation equally applies to multilateral institutions and national and multinational companies.
>
> The UDHR, due to its hierarchical superiority in the international judicial order, prevails over all treaties, including trade agreements or investment, and should explicitly respond to the principle of the Primacy of Human Rights. Signatory states of these agreements should unconditionally respect the regional instruments that establish civil and political rights as well as economic, social and cultural rights.
>
> They should work towards bringing to the public's attention violations of human rights caused by the implementation of neo-liberal measures such as free trade agreements; identify those responsible; seek sanctions and the payment of damages, as well as the adoption of measures

that ensure there will be no repetition of said violations (Regional Coordination Committee of the Hemispheric Social Alliance 1999).

As human rights NGO participation in the struggle against hemispheric integration continued to widen, SMOs and other NGOs started to resist the heavily legalistic agenda of human rights NGOs because these human rights NGOs had come late to an ongoing discussion (Herrera 2004).[9] Other NGOs reclaimed ownership of the discourse because they had joined the struggle earlier than human rights NGOs. By doing this, they asserted that the latter were not in any position to impose a citizen-oriented view of human rights that failed to consider other discourses and hence failed to articulate. In the end, SMOs and NGOs mobilized a variety of discourses that allowed for a diversity of human rights subject positions included in the rights of women, workers, and farmers.

Human rights NGOs' loss of control of the agenda was clearly expressed during the Second People's Summit held simultaneously to the Third State Summit in Quebec, Canada, in 2001. Notwithstanding the legalistic language resulting from human rights NGO participation (see for instance, 2001b), SMO and social NGO control over the agenda guaranteed that the Final Declaration mobilized socioeconomic discourses frequently used by SMOs and social NGOs (sustainable and economic development, food sovereignty, cultural identity, etc.), with specific human rights usually used as nodal points by the three different types of social agents analyzed here (see table 3). First, the rights that NGOs usually mobilize, such as free determination, food, health, access to water, land and resources, housing, decent living standard, culture, work and social security. Second, the rights that SMOs normally use, including ESCRs as a general reference, and the collective rights of indigenous peoples, migrants, children, and Afro-Americans. Finally, the rights usually referred to in the mainstream agenda of human rights NGOs, such as the rights to physical and psychological integrity and safety, and to nondiscrimination, information, and consultation (Alianza Social Continental 2001b).

The final declaration included human rights as one important discourse and thereby established the primacy of human dignity over trade and the duty of governments to make human rights the axis of free trade policy. According to the text, given the fact that free trade agreements led to widespread violations of human rights—income inequality, poverty, exclusion of indigenous people, destruction of agriculture, appropriation of indigenous knowledge, domestic violence, feminization of poverty, and so on—human rights law had to be more important than trade. The construction of human rights as the basis of free trade, highlighting the primacy of human dignity over commerce, can be seen in this quote from the Final Declaration. Here, social agents contrast a discourse of human dignity with one of neoliberal economic integration to construct a human rights view of free trade compatible with all social groups:

> ...The FTAA project is a statute of rights and freedoms for investors, consecrating the supremacy of capital over work, transforming life and the world into commodities, denying human rights, sabotaging democracy and undermining the sovereignty of States.
>
> We reject this trade liberalization and investment, deregulation and privatization project. We oppose a neo-liberal project that is racist, sexist, unjust and environmentally destructive.
>
> We propose the construction of new paths of continental integration based on democracy, equality, solidarity, respect for the environment and human rights.
>
> We wish to place human and collective rights first as they are established in international treaties for trade agreements. These rights should be respected without distinction or exclusion based on gender, sexual orientation, age, ethnicity, nationality, religion, political convictions or economic conditions.
>
> We want absolute respect for universal, equal and indivisible human rights...
>
> ...We want full respect for the fundamental rights of workers, and among these are the rights to free association, collective bargaining and the right to strike as well as the application of these to migrant workers.
>
> We want States that promote public well being and are capable of intervening actively to ensure respect for all human rights including, for women, freely consensual maternity; to strengthen democracy, including the right to communication; and ensure the production and distribution of wealth (Alianza Social Continental 2001b).

Legal and political human rights repertoires were included in the Declaration together with discourses appealing to a variety of subject positions. Consequently, human rights became an empty signifier fixing meaning in the anti-free trade struggle, that is, an empty signifier fixing meaning not only in terms of citizen participation in the formulation, implementation, and evaluation of social and economic policy, but also in terms of a wider idea of human dignity that created a sense of common interests among the social agents involved in the struggle. Free trade law was constructed as a type of law opposing human rights law, and reaffirmed the primacy of Inter-American human rights law over trade legislation. Therefore human rights finally articulated NGOs and SMOs, fixing meaning in terms of state duty and law enforcement for the protection of human dignity, which all subjects shared. For a chronology of events in the articulation against the FTAA, refer to table 4.

Table 4 Chronology of increasing human rights articulation in the Hemispheric Social Alliance

December 1994	Former U.S. president Bill Clinton called for the FTAA during the Americas Summit held in Miami, United States. Unions were the first to contest the possible consequences of an agreement mirroring NAFTA.
June 1995	Trade ministers met for negotiations in Denver, United States. Simultaneously, the First Labor Forum, Workers and Integration, organized by the Workers' Inter-American Organization, is held. The final declaration was constructed in terms of union rights rather than human rights. Therefore articulation was conducted with the mobilization of class as opposed to human dignity.
March 1996	Trade ministers met for negotiations in Cartagena, Colombia. Simultaneously, the ORIT called for the Second Labor Forum, Workers and Integration. The Final Declaration mobilized union and labor rights. Gender is added, but no references to human dignity are made. This articulates agents other than workers.
May 1997	The Third Trade Ministerial Summit takes place in Belo Horizonte, Brazil. Again, unions organize an alternative gathering, the Third Labor Forum, Workers and Integration. This time, however, they call on other sectors to join. Participation of NGOs leads to the inclusion of human rights repertoires in the Final Declaration.
September 1997	The Americas Solidarity Forum is held in Montreal, Canada. The Final Declaration mobilizes a variety of discourses such as environmentalism, migration, gender, and state duty-based human rights. The reference to human rights is not articulated around ideas of human dignity; it is only a means to call for state control of trade relations.
April 1998	The Second Americas Summit is held in Santiago, Chile. Simultaneously, the First People's Summit is held, marking the official setting up of the HSA. Multiple actor-specific forums are held, resulting in the first draft of the *Alternatives for the Americas*. The inclusion of NGOs and SMOs ensures the inclusion of human rights discourses and for the first time there are references to human dignity.
March 1999	The HSA's first hemispheric coordination meeting is held in San Jose, Costa Rica. Human rights discourse is prominent and legalistic.

Continued

Table 4 Continued

November 1999	A summit of trade ministers in Toronto, Canada. The first draft of *Alternatives for the Americas* is presented with a letter establishing articulation with human rights discourses. New drafts would be presented in 2001 and 2002, establishing the legal and political features of human rights repertoires.
April 2001	Second People's Summit is held simultaneously to the Third State Summit in Quebec, Canada. The final declaration includes human rights as an important discourse and thereby establishes the primacy of human dignity over trade and the duty of governments to make human rights the axis of free trade policy. There is full articulation with a legal-political human rights repertoire.

Alternatives for the Americas: Moving from Political to Legal-Political Human Rights Approaches

Articulation with human rights discourse was facilitated by SMO control of the human rights agenda, ensuring the inclusion of several discourses reflecting the specificities of SMO and NGO subject positions. However, this would not have been possible without the legal expertise of human rights NGOs. Articulation is achieved by the mobilization of several expert discourses such as development and ecology, together with references to the particularities of the chain of equivalence of human dignity—workers' and women's human rights, for instance. Nevertheless, the inclusion of more specific and expert references to legal texts, which SMOs and social NGOs include in their views of human rights as a hegemonic project, was the result of the expert knowledge of human rights NGOs in human rights law. Articulation is therefore achieved through a mixture of political and legal discourses, which appeal to both NGOs and SMOs.

SMO and NGO human rights articulation against the FTAA through striking a balance between legal and political discourses can be appreciated in the progressive transformation of the HSA's political platform and social agenda vis-à-vis free trade, *Alternatives for the Americas*. The first draft of *Alternatives for the Americas* was the product of the agent-specific forums held during the First People's Summit in Santiago de Chile. The document is comprised of a list of principles that should govern free trade and an inventory of their proposals corresponding to trade areas and subjects. Human rights discourse is not listed as the underlying principle but as an area related to the regulation of trade for the protection of people. While the principles are: democracy and participation, sovereignty and social welfare, reduction of inequalities, and sustainability; human rights are at the top of a list of "areas." The human rights list includes such issues as the environment, labor, migration, the role of the state, foreign investment, international finance, intellectual property rights, sustainable energy development, agriculture, access to markets and rules of origin, and dispute resolution. Human rights were not used as an empty signifier but as another discourse. The Introduction of *Alternatives for the Americas* shows that human rights discourse was mobilized in a series of "issues" rather than as an empty signifier articulating subjects:

> The document broaches the principal topics forming part of the official agenda of the FTAA negotiators (investment, finances, intellectual property rights, agriculture, access to markets and dispute resolution). Similarly, the document addresses topics of social relevance that governments have tended to ignore (human rights, the environment, labor, migration, the role of the state and energy). The problematic of other important groups, women and indigenous peoples, has been integrated into the completed document. The document opens with a chapter on the general principles underlying our alternative vision, followed by chapters that offer more concrete proposals. The topics and chapters complement each other, and for this reason it is considered important to read, study and discuss the document in its entirety (Alliance for Responsible Trade [ART-Estados Unidos] et al. 1998:11).

The human rights chapter contrasts the rights of people and the rights of corporations, and adopts a political rather than a legalistic approach to human rights as it refers to women's, workers', and indigenous subject positions and state duty, excluding law-making and enforcement through the courts from the discussion. Human rights as a framework was constructed in a letter attached to the first *Alternatives* draft, presented to the summit of trade ministers gathered in Toronto, Canada, in November 1999. Here, human rights were constructed as important issues not addressed by governments despite the fact they formed part of their international commitments:

> We are not opposed to the establishment of regulations for investment nor for international and regional trade. Neither do our criticisms of the dominant neo-liberal model of integration policies imply a desire to turn back the clock. But the current regulations have not helped our nations overcome or even reduce social and economic problems. We have proposed an alternative framework for labor which we continue to work on and develop. The proposal is summarized in the document *Alternatives for the Americas. Towards the Construction of a Hemispheric Accord of Peoples* which includes specific proposals for

those areas considered in the FTAA debates as well as for areas not considered and which should have been (such as human rights, labor rights, and environmental concerns).

...it is not possible to exclude trade and investment liberalization from the goals of "strengthening the democratic community," "eradicating poverty and discrimination" and "guaranteeing sustainable development." All of these principles form part of the agreement signed by the 34 nations attending the Americas Summit held in Miami in 1994. Neither is it possible to detach the discussion on investment and hemispheric trade from the commitment to human rights assumed by our governments when they signed the UDHR, the Inter-American Human Rights Agreement and other multilateral instruments (Alliance for Responsible Trade [ART-Estados Unidos] et al. 1998:17).

As mentioned above, in 1998 the participation of human rights NGOs was incipient and this can be seen in the scarcity of references to the legal implementation of human rights by the courts. Consider the following quote, where legalistic discourses are not mobilized at all and rights are not necessarily linked to human rights discourse:

The neo-liberal focus of free trade and hemispheric integration reaffirms both old and new rights for businesses. It speaks laterally of the rights of workers and says almost nothing about the social rights of the rest of the population. But the most serious deficiency is that it does not establish any link between them. The question of human rights and gender equity has in the past been integrated into regional or international trade agreements. Now they are subject to a critical broadside designed to show how they are nothing more than an obstacle to unimpeded trade. It is a strategy exclusively aimed at the promotion of economic growth at the cost of the social and economic well-being of large sectors of the population (Alliance for Responsible Trade [ART-Estados Unidos] et al. 1998:22).

In *Alternatives 2001*, by which time human rights NGOs had fully joined, the principles remained the same, but two new topics were added—gender and services—and human rights started to become more, although not predominantly, legalistic, making them more central in the elaboration of the framework and its underlying principles. For instance, while there is discourse with respect to human rights holism and state duty, the idea of "justice" is replaced by references to "norms." While referring to the human rights duties of transnational corporations and their obligations to the UDHR, it also includes references to the use of the legal mechanisms of the Inter-American system (courts and legal procedures). This quote from *Alternatives 2001* shows how more legalistic human rights discourses started to be mobilized:

> Ensure the right of all individuals affected by violations of their human rights to have access to simple, rapid and effective legal services that lead to restitution, compensation, rehabilitation, satisfaction, and the guarantee that the offending acts will not be repeated, according to basic guiding principles of the rights of victims of human rights violations and the international humanitarian right to reparation (UN document E/CN.4/1997/104). Affected individuals should also have the right to their choice of mechanism to achieve the most timely and effective response.
>
> Ensure the implementation of the decisions issued by the various agencies of the Universal and Regional Human Rights Protection System; collaborate in processes that handle and allocate sufficient economic resources for that systems' functioning. The member governments of the OAS are collective guarantors of said compliance, so they should ensure the objectives of investigations, sanctions for responsible parties, reparations for victims, and the adoption of measures so that the offending acts will not be repeated (Alianza Social Continental 2001a:29–30).

In *Alternatives 2002*, as women and environmentalists became more central subjects, gender was brought to the forefront, and new topics were included: natural resources, education, and communications. This meant that new discourses were mobilized in conjunction with human rights. However, at the same time human rights law enforcement was becoming increasingly central, as this quote shows:

> All mechanisms for conflict resolution in a trade or integration agreement should take into account international and regional human rights standards, as well as jurisprudence of the Inter-American Human Rights Commission and the Inter-American Court of Human Rights, in the process of resolving conflicts arising from claims concerning the violation of human rights principles established in these agreements.
>
> In its annual report for the General Assembly of the OAS, the Inter-American Commission will include a permanent chapter concerning measures and actions that guarantee that all trade and integration agreements respect the Inter-American and global instruments for the protection of human rights. In the preparation of said chapter, the Inter-American Commission will need to consider the contributions of civil society (Alianza Social Continental 2003:18).

The articulation of SMOs and NGOs with human rights discourse is realized here, since it combines state duty and law enforcement, while referring to the importance of making people the focus of trade due to the universality of human dignity, and to the rights of citizens to participate in economic decision-making. The rights of women, workers, and indigenous peoples are mobilized as nodal points in the areas of gender, labor, and the environment according to state duty. Fixing meaning with human rights refers to the primacy of human rights over trade regulations. It was a legal framework for lodging complaints in cases of abuses resulting from trade, including those perpetrated by corporations, in accordance with regional human rights mechanisms such as the Inter-American Convention.

To sum up, the HSA started as a workers' campaign that later included NGOs. However, at this point there was no articulation as such but only the sense of a common enemy—free trade. The campaign incorporated human rights discourse not as an empty signifier, but as one discourse mobilized together with many others, and fixed meaning politically rather than legally. The view of human rights became more legalistic as human rights NGOs joined fully. Although they tried to impose their view of human rights, SMO control of the agenda not only prevented this but also guaranteed a balance of legal and political perspectives that eventually permitted the hegemonic articulation of NGOs and SMOs with human rights. Articulation with human rights was realized only as the citizen subject positions of NGOs and the legalistic view of human rights NGOs were maintained simultaneous to the hegemonic articulation created by human dignity. NGOs and SMOs articulated as human rights were constructed as the regulatory framework for international trade that makes people, rather than capital, the center of development.

Nevertheless, as I shall discuss in the next section of the chapter, something more than a balance between law enforcement and state duty is needed to achieve hegemonic articulation in free trade using human rights discourse. The inclusion of different manifestations of subject positions and the mobilization of different discourses activists identify with are also central.

The Democratic Clause Project

Whereas the HSA started as a workers' campaign that progressively incorporated human rights discourses and articulated SMOs and NGOs, the DCP started as an NGO human rights articulation. This articulation saw articulatory potentiality in Article 1 of the Global Agreement, which stipulates that "Respect for democratic principles and fundamental human rights proclaimed by the Universal

Declaration of Human Rights, underpins the domestic and external policies of both Parties and constitutes an essential element of this Agreement" (Red Mexicana de Acción Frente al Libre Comercio et al. 2002b:1). NGOs made this reference to the UDHR a focus in their strategies to force the Mexican government to respect human rights in agreement with its international commitments. They have articulated with the democratic clause twice at different times, with different objectives and at different levels (national and transnational). These two different stages reflected the wider context and the expansion of human rights discourse in Mexico as discussed in the genealogy.

The First Stage: Articulating with Human Rights in Transition to Democracy

In 1996 the Mexican government and the European Union commenced negotiations for a comprehensive free trade and cooperation agreement. As is the case with most EU agreements with third countries, this included the so-called democratic clause. The Mexican government resisted its inclusion because human rights violations in the country were at a peak and it refused to be accountable for its actions to foreign governments (Margier 1997). Activists took advantage of this situation by centering their strategies on pressurizing European governments to make it a condition for signature of the accord. Anti-free trade, development, and human rights NGOs articulated by using a law-enforcement human rights discourse to form the underlying "democratic principles," arguing that a truly democratic government should agree to the democratic clause. If the Mexican government failed to accept it, its European counterparts had to refuse to sign the free trade agreement.

NGOs, like governments, saw the clause as a legal justification for termination of the agreement or the imposition of sanctions on the party seriously violating human rights—usually the third party. The human rights NGOs in the articulation mobilized the democratic clause to push the government to advance the CPR national agenda of the transition to democracy project, anti-free trade, and development NGOs attempting to influence transnational negotiations tried to draw attention to the antidemocratic behavior of the Mexican government that effectively prevented citizen participation in trade policymaking. For their part, trade NGOs believed that if they were prevented from participating in policy design, at least they could resist enforcement of the agreement and make the democratic clause a means for the implementation of CPRs and thus advance the democratic project, which in the end had the objective of establishing a democratic government that could reverse neoliberal economic policy.

In the end, neither signature (1999) nor enforcement of the agreement (2000) was prevented, but the Global Agreement did include a democratic clause—although this is nothing out of the ordinary since most EU trade agreements with third countries include such a clause. NGOs started to discuss a change in strategy according to the new scenario. On the one hand, anti-free trade, development, environmental, labor, and women's NGOs discussed the viability of establishing a citizen observatory to monitor the social and environmental performance of corporations, together with the establishment of more formal means of citizen participation, according to the "evolution" of the agreement. This is explained by the fact that the Global Agreement itself is more than a trade treaty since it includes political relations and cooperation in several areas. In serving its political and cooperation objectives, parties may modify the agreement—therefore it can "evolve." They believed that by directly pointing out the shortcomings and social impact of free trade, they could influence the parties to modify the agreement.

On the other hand, for human rights NGOs the notion of "implementation" was constructed by mobilizing two typical NGO discourses: citizen participation and legal enforcement. Consequently, failing to have "mechanisms for implementation" meant a lack of machinery for human rights justiciability (courts, rules, protocols, etc.) and formal means of participation (committees, consultations, etc). Basing their actions mostly on articles of the Global Agreement, human rights NGOs demanded either the expansion of cooperation toward supplementary accords on the environment and labor; a supplementary accord on human rights with legal mechanisms for implementation; mechanisms linked to the universal system of implementation; a human rights office formed by independent experts and recognized by both Mexico and the EU; a working committee on human rights; or the possibility of sanctions and individual communications (Arroyo and Peñaloza Méndez 2000, Red Mexicana de Acción Frente al Libre Comercio et al. 2001). Mobilizing a law-enforcement view of human rights, human rights NGOs suggested that if the democratic clause was provided with legal mechanisms for implementation it would have the potential to unite social agents. The following quote demonstrates this:

> If having incorporated a democratic clause into the Global Agreement seemed an advance, civil organizations who have followed up on the

Agreement share the belief that the clause must be given content, as is the case with other clauses, and make it an umbrella instrument for the protection and promotion of civil, political, economic, social and cultural rights (Red Mexicana de Acción Frente al Libre Comercio et al. 2002a:2).

In spite of the discussions, activists did not reactivate the DCP in the short term because the context was changing. The democracy hegemonic project was drawing to a close after a change of party in the presidential office. Therefore the human rights panorama that encouraged some human rights NGOs to take action in the DCP had changed drastically, particularly regarding the government's attitude toward international human rights law. Unlike its predecessors from the PRI, the new government from the PAN was willing to sign and ratify conventions and protocols that made the use of such options as a democratic clause for general human rights implementation increasingly unnecessary. Simultaneously, however, the new administration was enforcing a conservative economic program that was bringing the neglected socioeconomic rights agenda to the fore. Social conflict moved from the political to the economic sphere as a consequence of the new president's democratic commitments and conservative economic agenda. While access to human rights mechanisms was improving, violations of ESCRs were on the rise. The changing scenario is referred to in this quote in which the "Miguel Agustín Pro Juárez" Human Rights Center (Prodh Center) mobilizes a legal discourse to construct the changes characterizing the new situation:

> …The human rights situation in our country was alarming and the forums for citizen complaints and for the Mexican State to issue its reports were extremely limited.
>
> …To assert human rights as an "essential element" of the agreement was seen as a great opportunity to construct alternatives. Nevertheless, from 1997 to the present, although the human rights situation in Mexico is not radically different, we have seen a series of changes that modify expectations concerning the possible putting into practice of the democratic clause, as well as the interpretation of precisely what is meant by the assertion that the Universal Declaration is an "essential element" in a trade agreement.
>
> …Among these changes there are two which stand out: greater ease and effectiveness in gaining access to international human rights systems for Mexico, and the increasing penetration of European capital which is subject to little or no regulation, particularly with respect to the environment and labor rights (Centro de Derechos Humanos

"Miguel Agustín Pro Juárez and Iniciativa de Copenhague para Centroamérica y México, 2002:1–2).

The Second Stage: The "Positive Dimension" of the Clause and Transnational Collective Action

The second stage of the DCP commenced in 2002 as the RMALC, development NGO DECA-Equipo Pueblo and the Prodh Center articulated to form an advocacy group that could "revamp" the project in the light of the new context. They agreed to make the democratic clause functional in the terms of previous discussions by establishing legally binding mechanisms. Activists mobilized a law enforcement discourse that constructed the new objective of the democratic clause as a series of legally binding mechanisms aimed at observing respect for human rights, gender equality, and the environment. Therefore they agreed to lobby for the setting up of a citizen committee and a social observatory that could observe human rights in relation to trade and investment activities. Again, they were confident that a human rights legal approach would articulate subjects, not in pursuit of "transition to democracy," but in pursuit of the broader objective—this time related to transnational collective action—of observing human rights within trade and investment activities, as this quote shows:

> Those of us proposing this Common Strategy believe that we can contribute to the improvement and modification of the Agreement by means of changes to the limitations indicated and the avoidance of negative impacts, with the participation of organizations from civil society. It is necessary that the Global Agreement be given content and mechanisms to enforce the very principles it stipulates and, in effect, ensure that relations between Mexico and the European Union serve as a watershed in the creation of international agreements that, beyond the promotion of free trade and the deregulation of investment, promote respect for Human Rights in terms of their indivisibility, gender equity, respect for the environment, the active participation of civil society, democracy and peace between peoples (Red Mexicana de Acción Frente al Libre Comercio, 2002b).

Articulation with human rights on this occasion was not meant to advance transition to democracy but to promote law enforcement in trade and investment, especially in terms of making corporations accountable to domestic law and dealing with the preferential treatment they received. The human rights discourse mobilized was still legalistic but used ESCRs as nodal points fixing meaning more specifically. NGOs mobilized a legal discourse in order to construct legal enforcement pertinent to corporations for the protection of ESCRs, as this quote demonstrates:

> Despite the increasing penetration of European capital and the fact that in Mexico European corporations are not subject to environmental and labor norms, or questions of social responsibility as in Europe, reports by the State concerning what is done to monitor the performance and operations of European corporations are not registered in detail with respect to human rights, and with the limitations of universal and regional monitoring organizations in terms of economic, social and cultural rights, these particularities are diluted.
>
> In addition, given greater access for the presentation of claims concerning the violation of civil and political rights before universal and regional systems, the next step would be to increase possibilities with respect to economic, social and cultural rights, not only in international systems but also in the new organs of global governance, such as trade agreements and other economic and financial institutions. In the case of trade agreements the objective would be to oblige trading partners to issue reports concerning violations of human rights in the context of their trade relations and according to their own mechanisms and institutions (Centro de Derechos Humanos "Miguel Agustín Pro Juárez" 2002:4).

Since on this occasion the democratic clause was focused on the objective of fairer trade rather than on the prevention of human rights violations in Chiapas or electoral fraud at the national level, NGOs again mobilized a legal approach focused on citizen participation to forward the idea of a "positive dimension" as opposed to a "negative dimension" to the clause. The positive dimension required positive measures for the establishment of the "appropriate mechanisms" to guarantee respect, protection, and promotion of human rights, and the state duty to prevent corporations from violating human rights, not only with respect to CPRs as had happened up to that point, but also in relation to ESCRs. NGOs contrasted discourses of ECSRs and CPRs, and incorporated a citizen participation discourse in order to construct the positive dimension of the clause:

> ...In its documents, the EU recognizes that a positive dimension of the clause exists, that is, a willingness to take affirmative actions with regard to human rights. Nevertheless, up until now this has been limited to assistance for the strengthening of democratic institutions and is based on a very limited interpretation of article 39, regarding co-operation with respect to human rights and democracy, because it circumscribes human rights to democratic freedoms and it limits civil society to being an object and not subject to the implementation of the measures.

To recognize the active role of civil society and, based on the essential element of the agreement, to call on organized expressions of civil society from both sides involved in promoting respect for human rights is indispensable. That is why a broader reading of this article is necessary (Red Mexicana de Acción Frente al Libre Comercio et al. 2002b).

A positive dimension was therefore constructed as the means to implement human rights in the agreement as a whole: in cooperation human rights would be implemented through the establishment of a social observatory; in political dialogue it would be implemented through the creation of a Mexican-European citizen committee. Implementation of human rights in trade would be established with appropriate modifications to the agreement resulting from consultations with the citizen committee and reports from the social observatory (Red Mexicana de Acción Frente al Libre Comercio and Iniciativa de Copenhague para Centroamérica y México 2003). Human rights in this new interpretation of the democratic clause meant the establishment of legally binding mechanisms for human rights observation and citizen participation, as this quote demonstrates:

> A more comprehensive reading of this article permits greater harmony with other elements of the agreement which deal more directly with the impact of the relations between Mexico and the EU on economic, social and cultural rights and society participation, such as co-operation with regard to social matters, development and the environment, as well as political dialogue.
>
> Drawing from five years of work and experience in the EU-Mexico Civil Society Dialogue, our proposal is to give a positive dimension to the democratic clause based on these ideas. This means that the positive dimension of the democratic clause would express itself in an organic way in each of the three general aspects of the Global Agreement: political dialogue, co-operation and commercial and economic relations (Red Mexicana de Acción Frente al Libre Comercio et al. 2002b).

Consequently, the human rights legal approach underpinning the democratic clause became the only empty signifier fixing meaning in the whole of the agreement, not only in terms of CPR accountability as on previous occasions but, most importantly, in terms of three new aims: observation of the impact of the agreement on people, modification of the agreement for the improvement of the human rights record, and civil society participation in the first two. As a legalistic, citizen participation-oriented human rights discourse became the only empty signifier fixing meaning, subject positions were reduced exclusively to that of citizens.

The DCP thus conceived served to articulate development, human rights, and free trade NGOs during the First Forum for the Dialogue with Civil Society Mexico-European Union held in Brussels, Belgium, November 26, 2002 (Red Mexicana de Acción Frente al Libre Comercio and Iniciativa de Copenhague para Centroamérica y México 2002). Here some SMOs—GyE, FAT, and the Farmers' Democratic Front (FDC, the Spanish acronym for Frente Democrático Campesino)—joined the articulation to demand mechanisms for the observation of the human rights situation under the trade agreement, and citizen participation in trade policy and decision-making. They called on other SMOs and NGOs from all sectors—indigenous people, the poor, women, workers, and so on—to support the proposal of setting up a citizen committee and a social observatory to observe human rights implementation in the context of European and Mexican trade and investment activities. Mobilizing a legal discourse that makes Article 1 of the agreement the basis of all EU-Mexico political and economic activities, SMOs and NGOs articulated by demanding implementation of the democratic clause that was constructed as an article covering everyone's interests:

> The clause gains enforceability and legal force through its inclusion as an "essential element of the agreement" meaning that not only is it inherent to the agreement as one of its pillars, but that its implementation also has to be projected and developed. The democratic clause extends itself in other articles of the agreement, which develop a comprehensive vision of human rights referring to poverty alleviation, labor, the environment and marginalized groups...(Centro Prodh et al. 2002).

However, after 2002, articulation with human rights became difficult because this change of approach moved the human rights debate from the "transition to democracy" field, mostly populated by NGOs, to the socioeconomic field, mainly dominated by SMOs and social NGOs representing a complex array of subject positions. This obliged NGOs to articulate SMOs in the human rights chain of equivalence, but articulation became difficult because in the project as a whole, meaning was fixed according to the subject position of NGO activists, that is, from the perspective of citizen participation in the design, implementation, and assessment of policy. Interpretation of the democratic clause through the construction of the NGO subject position as citizens is reflected in a communiqué sent to the Joint Committee in May 2002:

> While in other economic integration processes evaluations of the impact of the Agreement have been conducted, for Mexico there is no balance of its effects. For this reason we call for the creation and formalization of mechanisms and instruments of participation for civil society and social sectors represented in State authorities which have been excluded until now, concretely the legislatures. By this means we request that during the meeting of the Joint Council in Brussels next May:
>
> 1. The parties call for an increase in their representation before the Legislative Powers of both.
>
> 2. The Mexican and European parties draw up a Joint declaration for the creation of a Mixed Consultative Committee (CCM—acronym in Spanish), under the protection of Article 49 of the Global Agreement, which establishes the ability of this organ to make decisions concerning the creation of special committees or organisms which provide assistance in the completion of its tasks.
>
> …Through the CCM, which will be formed by members of the Economic and Social Committee of the EU and members drawn from Mexican social, economic and civil sectors, we propose the establishment of many of the mechanisms described in the Report by the Economic and Social Committee of the EU on the subject of organized European civil society—a contribution of the Committee to the drawing up of the White Book. In particular we refer to establishment of the judicial basis for participation and consultation—in the broadest sense of the conceptualization developed in the report—via social dialogue, civil dialogue, public protests, audiences and reports (Red Mexicana de Acción Frente al Libre Comercio et al. 2002c:2).

The Difficulties of SMO-NGO Articulation and Transnational Articulation

Notwithstanding the successful experience of the First Forum for Dialogue with Civil Society Mexico-European Union, further articulation using the democratic clause proved increasingly difficult. This was due to factors concerning SMO and NGO differences (see table 2) and contesting constructions of human rights in Mexico and Europe.

SMO and NGO Differences

Articulation with the democratic clause became increasingly difficult because the positive dimension of the democratic clause made human rights an empty signifier fixing meaning in all areas of the agreement—from the political to the economic and cooperation spheres.

This included institutional citizen participation, which is properly the field of NGOs, but also observation and negotiation in fields more related to SMOs, especially labor and the environment. This was problematic because SMOs not only have different subject positions but also construct human rights notions through the mobilization of a variety of discourses together with human rights as nodal points, depending on the different effects of meaning they want to achieve. SMOs do not articulate using a general understanding of human rights as a single empty signifier (see table 3). This construction had implications on two levels.

Firstly, a focus on citizen subject positions—citizen participation via the committee and the social observatory—was a problem because SMO activists construct their subject positions differently. While NGOs are aware of their lack of representation and hold a citizen subject position, SMOs are concerned with the issues affecting them directly. NGOs are more concerned with fixing meaning in policy design and lobbying agendas, which are in turn aimed at tackling the issues faced by the movements they work with—women, workers, farmers, indigenous peoples, environmentalists (see table 3). SMOs considered these mechanisms to be abstract and to contribute little to solving the problems that they face in their daily lives. This view came to the surface during a workshop held in Brussels in 2003 (June 16–17, 2003) which was aimed at developing the social observatory and citizen committee proposals, as well as introducing the project to women and workers invited by the project sponsors (German organizations linked to the Socialist and the Green Parties, the Friedrich Ebert Foundation and the Heinrich Böll Foundation, respectively). Here, working women plainly stated that the social observatory and the committee made no sense whatsoever if they lacked mechanisms by which workers could directly complain about corporate abuse and receive a concrete response. NGOs claimed that a trade agreement could not become a human rights covenant and that formal mechanisms for citizen participation were needed in order to achieve human rights implementation. This explanation only served to disappoint them and, in the end, they avoided commitment to further participation.

Second, since SMOs prefer political to legal approaches to human rights, their articulation required a definition of the project in the terrain of the political as well as the legal, that is, it required an appeal to state duty as well as to law enforcement through the courts. However, fixing meaning with a balance of political (state duty) and legal (law enforcement) approaches was not achieved. This was because NGOs shifted from mobilizing discourses of law enforcement via the courts to mobilizing discourses of law enforcement via citizen participation, which, rather than providing a political dimension, reduced the discourses mobilized for the construction of subject positions. European activist Helen Rupp pointed out the sudden change from law enforcement through the courts, an issue advanced by human rights NGOs from 2000 to 2001, to law enforcement via citizen participation, which she refers to as a "political route":

> During the first session of the Meeting in November of last year, Human Rights and the Democratic Clause, *"two routes"* were spoken of to achieve objectives with respect to the democratic clause. I believe that the proposals summarized in this document are related to what would be the *"first route"* which could be called the *"legal route"* as they refer to legal interpretations, of demands based on these interpretations, of modifications/extensions to the agreement or even of an additional agreement for human rights. *It seems to me that this route is not related to the common strategy without there being detailed discussion*...This would be to approach the subject from a less legal perspective, that is, something we could call a "political route," and I would like to propose certain reflections on this subject. From this perspective it is not so much a "legal problem" (how to apply the law and what mechanisms to apply in sanctioning HR violations) as an essentially political question: how much pressure can be exerted through denouncing HR violations and contrasting these with the promises of governments concerning respect for, and guarantees and protection of, HRs...(Rupp 2002).

Recently, NGOs have deployed a more balanced view of law enforcement and state duty, together with the inclusion of SMO discourses. For instance, during the Second Forum for Dialogue with Civil Society Mexico-European Union, held in Mexico City from February 28–March 1, 2005, NGOs continued to propose the social observatory and the citizen committee (Red Mexicana de Acción Frente al Libre Comercio and Iniciativa de Copenhague para Centroamérica y México 2005), but the democratic clause began to adopt a more balanced view of political and legal approaches, as the following quote from the final Declaration demonstrates:

> We again call on Mexico and the European Union to respond to the repeated proposal of making the clause subject to demands and legal application in terms of human rights, particularly with respect to the impact of trade and investment. We repeat that in accordance with the priority of human rights, founded on the United Nations Charter (103), the principal responsibility of States is to respect, promote and

guarantee integral rights above commercial rights (Red Mexicana de Acción Frente al Libre Comercio et al. 2005).

Furthermore, during this summit human rights ceased to be the only empty signifier as more discourses appeared, including that of social cohesion, which became increasingly central, as this quote, also from the final statement, demonstrates:

> We confirm our determination to contribute to stimulation of the process of association and integration of Mexico-EU which effectively strengthens the defense of human rights, preservation of the environment, equity, promotion of social cohesion and strengthening of democracy and the rule of law, and we demand that authorities urgently attend to the numerous cases of violations of the Human Rights of Indigenous Peoples, of the Human Rights of those detained in Guadalajara during the Heads of State Summit in May, 2004 and of the indigenous people detained in Oaxaca (Red Mexicana de Acción Frente al Libre Comercio et al. 2005).

However, the delay in including political approaches and specific nodal points mobilized by SMOs has prevented articulation between the two.

Contesting Human Rights Views in Transnational Collective Action

Although it proved problematic for SMO and NGO articulation, the positive dimension of the democratic clause led to the reformulation of activist views of international power relations. In contrast to the first stage of the project, in which the democratic clause articulated NGOs pursuing changes in the Mexican political system, in this second stage the reduction in scope—ESCRs within the trade and investment agreement—meant calling into question the performance of European states as much as the Mexican state. It therefore shifted the focus from the performance of the Mexican government to the performance of European capital and of European government control of this capital, as the following quote shows:

> ...it is very important that civil organizations begin to call for the establishment of mechanisms permitting the participation and consultation of civil society in the monitoring of human rights, not in a general sense, because that is already being done in the universal and regional systems by means of the changes mentioned above, but in terms of the bilateral relationship, specifically in terms of investment and trade. Consequently, if the possible mechanisms remain at

the level of generalities then human rights violations resulting from European investment will be diluted (Centro de Derechos Humanos "Miguel Agustín Pro Juárez" 2002:2).

This view was very different to the more traditional view involved in strategies intended to mobilize international pressure in order to force a state to end CPR abuse.[10] These strategies focus on the performance of weak states and assume that Western democracies have the authority to judge the human rights performance of others. European human rights NGOs resisted any shift in focus from habitual strategies, based on putting pressure on weak states, to strategies that included greater awareness of power relations in free trade negotiations. Europeans did not believe that any power issues were involved and preferred a purely legalistic approach to the assessment of all rights—making the agreement a mini-human rights commission.[11] Mexicans and Europeans had contesting views of the ways to fix meaning with human rights in international trade agreements. Consequently, Mexicans had to look for support from the wider human rights movement in order to convince Europeans that the change from a legal to a political approach had the support of most Mexican human rights NGOs. Nevertheless, as previously mentioned, there was also some resistance from Mexican NGOs.

The heavily Western-biased view of human rights is not unique to European human rights NGOs. Some Mexican NGOs also demonstrate this bias, as do more radical European groups. They all share the same view of human rights, although they see them as a problem rather than an advantage since they construct human rights as a discourse grounded on the authority of Western democracies. They therefore *assume* that human rights are not an adequate tool *for countries like Mexico*. This was evident during the Organized Civil Society's Third Meeting EU-Latin America-The Caribbean (April 13–15, 2004, Guadalajara, Mexico). At this meeting there was a confrontation between Mexican NGOs and some European anarchist groups that wanted human rights out of the picture because it was "a Western discourse."

Despite the fact that during the summit the "social statement" was entitled "People's rights are first," few references to human rights were included because there was no agreement between European and Mexican organizations as to what actually constituted human rights. In the end human rights were used only minimally as a nodal point fixing meaning in the declaration: they were referred to in terms of ESCR (their primacy over commercial trade), the protection of labor rights according to the ILO, discrimination toward migrants (especially in terms of their civil rights), and indigenous peoples (in terms of access to land and resources, and protection of their knowledge, Covenant 169).

European social NGOs also wanted to see a shift from a human rights discourse to one of "social cohesion," which is the discourse now used by the EU. This concept reduces the rights issue to public policy in cooperation rather than engaging in the treatment of structural issues concerning fundamental changes in the terms of the agreement. The declaration was therefore constructed in terms of development and social cohesion. Human rights virtually disappeared (2004b).

While NGO-SMO articulation was difficult because of the different discourses mobilized by the different types of organizations, transnational collective action became difficult because of the contesting views of human rights on both sides of the Atlantic.

To sum up, articulation with human rights using the democratic clause of the Global Agreement is mostly an NGO project in which human rights articulate many types of NGOs but have failed to articulate SMOs because they do not include subject positions expressing different kinds of interests that move beyond citizen participation, and failed to provide a balance between law enforcement and state duty approaches. Articulation at the transnational level has also been difficult because of contesting views of human rights in Mexico and Europe. For a chronology of the articulation against the Global Agreement, refer to table 5.

Table 5 Chronology of the first and second stages of the Democratic Clause Project

	First stage
1996	The Mexican government and the EU commence negotiations for a comprehensive free trade and cooperation agreement, which includes a democratic clause. Human rights and anti-free trade activists articulate around it to put pressure on the government to cease violations of civil and political rights and to not sign the agreement. Human rights discourse used is heavily liberal and focused on civil and political rights.
1999	The two parties sign the Global Agreement, which includes the democratic clause, inspired in the UDHR.
2000	The Global Agreement is enforced. Activists evaluate the impact of the previous three-year campaign and the direction to be taken. After 70 years in power, the PRI is replaced by the PAN, which campaigned with a liberal political agenda but a very conservative economic and social policy. The government-civil society relationship changes fundamentally.
	Second stage
January 2002	Two years after enforcement of the agreement and in the context of conservative economic policy, activists relaunch the DCP. The focus this time is making the democratic clause functional by establishing

Continued

Table 5 Continued

	legally binding mechanisms. Decision to lobby for a citizen committee and a social observatory for observing human rights in relation to trade and investment activities. This is referred to as a positive dimension as opposed to a negative dimension to the clause. Some organizations, especially those from Europe, oppose this turn because it moves away from the liberal approach they were familiar with. The discourse mobilized is heavily legal.
November 2002	After six years of demanding consultation, NGOs manage to get the governing parties to organize the First Forum for the Dialogue with Civil Society Mexico-European Union in Brussels, Belgium. SMOs join the network and articulation around the democratic clause is achieved. The legal human rights discourse becomes political in order to articulate SMOs.
April 2004	The Organized Civil Society's Third Meeting EU-Latin America-The Caribbean was held in Guadalajara, Jalisco. Europeans oppose the human rights interpretation that Mexican activists were giving to trade.
March 2005	The Second Forum for Dialogue with Civil Society Mexico-European Union is held in Mexico City. NGOs continue to propose the social observatory and the citizen committee, with a focus on both law and politics. However, SMOs are no longer very interested.

Conclusion

This chapter has assessed two NGO and SMO campaigns against free trade. On the one hand, the HSA, which was an initiative of workers, initiated opposition to the FTAA and eventually requested the participation of NGOs. The campaign incorporated human rights discourse, although not as an empty signifier but as one discourse mobilized together with many others, and fixed meaning politically rather than legally. Human rights NGOs wanted to dominate the discussions but subjects using more political approaches to human rights reclaimed their right to define meaning while using human rights as a nodal point. Nevertheless, human rights NGOs became increasingly important actors and their growing participation in defining discourse is seen in the legalistic features of human rights in the agenda. Articulation with human rights, however, was only achieved when the citizen subject positions of NGOs and the legalistic view of human rights NGOs were maintained simultaneous to the chain of equivalence created by human dignity. NGOs and SMOs articulated as human rights were constructed as the regulatory framework for international trade that makes people, rather than capital, the center of development.

On the other hand, the DCP is an NGO-led articulation bringing together anti-free trade, development, and human rights NGOs. It was first aimed at articulating NGOs, but eventually needed to articulate SMOs, with the human rights principles underlying the so-called democratic clause, in order to demand the formal recognition of a citizen committee and a social observatory as the means to comply with the government's human rights commitments. However it failed to articulate SMOs and NGOs because it focused on citizenship and failed to achieve a balance between law enforcement and state duty approaches. At the transnational level, contesting views on human rights strategies have also been a problem.

In chapter five we argued that whereas NGOs identify with human rights in terms of citizens and seek a balance between political and legal approaches, SMOs identify with a variety of subject positions expressed in different group rights, for example women's rights, and prefer a political rather than a legal human rights approach. Here I conclude that the HSA manages to articulate SMOs and NGOs as it achieves a balance of political and legal approaches, and includes a variety of subject positions including citizens. In contrast, the DCP manages to articulate only NGOs as it fails to mobilize more discourses and achieve a balance between legal and political approaches. These differences can be observed in table 6.

Table 6 Differences between the Hemispheric Social Alliance and the Democratic Clause Project

	HSA Starts	HSA Ends	DCP Starts	DCP Ends
Articulation	SMO	SMO-NGO	NGO	NGO
Subject positions	Workers	Citizens, workers, women, indigenous peoples, farmers	Citizens	Social groups and citizens
Hegemonic project	State duty	Balance between state duty and law enforcement	Law enforcement (via courts and citizen participation)	Balance between state duty and law enforcement
Human rights fixing meaning	Workers rights	Group rights, ESCR, citizen's rights to participation	Civil and political rights (democracy)	ESCR and CPR (free trade and investment)

Conclusions

The principal objective of this study was to demonstrate that the specific potential of human rights discourse for collective action is its ability to unite social agents that express divergent interests and identities in particular transnational contexts such as the anti-free trade struggle. Most studies of the politics of human rights have largely focused their attention on political change and the changes in norms that result from pressure exerted by social movement. The current study was more concerned with two sociopolitical issues: the structural and subjective factors making human rights an insurrectionary practice; and the strategic use of human rights discourse by social agents to find common ground for collective action in specific contexts.

A combination of different poststructuralist views of discourse and discourse analysis have therefore been employed here to provide a framework, facilitating an assessment of the structural/subjective factors permitting two things: 1) human rights discourse to emerge and develop in Mexico, and 2) an analysis of the discursive practices used in contemporary struggles against free trade. In these struggles, agents have established common ground through the use of human rights discourse. This discursive approach has demonstrated that human rights language and institutional frameworks constitute sites where political projects and worldviews can be negotiated. It must be pointed out, though, that this usually depends on the political context and the way the particular issue at stake relates to other discourses.

More specifically, through applying this framework to the case of Mexico, it has been possible to identify how the economic discourses shaping globalization, such as neoliberalism and free trade, have exerted an influence on human rights discourse. This expansion is evidenced by the addition of economic issues to the agenda. The use of economic discourse has also influenced the construction of agency since the multiplication of subjects has effectively led to a replacement of the Marxist discourses previously used for articulation, with the discourse of transition to democracy. It was this discourse of transition to democracy that formed the basis for the emergence and development of human rights discourse in Mexico. This shift toward more symbolic issues indicates that social movements are now concerned with a range of issues in addition to questions of material well-being. Having said this, a focus on symbolic issues such as human dignity does not necessarily undermine the construction of socioeconomic demands identified with social movements as class and material interests become part of a wider articulation identifying with human dignity.

As a result of the changes indicated above, human rights discourse has been increasingly used in Mexico to articulate anti-free trade struggles and has allowed groups to coordinate their actions with transnational organizations. Analysis of the discursive practices of NGOs and SMOs in contemporary anti-free trade articulations demonstrates that the construction of subject positions, hegemonic projects, and the use of mobilization help to provide unity and facilitate collective action in specific contexts.

However, while human rights discourse can potentially unite different subjects through its inclusion of numerous issues focused on the question of human life, certain limitations can be identified in the uses of such discourse. These limitations are linked to the discursive choices made by agents and the failure of some agents to design alternative strategies. Once this potential for human rights discourse to facilitate collective action against free trade has been established, a number of related factors come to the fore, such as the important role of structural change in establishing such discourse as a tool for collective action; the sociopolitical potential of human rights discourse to provide symbolic ground and advance material interests; and the limitations of this discourse. I shall now discuss these three issues in more detail.

Structural Change, Subjectivity and Human Rights Discourse

The examination of structural and subjective factors in Mexico has shown that the assessment of structural and subjective issues helps to identify the specific circumstances that permit human rights discourse to be used strategically for collective action in Mexico. The discussion of global structural change and the related emergence and multiplication of new social actors has shown that the emergence and development of human rights as an insurrectionary practice in anti-free trade struggles is context-specific.

Nevertheless, two issues related to structural change can be said to be more general. First, the influence of global change on international human rights discourse can be identified in the expansion of its rubric to include issues related to free trade and in the strengthening of mechanisms related to economic and social rights. These changes have made international human rights discourse a suitable tool for use in struggles related to the global political economy. Secondly, structural political change has also made internationalization of the human rights regime possible and contributed to the spread of democracy discourse. This is not to say that neoliberalism was promoted in order to make democracy and human rights the means to resist socioeconomic exploitation, but that the internationalization of these two discourses converted them into sites of power relations in Mexico. The battle in Mexico between existing power structures and social movements has been focused on defining the nature of hegemonic projects whereby human rights and democracy are employed in the service of either the interests of capital or of human life and nature.

In the specific case of Mexico, the imposition of neoliberalism can be seen in a trade discourse that favors business and demands that states abandon their participation in economic and social policy, at the same time relaxing legislation designed to support the local economy and protect labor, women, and nature. Accordingly, social agents constructed their structural positions in accordance with the state's failure to protect human life and nature and its inability to assume control of economic and social policy. As structural changes had a negative impact on the daily lives of many Mexicans, subjects replaced Marxist discourses with the discourse of transition to democracy and this in turn established the basis for the emergence and development of human rights discourse. Human rights discourse therefore served as an appropriate tool for transnational collective action as the rubric was expanded and it became internationalized.

Analysis of different cases in the Latin American region show that while some similarities can be identified in the emergence of liberal discourses for articulation, the specific political context and the particularities of corporatism in Mexico led to human rights discourse developing more slowly—although the discourse became evident in the 1980s, it had been used since the mid-1970s in both South and Central America. In addition, the specific characteristics of the transition to democracy project in Mexico delayed the construction of ESCRs discourse and the inclusion of disciplines other than law and politics during the decade of the 1990s, a period when transition to democracy had been replaced as a discourse throughout the region.

It is the conjunction of these two factors that established the necessary conditions for human rights discourse to not only become a means for subjects to achieve unity in their mobilizations, but also a useful tool in the design of agendas demanding the state become more involved in trade policy and the protection of human life and nature in general. This study therefore shows that, in the case of Mexico, the availability of international human rights as a discourse facilitating collective action in anti-free trade struggles was not a question of chance. Rather, it was the result of interaction between structural change and the identification of subjects with liberal principles and values in specific political contexts. These factors helped to establish the symbolic common ground necessary for creating the universality that, in Marxist terms, class is expected to establish.

What this specific case demonstrates, therefore, is that in cases where antagonisms develop differently, human rights discourse may not become an insurrectionary practice in the way it has in Mexico. The reluctance of some European NGOs to use human rights discourse may therefore be related to the specificities of the development of human rights discourse in Europe and the specific choices made by groups to employ a discourse focusing on New Conservatism rather than liberalism. It would therefore be interesting to see more research conducted on the structural and subjective particularities allowing for the development of human rights struggles in Asian, African, and European countries, or even in Latin American countries such as Venezuela, where democracy has existed since the late 1950s, to develop this idea of context determining whether human rights discourse comes to constitute an insurrectionary practice.

The Political Potentiality of Human Rights Discourse

The study of the structural and subjective factors allowing for the emergence and development of human rights as an insurrectionary practice showed the context-specific issues that allow human rights discourse to articulate collective action in Mexico. The analysis of SMO and NGO discursive practices allowed us to demonstrate how human rights discursive constructions facilitate unity in social struggles. The analysis of categories adapted from hegemony theory and the insights offered by interpretative repertories allowed us to examine how human rights discourse is used in the discursive practices of the social field to achieve common understanding, create a sense of sameness, and reach agreement in the design of agendas and the organization of mobilization.

Focusing human rights discourse on the question of humanity leads to the hegemonic articulation of the different social agents who come to identify with their fellow humans or citizens regardless of their status as workers, women, farmers, human rights defenders or developers. Articulation facilitates solidarity and the negotiation of agendas between different social groups. At the same time, through focusing human rights discourse on the state, SMOs and NGOs are able to tackle the problems introduced by free trade. These problems, related to the enforcement of free trade agreements, are perceived as fundamentally linked to the state's failure to engage in economic and social policy, and its unwillingness to prevent corporate abuse with regards to labor, women, and the environment. Through their identification with fellow human beings and the fixing of meaning with state duty and law enforcement, activists find common ground for the negotiation of agendas through the rubric of specific human rights. For example, the right to development or the right to food allows activists to fix meaning in the design of subject-specific agendas.

As a result of this analysis, it can be concluded that human rights discourse possesses not only legal but also political potential. The intertextuality of human rights facilitates articulation as well as the strategic use of rights for addressing the demands of social movements outside the courts. I discussed the claims of Baxi to the effect that human rights could become an important "insurrectionary practice" given the intertextuality of human rights values and instruments, and that this occurs when people involved in struggles expand the rubric of rights (Baxi 2003). I also explained that in Critical Legal Studies, intertextuality refers to the way texts are never completely new or self-evident, but formed by the conjunction of previous texts and their particular social contexts. Despite the fact that this intertextuality of human rights is a strategy usually employed in legal defense, this book has demonstrated that intertextuality as described by Baxi is a tool that can be used for the political as well as legal interpretation of human rights at the international level in such forums as the Global Agreement or FTAA in two ways. For instance, the report on farmers' rights cited in chapter five established the formulation of the "right to be a farmer," which is achieved through combining arguments related to two existing rights: the right to work and the right to culture. According to this formulation, being a farmer is not only a job, it is also an activity linked to a cultural identity (Centro de Derechos Humanos "Miguel Agustín Pro Juárez").

Intertextuality, as used in Mexican anti-free trade struggles, therefore, has political potential because it carries a surplus of political meaning that is expressed in the legitimacy of human rights law and the establishment of a wider political platform that offers the means to tackle the problem of human suffering. Take the case of the HSA, which has established a program of action based on a human rights understanding of free trade that addresses the demands of environmentalists, women, workers, farmers, and developers, among other social agents.

However, it should be noted that this potential varies according to whether articulation is mostly led by NGOs or SMOs, the categories of organization studied here at the empirical level. This research has shown that NGOs and SMOs have different concerns and that their strategies do not necessarily converge sufficiently to achieve articulation. These differences can also be used to identify different approaches to the use of human rights as an insurrectionary practice, that is, how human rights are used by subjects with different identities and material interests in order to find common ground. While both NGOs and SMOs manage to articulate with human rights, their construction of subject positions, formulation of agendas, and mass mobilization strategies are different. This means that articulation is used to incorporate an array of differing identities and interests in distinct ways, as the cases of the HSA and the DCP show. NGOs, especially human rights NGOs, tend to be less inclusive when dealing with different subject positions and usually fail to join SMO strategies, thereby reducing the scope for articulation.

The Limitations of Contemporary Human Rights Struggles against Free Trade in Mexico

Although the legitimacy and intertextuality of human rights have proved to be very useful in the cases analyzed, contemporary human rights struggles against free trade in Mexico also demonstrate certain limitations. These limitations are related to the following: the failure of activists to critically assess the human rights discourses they use in their strategies; the top-down nature of human rights strategies; and the incapacity of human rights NGOs to play a more active role in making human rights discourse more accessible to SMOs.

First, NGO and SMO activists tend to use human rights discourses without critically assessing their basic assumptions. The implications of this failure are twofold. On the one hand, since NGOs, especially human rights NGOs, rely on versions of human rights that are individualistic and focused exclusively on CPRs, the development of strategies for, and approaches to, ESCRs has been slow. To date, human rights NGOs have relied on human rights discourses that effectively prevent them from including a wider variety of disciplines in their approach, thereby limiting their ability to articulate with organizations working on ESCR-related issues. Since the limited production of academic literature on human rights in Mexico could account for the lack of systematic reflection on human rights discourses by activists, a greater number of sociological analyses of human rights theories and legal practices need to be produced.

On the other hand, while organizations do question the limitations of state-centered approaches to human rights, in their discursive practices they continue to identify state duty as one of the central features of human rights discourse. This is explained, and justified, by the cultural specificities of the region and Mexico's reduced power bargaining in the global political economy. Nevertheless, such emphasis should not become an obstacle to the political potential of human rights beyond national frontiers. The intertextuality of human rights discourse provides a unique opportunity for deployment of the discourse beyond state borders while a continued focus on the state prevents the rubric being expanded to include non-state actors—it has expanded considerably in terms of issues but little in terms of the agents responsible for human rights violations. Highlighting the responsibility of corporations toward human rights, for example, would make a significant contribution to the support of specific struggles.

Second, the use of human rights discourse for collective action in such transnational instances as free trade is predominantly top-down. This means that it is mostly social movement leaders and NGO activists involved in advocacy and lobbying who use human rights discourse to fix meaning in the construction of subject positions, hegemonic projects, and mobilization. Most grassroots SMOs are not familiar with human rights discourses. This presents an obstacle to their use for mass mobilization and the formulation of local human rights strategies.

Third, and this point is related to the top-down character of the use of human rights discourse, there is the failure of human rights NGOs to work more closely with SMOs and join them in their activities. This is partly explained by the reluctance of human rights NGOs to reassess the efficiency of their legal strategies when dealing with ESCRs, but is also explained by their failure to articulate with SMOs since they have so far failed to acknowledge alternative discourses and the importance of different subjectivities.

To sum up, analysis of the use of human rights discourse for collective action has shown that human rights develop as an insurrectionary practice in accordance with the specific structural and subjective conditions of a given context. It has also shown that human rights discourse has political potentiality for social movements working in this field as it serves to establish common ground where SMOs and NGOs can forward their particular agendas and provides the discursive means to address issues related to state duty and corporate responsibility.

This conclusion, however, does not ignore the limitations of the approach and recognizes the obvious need for similar research to be conducted in other regions and with reference to transnational collective action. This is of particular importance when we consider the dynamic nature of globalization, which requires not only local but also transnational solidarity. Human rights approaches to transnational collective action will be successful only when they establish common ground for diverse struggles. Research on the intertextuality of human rights discourse in transnational contexts such as the negotiation of external debt for poor countries or European policy for international migration would therefore reveal interesting features of the political potentiality of human rights intertextuality in transnational collective action. Further research in the area would also facilitate more constructive cooperation and go some way to address the necessary revision of methodologies and approaches in the context of a dynamic global political economy where the nature of the human rights struggle is subject to constant change.

NOTES

INTRODUCTION: A DISCURSIVE AND SOCIOPOLITICAL APPROACH TO FREE TRADE AND HUMAN RIGHTS

Some of the ideas used in this chapter were first published in the article "Derechos humanos y sociedad civil global: un aborde discursivo," in *Revista Iberoamericana de Derechos Humanos* (3), Autumn 2007 (ISBN: 970-07-6877-5). They are reproduced here with their permission.

1. Others did it long before. See, for example, Lefort, C. and Thompson, J.B. (1986). *The Political Forms of Modern Society: Bureaucracy, Democracy, Totalitarianism*. Cambridge: Polity Press; Fields, A.B. and Narr, W. (1992). Human Rights as a Holistic Concept. *Human Rights Quarterly*. 1992. 14 (1): 1–20; Aziz, N. (1995). The Human Rights Debate in an Era of Globalization: Hegemony of Discourse. *Bulletin of Concerned Asian Scholars*. 4 (27): 9–23; Hunt, A. (1990). Rights and Social Movements: Counter-Hegemonic Strategies. *Journal of Law and Society*. 17 (3): 309–328; Keck, M.E. and Sikkink, K. (1998b). Transnational Advocacy Networks in International Politics: Introduction. In *Activists beyond Borders*. Ithaca: Cornell University Press; Kusý, M. (1985). Chartism and "Real Socialism: Citizens against the State in Central-Eastern Europe. In Keane, J. Ed. *The Power of the Powerless*. London: Hutchinson; Stammers, N. (1993). Human Rights and Power. *Political Studies*. March 1993. 41 (1): 70–82; Aldana, J.C. and Vázquez Ortega, J.J. (2005). La ilegalidad de la legalidad: el discurso de los derechos humanos a fiscalización. In López Gutiérrez,C., Vázquez Ortega, J.J., and Uribe Patiño, F.J. Eds. *Globalización, violencia y derechos humanos. Entre lo manifiesto y lo oculto*. Mexico: UAM-Itaca.

2. The American School of Social Movements focuses on the situational (as opposed to structural) contexts that facilitate mobilization. Mobilization is considered a process by which instrumentally rational collective actors control the resources available to them in order to pursue collective goals and interests. There are three theoretical models elaborated as part of this approach: entrepreneurial mobilization theory (Mcadam et al. 1996, Zald and McCarthy 1979), the political process model (McAdam et al. 1996, Tilly 1978), and framing (Snow 1992, Tarrow 1992). First, drawing on organizational theory and rational choice political theory, entrepreneurial mobilization establishes that activists are rational actors

making their choices on the basis of a cost-benefit calculus: they invest resources (time, money, status) in order to lobby their demands. They adopt the form of organizations in order to systematize resources and guarantee the survival of the movement. Second, the political process model focuses on the state as a center of political conflict and mobilization depends on political timing because at certain times the state is more receptive or vulnerable. Therefore, in addition to resources, activists require political opportunities in order to act. Finally, framing is a response to the emphasis New Social Movement Theory places on identity and proposes a new focus on collective identities, core discourses, and frames of meaning that link members of social movements and movement networks to one another. Frames are concerned with how ideological messages mediate between "pre-figurative" and "strategic" politics and serve as a means to present the ideas and demands of activists (Snow 1986, 1992). See: Mcadam, D., Mccarthy, J.D., and Zald, M.N. Eds. (1996) *Comparative Perspectives on Social Movements. Political Opportunities, Mobilizing Structures, and Cultural Framings*. Cambridge: Cambridge University Press; Zald, M.N. and Mccarthy, J.D. (1979). *The Dynamics of Social Movements: Resource Mobilization, Social Control, and Tactics*. Cambridge, Mass.: Winthrop Publishers; Snow, D.A. (1992). Master Frames and Cycles of Protest. In Morris, A.D. and McClurg Mueller, C. Eds. *Frontiers in Social Movement Theory*. London: Yale University Press; S.Tarrow. (1992). Mentalities, Political Cultures, and Collective Action Frames: Constructing Meanings through Action. In A.D. Morris and C. McClurg Mueller. Eds. *Frontiers in Social Movement Theory*. London: Yale University Press; Tilly, C. (1978). *From Mobilization to Revolution*. Massachusetts: Addison-Wesley Publications.

3. North American Free Trade Agreement (1993); Bolivia (1995); Costa Rica (1995); The Group of Three (Venezuela, Colombia, Mexico) (1995); Nicaragua (1998); Chile (1999); Israel (2000); Global Agreement with the European Union (2000); Free Trade Agreement with the Northern Triangle (Norway, Iceland, Switzerland, Liechtenstein) (2001); El Salvador, Guatemala, and Honduras (2001). The most recent one was signed in 2005 with Japan. See: Secretaría de Economía (2006a) *Acuerdos y Negociaciones* [online]. Gobierno de México. Available from: http://www.economia.gob.mx. (January 18, 2006).

4. This tendency was already clear in 1993 when NAFTA was signed and has only increased—in 1993 exports represented 82.6 percent of the total (42,850.9 million dollars of a total of 51,832), and imports 69.29 percent (45,294.7 million dollars of a total of 65,366.5). By 2000 exports had already reached 88.7 percent (147,685.5 million dollars of a total of 166,454.8), and imports 61.81 percent (127,534.4 million dollars of a total of 174,457.8). While Mexico has increased its imports from China (from less than 1 percent in 1993 to 5.49 in 2003) and Japan (from 6 percent in 1993 to 11.6 percent in 2003), it has not

managed to export more to these countries. Exports to the EU have decreased from 5.38 percent in 1993 to 3.80 in 2003, and imports have remained almost the same (11.9 percent in 1993 and 10.44 in 2003) in spite of the trade agreement signed in 2000. Exports and imports with other groups of countries are not significant in statistical terms. Figures taken from the table of exports (1993–2004) and the table of imports (1993–2004). Secretaría de Economía (2006b) *Estadísticas de Comercio e IED. Tabla de Exportaciones y Tabla de Importaciones* [online]. Gobierno de México. Available from: http://www.economia.gob.mx/?P=2261. (January 25, 2006).
5. For an economic assessment of the commercial outcomes of Mexico's trade policy, see the work of RMALC at http://www.rmalc.org.mx, and García Alba, P., Gutiérrez, L., and Torres Ramírez, G. Eds. (2004). *El Nuevo Milenio Mexicano.* México y el Mundo I. Mexico: UAM Azcapotzalco.
6. The employment situation in Mexico is complex and cannot be analyzed solely in the light of free trade. Official figures show that between 1991 and 2003 the unemployment average was between 2 and 3 percent— the exception was 1995, after the financial crisis when unemployment reached 5 percent of the workforce—but these figures fail to provide information about the quality of the jobs, which could be badly paid or even exist in the informal economy. However, there is no direct link established between unemployment and free trade. Liberalization and stabilization policies in the 1980s contributed to unemployment, as the privatization of state industries led to massive redundancies, but more recently free trade is more related to low wages and the erosion of collective labor rights as part of labor flexibility, known in Mexico as the "restructuring of productivity." For a comprehensive analysis of employment in Mexico from the 1970s onward see: Oficina Del Alto Comisionado de las Naciones Unidas para Los Derechos Humanos en México. (2003). *Diagnóstico sobre la Situación de los Derechos Humanos en México.* Mexico: ONU. For an analysis of employment during the implementation of structural adjustment programs and stabilization policies, see: Gutiérrez Garza, E. (1990). La crisis laboral y la flexibilidad del trabajo. México 1983–1988. In Gutiérrez Garza, E. Ed. *Los saldos del sexenio (1982–1988).* Testimonios de la crisis IV. Mexico: Siglo XXI Editores. For an assessment of union activity during the 1980s and 1990s, see: Bizberg, I. (2003). Estado, organizaciones corporativas y democracia. In *México al inicio del siglo XXI. Democracia, ciudadanía y desarrollo.* Mexico: CIESAS-Porrúa; Ortega, M. and Solís, A.A. (1990). Estado, Capital y Sindicatos, México 1983–1988. In Gutiérrez Garza, E. Ed. *Los saldos del sexenio (1982–1988).* Testimonios de la crisis IV. Mexico: Siglo XXI. Unemployment figures have been calculated based on figures from the National Employment Survey provided in tables (economically active population 1991–2004 and unemployed population 1991–2004), at: INEGI (2006) *Encuesta nacional de ocupación*

y empleo [online]. Gobierno de México. Available from: http://www.inegi.gob.mx/est/default.asp?c=5213. (January 20, 2006).
7. A comprehensive study of the dismantling of Mexico's agricultural sector through stabilization and liberalization policies can be found in: Arroyo Picard, A., Gómez Cruz, M.A., Schwentesius Rindermann, R., Ranney, D., Dillon, J., and Hansen Kuhn, K. (2003). *Lessons from NAFTA: The High Cost of "Free" Trade.* Mexico: ASC.
8. For an interesting discussion on the thinkers of New Spain, see: Beuchot, M. (2000). *Filosofía social de los pensadores novohispanos.* México: IMDOSOC. Ibargüengoitia, A. (1994). *Filosofía social en México, siglos XVI al XX.* México: Universidad Iberoamericana. For the adoption of liberalism in Mexican thought see: Reyes Heroles, J. (1978). *México. Historia y Política.* Madrid: Tecnos. Hale, C.A. (2005). *El liberalismo mexicano en la época de Mora.* México: Siglo XXI.
9. Genealogical views of human rights have been developed by Baxi himself in his distinction between modern and contemporary human rights, and by A. Woodiwiss in relation to the idea of universal human rights at the United Nations. See: Baxi, U. (2002). *The Future of Human Rights.* New Delhi: Oxford University Press; Woodiwiss, A. (2002). Human Rights and the Challenge of Cosmopolitanism. *Theory, Culture and Society.* February–April. 19 (1–2): 139–155.
10. Critical Legal Studies is a current of thought in the study of law, with expressions in both the United Kingdom and the United States, which has adopted Jacques Derrida's notion of deconstruction to call attention to how some legal doctrines are based on unjust assumptions that discriminate against particular social groups. This current emphasizes the use of deconstruction techniques to gain political insight into the law—with politics understood here as morals and justice—and allows for the inclusion of The Other. In the words of M. Rosenfeld, "... legal discourse—and particularly modern legal discourse with its universalist aspirations—cannot achieve coherence and reconciliation so long as it produces writings that cannot eliminate from their margins ideological distortions, unaccounted for differences, or the lack of full recognition of any subordinated other." Rosenfeld, M. (1998). *Just Interpretations: Law between Ethics and Politics.* Berkeley: University of California Press. p. 14. For a general discussion of the use of deconstruction in Critical Legal Studies and other related currents, see: Balkin, J.M. (2005). Deconstruction's Legal Career. *Cardozo Law Review.* 27 (2): 101–122.
11. The role of human rights NGOs in text construction at the international level could be traced in some studies examining the influence of these groups in norm making. See: Risse, T., Ropp, S.C., and Sikkink, K. (1999). *The Power of Human Rights. International*

Norms and Domestic Change. Cambridge: Cambridge University Press; Korey, W. (1998). *NGOs and the Universal Declaration of Human Rights: A Curious Grapevine.* New York: St. Martin's Press.

12. This reinterpretation of human rights law through intertextuality is mostly related to the authoritative interpretation of human rights law in judicial institutions for the production of jurisprudence and legal defense. In legal studies there is a large body of literature addressing the issue of the nature of legal authority and how this should be interpreted when defending cases or establishing jurisprudence. Some argue that the law should be interpreted in the light of lawmakers' intentions, while others argue that interpretation should be validated in terms of the benefit it brings to the defendant. For Critical Legal Studies scholars there is no single answer to this: "...no theory or legal interpretation can be foundational in the sense of offering a primary or central method. None of the familiar methods of legal interpretation—canons of textual construction, history, structure, precedent, consequences, or natural justice—can stand as a self-sufficient ground for legal interpretation. Nor can any one be elevated above the others as a general rule. Rather, deconstruction argues that interpretation is a pragmatic enterprise drawing on each of these modes of argument in a creative tension. The art of legal interpretation is the art of using the multiple tools of interpretation without being able to rely on any single tool as foundational." Balkin, J.M. (2005). Deconstruction's Legal Career. *Cardozo Law Review.* 27 (2): 101–122. For different approaches to interpretation, including the influential proposals of R. Dworkin and H.L.A. Hart, see: Marmor, A. (1997). *Law and Interpretation: Essays in Legal Philosophy.* Oxford: Clarendon Press.

13. The realization of this twofold surplus of political meaning can be appreciated in the literature on Charter 77, which was set up in 1976 in Czechoslovakia as a response to the repression of an underground rock band that wrote critical songs about socialist society and politics, but mainly challenged the state monopoly of art and culture. As members of the band were jailed and subjected to unfair trials, a group of Czechoslovakian citizens that had been critical of the lack of liberty in their country demanded that the socialist government comply with the human rights norms it committed to when accepting the Helsinki Act. This was the beginning of a long struggle for human rights in Czechoslovakia that ended with the country's democratization. Skilling, H.G. (1981). *Charter 77 and Human Rights in Czechoslovakia.* London: Allen & Unwin; Einhorn, B., Kaldor, M., and Kavan, Z. (1996). *Citizenship and Democratic Control in Contemporary Europe.* Cheltenham: Brookfield US/Edward Elgar. For the impact of the Helsinki Act commitments on democratization in the whole of Eastern Europe, see Thomas, D.C. (2001). *The Helsinki Effect: International Norms, Human Rights, and the Demise of Communism.* New Jersey: Princeton University Press.

14. See discussion in: Baxi, U. (2002). *The Future of Human Rights.* New Delhi: Oxford University Press.
15. Laclau and Mouffe are concerned with the social as a system of meaning. They focus little attention on how entities within this system construct meaning. For these authors, discourse is practice, but they do not describe the empirical world and are therefore more concerned with a formulation of theoretical discourses than with descriptive activities of the actual social fields. This is related to Laclau's argument that the operation of separating language from the social is impossible, as they are constitutive of each other. Although in general terms I agree with this argument, a conceptualization of human rights as the one used here, although idealistic in its epistemology, requires a more realistic ontological approach because it is interested in the social practices through which discursive formations are structured locally. The examination of human rights discursive practices is beyond Laclau and Mouffe's immediate ontological scope, but their framework is still useful to understand such issues as the partial definition of meaning when using specific discourses. See Laclau and Mouffe's own explanation of their ontology in: Laclau, E. and Mouffe, C. (1987). Post-Marxism without Apologies. *New Left Review.* 1 (166): 79–106.
16. The multiplication of identities, as well as new forms of solidarity, cooperation, and collective identities in late capitalism has been advanced by the proponents of the New Social Movement theory (NSM). NSM emerges as a critique of classic Marxist analysis as applied to collective action, analysis that identifies the relations of production as the principal cause of conflict and the working class as the privileged subject leading the struggle for progressive social change. NSM shifted the emphasis from class to the symbolic features of social movements and the role they play in the new contexts of macro-sociological transformations arising in the late twentieth century, in particular the emergence of postindustrial societies. Instead of identifying the relations of production as the main source of collective action, NSM focuses on the symbolic action/cultural sphere, politics, and ideology, and shifts its attention from material interests to values. It is argued that identities are socially constructed rather than inherent to structural location, and that collective action is contingent. Furthermore, NSM proponents focus on the processes that promote autonomy and self-determination, although in their analyses they provide a model of society that works as the general structural context for collective action, that is, postindustrial society, post-Fordism, and so on. The former issue is one of the major characteristics of the NSM as it establishes a basis for the qualification of social struggles as "new social movements" as opposed to "old social movements." According to Escobar, the Latin American experience is different in the following way: "In the Third World, the

hegemonic formation took the form of development. Development resulted in a multiplicity of antagonisms and identities (differentiated peasants, urban marginals, 'traditional' groups, women and the like) who, in many instances, are becoming the subjects of struggles in their respective domains" (Escobar 1992:80). See: Escobar, A. (1992). Culture, Economics and Politics in Latin American Social Movements Theory and Research. In Escobar, A. and Alvarez, S. Eds. *The Making of Social Movements in Latin America: Identity, Strategy, and Democracy.* Boulder: Westview Press. For NSM see: Scott, A. (1995). Political Culture and Social Movements. In Allen, J. Ed. *Political and Economic Forms of Modernity.* London: Open University Press, Buechler, S.M. (1995). New Social Movement Theories. *The Sociological Quarterly.* 1995. 36 (3): 441–464.

17. Because I will be using only some insights of Laclau's sophisticated theoretical work, and for the sake of methodological clarity, his extremely complex ontology was simplified to its maximum here. The discursive theoretical framework that Laclau calls *hegemony theory* is the product of a still ongoing theoretical construction that has gone through three stages (Andersen 2003, Howarth 2000, Torfing 1999). The first stage is consistent with the Marxist tradition and focuses on workers as a "fundamental class" pursuing hegemony; the second is detached from Marxism and establishes the ways different identities join together contingently in a common political project aimed at creating a new order (developed in *Hegemony and Socialist Strategy* [Laclau and Mouffe 2001]); and the third, and most recent, focuses on the complexities of subjectivity and thus on the construction of identities (developed from *New Reflections on the Revolution of Our Time* [Laclau 1990] onward [Laclau 1994, 1996, 2000a, 2000b, Laclau and Zac 1994]). See: Laclau, E. (2000a). Constructing Universality. In Butler, J., Laclau, E., and Zizek, S. Eds. *Contingency, Hegemony, Universality. Contemporary Dialogues on the Left.* London: Verso; Laclau, E. (1993). Discourse. In Goodin, R.E. and Pettit, P. Eds. *A Companion to Contemporary Political Philosophy.* London: Blackwell; Laclau, E. (1996). *Emancipation (s).* London: Verso; Laclau, E. (2000b). Identity and Hegemony: The Role of Universality in the Constitution of Political Logics. In Butler, J., Laclau, E., and Zizek, S. Eds. *Contingency, Hegemony, Universality. Contemporary Dialogues on the Left.* London: Verso; Laclau, E. (2006). *Las identidades políticas en un mundo globalizado.* Mexico: Colegio de México; Laclau, E. (1990). *New Reflections on the Revolution of Our Time.* London: Verso; Laclau, E. (2005). *On Populist Reason.* London: Verso; Laclau, E. (1977). Politics as the Construction of the Unthinkable. Article. The Department of Government, University of Essex; Laclau, E. (1994). Why Do Empty Signifiers Matter to Politics? In Weeks, J. Ed. *The Lesser Evil and the Greater Good. The*

Theory and Politics of Social Diversity. Cornwall: Rivers Oram Press; Laclau, E. and Mouffe, C. (2001). *Hegemony and Socialist Strategy. Towards a Radical Democratic Politics*. London: Verso; Laclau, E. and Mouffe, C. (1987). Post-Marxism without Apologies. *New Left Review*. 1 (166): 79–106; Laclau, E. and Zac, L. (1994). Minding the Gap: The Subject of Politics. In Laclau, E. Ed. *The Making of Political Identities*. London: Verso. Full application of hegemony theory: Smith, A.M. (1994b). Rastafari as Resistance and the Ambiguities of Essentialism in the "New Social Movements". In Laclau, E. Ed. *The Making of Political Identities*. London: Verso; Smith, A.M. (1994a). *New Right Discourse on Race and Sexuality: Britain 1968–1990*. Cambridge: Cambridge University Press. Studies on Laclau: Torfing, J. (1999). *New Theories of Discourse*. Oxford: Blackwell Publishers; Howarth, D. (2000). *Discourse*. Buckingham: Open University Press; Howarth, D. (2004). Hegemony, Political Subjectivity, and Radical Democracy. In Critchley, S. and Marchart, O. Eds. *Laclau: A Critical Reader*. London: Routledge; Andersen, N.A. (2003). *Discursive Analytical Strategies. Understanding Foucault, Koselleck, Laclau, Luhmann*. Bristol: The Policy Press; Butler, J., Laclau, E., and Zizek, Slavoj (2000). *Contingency, Hegemony, Universality. Contemporary Dialogues on the Left*. London: Verso.

18. This study is based on the examination of the archives of the following pioneering human rights organizations: "Miguel Agustin Pro Juárez" Human Rights Centre (Prodh Centre), the "Fray Francisco de Vitoria" Human Rights Centre (Vitoria Centre), and the Mexican Academy of Human Rights (the Academia which stands for Academia Mexicana de Derechos Humanos). I also consulted the archives of the Mexican Free Trade Action Network (RMALC), which is the NGO network concentrating historical data about the struggle against free trade in Mexico. The documents included bulletins, press releases, annual reports, and internal work documents. The study also includes interviews with NGO and SMO activists. See their names in the list of references.

1 THE NEOLIBERAL PARADOX: CONSERVATIVE ECONOMIC CHANGE AND THE RISE OF DEMOCRATIC POLITICS

1. For discussions of import-substitution policy, see: Kay, C. (1989). *Latin American Theories of Development and Underdevelopment*. London: Routledge; Castañeda, J.G. (1993). *Utopia Unarmed. Latin America Left after the Cold War*. New York: Alfred A. Knop; Rist, G. (1997). *The History of Development. From Western Origins to Global Faith*. London: Zed Books; Kaplan, M. (2002). El Estado latinoamericano: crisis y reformas. In Basave, J., Dabat, A.,

Morera, C., Rivera Ríos, M.Á. and Rodríguez, F. Eds. *Globalización y alternativas incluyentes para el siglo XXI*. Mexico: Facultad de Economía-UAM-I; Isin, E.F. and Wood, P.K. (1999). *Citizenship & Identity*. London: Sage; Gutiérrez Garza, E. (1988). Introducción. In Gutiérrez Garza, E. Ed. *La crisis del Estado de Bienestar*. Testimonios de la crisis II. Mexico: Siglo XXI-UNAM; Durán Juárez, J.M. and Partida, R. (1992). Modelo económico, regionalización y nuevo Estado mexicano (1940–1990). In Alonso, J., Aziz Nassif, A. and Tamayo, J. Eds. *El nuevo Estado mexicano*. I. Estado y economía. Mexico: Nueva Imagen; Calderón Rodríguez, J.M. (1988). La ruptura del colaboracionismo de clases y las perspectivas de la democracia. In Gutiérrez Garza, E. Ed. *La crisis del Estado de Bienestar*. II. Mexico: Siglo XXI-UNAM; Kitching, G. (1990). *Development and Underdevelopment in Historical Perspective. Populism, Nationalism and Industrialization*. London: Routledge; Soria, V.M. (1988). La crisis de la protección social en México. Un análisis de largo plazo con énfasis en el periodo 1971–1985. In Gutiérrez Garza, E. Ed. *La crisis del Estado de Bienestar*. II. Mexico: Siglo XXI-UNAM; Green, D. (1995). *Silent Revolution: The Rise of Market Economics in Latin America*. London: Cassell: LAB.
2. The Austrian School of Economics is a liberal economic trend that appeared as a counterbalance to Marxist ideas in the late nineteenth century. It was not very popular among mainstream economists because of its subjectivist approach to economics. Before the Second World War it was identified by six central ideas: methodological individualism; methodological subjectivism; marginalism; the influence of utility on demand and thus of market prices; opportunity costs; and the time structure of consumption and production. After the 1940s, two important ideas were added by Ludwig von Mises and Friedrich Von Hayek: markets and competition as processes of learning and discovery; and the individual decision as an act of choice in an essentially uncertain context. The Austrian School came to be well known in the mainstream Anglo-Saxon liberal economic tradition only recently, thanks to the work of Hayek, who moved to the United States in 1950 after working for a few years as a lecturer at the London School of Economics. The revival of Austrian economics is located in time in 1974, during the South Royalton Conference, shortly before Hayek was awarded the Nobel Prize for Economics. Friedman was also awarded this prestigious prize in 1976. A few years later he would become an adviser to Margaret Thatcher. Friedman's first opportunity to work with a "real" national economy was with dictator August Pinochet in Chile; this is one of the reasons for Thatcher's admiration of Pinochet. Kirzner, I.M. (1992). *The Meaning of Market Process. Essays in the Development of Modern Austrian Economics*. New York: Routledge.
3. See discussions of the methodological inaccuracies of neoliberal economics in: Chang, H.-J. (2002). Una perspectiva institucional

sobre el papel del Estado: hacia una política económica institucional. In Basave, J., Dabat, A., Morera, C., Rivera Ríos, M.Á., and Rodríguez, F. Eds. *Globalización y alternativas incluyentes para el siglo XXI.* Mexico: Facultad de Economía-UAM-I; Shand, A.H. (1990). *Free Market Morality.* London: Routledge; Toye, J. (1993). *Dilemmas of Development.* 2nd. Oxford: Blackwell.

4. The analysis of Structural Adjustment Programs was popular in the 1990s with many interesting studies being produced, such as: Román Morales, L.I. (1992). *¿Qué es el ajuste estructural?* Mexico: ITESO y Proyecto CONACYT-SIMORELOS; Dasgupta, B. (1998). *Structural Adjustment, Global Trade and the New Political Economy of Development.* New York: Zed Books.

5. From the 1930s to 2000, Mexican presidents belonged to the PRI, which was first set up in 1929 as the National Revolutionary Party by President Plutarco Elias Calles, a general from the times of the Mexican Revolution. The party was set up as a means to solve political conflict between *caudillos* (charismatic leaders) in the aftermath of the 1910 Mexican Revolution and to legitimize the government created by the 1917 Constitution. It changed its name to the Party of the Mexican Revolution in 1939, and became the PRI in 1946. The PRI ruled the country in continuous six-year administrations until 2000 when, following at least 12 years of slow political change triggered by both internal and external dynamics, a president from a different party—the conservative PAN, which was set up in 1939—was elected in a less-questioned electoral process. There is general agreement that the PRI managed to stay in power for so long because of its corporatist and clientelistic politics. Camp, R.A. (1996). *Politics in Mexico.* 2nd. New York: Oxford University Press.

6. For broader discussions of Mexican corporatism see: Ramírez Saiz, J.M. (2003). Organizaciones cívicas, democracia y sistema político. In Aziz Nassif, A. Ed. *México al inicio del siglo XXI. Democracia, ciudadanía y desarrollo.* Mexico: CIESAS-Porrúa; Malloy, J.M. (1977). Authoritarianism and Corporatism in Latin America: The Modal Pattern. In Malloy, J.M. Ed. *Authoritarianism and Corporatism in Latin America.* Pittsburgh: University of Pittsburgh Press; Taggart, P. (2000). *Populism.* Buckingham: Open University Press; Camp, R.A. (1996). *Politics in Mexico.* 2nd. New York: Oxford University Press; Fox, J. (1995). Mexico's Difficult Democracy: Grassroots Movements, NGOs, and Local Government. In Reilly, C.A. Ed. *New Paths to Democratic Development in Latin America. The Rise of NGO-Municipal Collaboration.* Boulder: Lynne Rienner.

7. Analysts of corporatism share the opinion that corporatism, as it was known until the 1980s, no longer exists and it is not the only form of social organization as was previously the case. Nevertheless, this is not to say it has disappeared. Corporatism observers share the opinion that we are facing a different form of corporatism that

responds to the necessities of the "neoliberal project"—neocorporatism. The monopoly of representation is one of the characteristics lost in the reform. While this is dealt with later in the chapter, see also: Mondragón Pérez, Y. (1997). La recomposición neocorporativa entre Estado y sindicatos: los límites a los proyectos sindicales de interlocución, el caso del STRM. In Zermeño, S. Ed. *Movimientos sociales e identidades colectivas. México en la década de los noventa.* Mexico: La Jornada-CIICH; Calderón Rodríguez, J.M. (1988). La ruptura del colaboracionismo de clases y las perspectivas de la democracia. In Gutiérrez Garza, E. Ed. *La crisis del Estado de Bienestar.* II. Mexico: Siglo XXI-UNAM; Bizberg, I. (2003). Estado, organizaciones corporativas y democracia. In Aziz Nassif, Alberto, Ed. *México al inicio del siglo XXI. Democracia, ciudadanía y desarrollo.* Mexico: CIESAS-Porrúa.
8. Translation of Monsiváis on page 224 of Castañeda, J.G. (1993). *Utopia Unarmed. Latin America Left after the Cold War.* New York: Alfred A. Knop. See Monsiváis, C. (2000). Prólogo. Lo marginal en el centro. In Monsiváis, C. Ed. *Entrada libre. Crónicas de la sociedad que se organiza.* Mexico: Era.
9. Commentators argue that actual independent organization during the period of PRI rule started as the result of governmental repression against student movements on two occasions. During the first, on October 2, 1968, dozens of students were killed two weeks before the Olympic Games in Tlatelolco Square, Mexico City, by police and army officials dressed as civilians who mixed with the crowd at a demonstration against police repression of previous student mobilizations. The massacre put an end to two months of student activism against repression. Three years later, on June 10, 1971, under the "leftist" government of Luis Echeverría, another massacre took place. After that, dozens of students joined the guerrilla movements operating in Mexico City, southern and northern Mexico. Guerrillas were persecuted and their members were victims of forced disappearance, torture, imprisonment, or execution. Those who did not join guerrillas joined popular movement organizations or set up NGOs. According to Jorge Castañeda, independent urban movements from the 1970s were easily coopted, corrupted, and repressed. More successful independent organizations were the ecclesiastic base communities (*comunidades eclesiales de base,* CEBs), which were widespread throughout Latin America in the 1970s and encouraged by liberation theologians. See Castañeda, J.G. (1993). *Utopia Unarmed. Latin America Left after the Cold War.* New York: Alfred A. Knop; Foweraker, J. Ed. (1990) *Popular Movements and Political Change in Mexico.* London: Lynne Rienner Publishers.
10. The election of the PRI's presidential candidate was a very important political ritual because it meant that the one chosen would in fact be

the next Mexican president. The president in turn would choose the candidate from his cabinet. Before the neoliberal turn, the Interior Secretary would often be the one appointed, but neoliberals tended toward those in charge of the Treasury or the Finance Secretariat. A discussion appropriate for those unfamiliar with Mexican politics can be found in Camp, R.A. (1996). *Politics in Mexico*. 2nd. New York: Oxford University Press.

11. The best example of a neocorporatist union is the formerly state-run telecommunications company Telmex. As Telmex was to be privatized in the early 1990s, Salinas launched a Union Modernization Project that established the new rules. The union of the still state-run Electricity Company, the SME, and the union of Volskwagen Mexico later adopted the new model. A detailed account of the Telmex union case is presented in: Mondragón Pérez, Y. (1997). La recomposición neocorporativa entre Estado y sindicatos: los límites a los proyectos sindicales de interlocución, el caso del STRM. In Zermeño, S. Ed. *Movimientos sociales e identidades colectivas. México en la década de los noventa*. Mexico: La Jornada-CIICH. General discussions of neocorporatism can be found in: Bizberg, I. (2003). Estado, organizaciones corporativas y democracia. In *México al inicio del siglo XXI. Democracia, ciudadanía y desarrollo*. Mexico: CIESAS-Porrúa.

12. For a broader discussion of the case of the Comité de Defensa Popular see Haber, P.L. (1997). ¡Vamos por la dignidad de Durango! Un estudio del poder sociopolítico. In Zermeño, S. Ed. *Movimientos sociales e identidades colectivas. México en la década de los noventa*. México: La Jornada-CIICH.

13. Pronasol's political aims were clearly revealed in its incorporation into, and eventual elimination from, the bureaucratic layer. It was first set up as a Program in 1989 and was incorporated into the then new Secretariat of Social Development, the chairperson of which, Luis Donaldo Colosio Murrieta, became the next PRI presidential candidate and was assassinated during his electoral campaign in 1994. His successor and eventual president Ernesto Zedillo eliminated it altogether in 1994 as soon as he took office. For interesting discussions on the political role of Pronasol see: Kaufman, R.R. and Trejo, G. (1997). Regionalism, Regime Transformation and Pronasol: The Politics of the National Solidarity Programme in Four Mexican States. *Latin American Perspectives*. October 1997. 29 (3): 717–745; Morris, S.D. (1992). Political Reformism in Mexico: Salinas at the Brink. *Journal of Interamerican Studies and World Affairs*. Spring 1992. 34 (1): 27–57.

14. Between the 1950s and 1960s the Catholic Church played a crucial role in founding NGOs through providing credit funds, popular education, food distribution, health, and solutions to urban problems. However, it was not until the 1970s that NGOs multiplied. These were set up by the progressive Church advancing liberation theology

and intellectuals of the social left and were based on the ideas of popular pedagogy and dependency theory. Hernández, L. and Fox, J. (1995). Mexico's Difficult Democracy: Grassroots Movements, NGOs, and Local Government. In Reilly, C.A. Ed. *New Paths to Democratic Development in Latin America. The Rise of NGO-Municipal Collaboration.* Boulder: Lynne Rienner. p. 192.

2 The Emergence of Human Rights Discourse in Mexico

Some parts of this chapter appeared in the article "Transición a la democracia y derechos humanos en México: la pérdida de la integralidad en el discurso," in *Andamios. Revista de Investigación Social* 3 (6), June 2007, Mexico (ISSN: 1870-0063). They are reproduced here with their permission.

1. Latin American dependency theory advances the idea that development and underdevelopment form a single process whereby the center (rich countries) and the periphery (poor countries) form part of a world economy that reproduces the disparities between the two through international trade. Third World countries remained underdeveloped because the First World has prevented them from acquiring economic surplus (defined as the difference between production and consumption), through the imperialist practices of monopoly capitalism, which is characterized by the control of markets by large transnational corporations informed by both industrial and finance capital. The "periphery" was actively underdeveloped because it only exported raw materials to the "core," which used them to manufacture goods that were reexported to the periphery with value added. The core, they claimed, was entirely dependent upon the periphery's resources. Concerned with the implications of this phenomenon for the social structure (domination was reproduced in the internal structure), the *dependentistas* argued that this led to structural economic distortions and growing social inequality. See: Kay, C. (1989). *Latin American Theories of Development and Underdevelopment.* London: Routledge; Rist, G. (1997). *The History of Development. From Western Origins to Global Faith.* London: Zed Books.

2. The national security doctrine supported repression by military juntas in the Southern Cone. It "views 'geopolitics' as occupying a central place within human knowledge...Geopolitics holds that individuals and groups must be subordinate to the state, which it views as a kind of organism and as the ultimate source of values. There is a basic Hobbesian assumption that all states are permanently at war with one another, although they may form alliances against common enemies. The whole art of governance is understood as synonymous with strategy; the greatest good is national security. Even economic growth is first justified in terms of security. The welfare of citizens

is subordinate to security, although it is admitted that beyond a certain point unmet needs themselves threaten security if they generate unrest... The agents of development are elites, both military and technocratic... The remaining groups in the nation, including peasants, labor unions, and university students and faculty, are seen as minors still needing tutelage... Another assumption of national security is that the nation is allied with the United States in the East-West Conflict. Religion is seen from this perspective. Western Christian civilization is threatened by Marxist atheism in the East." Berryman, P. (1987). *Liberation Theology. Essential facts about the Revolutionary Movement in Latin America and Beyond.* London: I.B. Tauris.
3. See, for instance, González Casanova, P. (1989). Pensar la democracia. In González Casanova, P. and Cadena Roa, J. Eds. *Primer informe sobre la democracia: México 1988.* Mexico: Siglo XXI-CIICH.
4. See, for instance, González Casanova, P. (1989). Pensar la democracia. In González Casanova, P. and Cadena Roa, J. Eds. *Primer informe sobre la democracia: México 1988.* Mexico: Siglo XXI-CIICH; Woldenberg, J. (1989). La negociación político-social en México. In González Casanova, P. Ed. *Primer informe sobre la democracia: México 1988.* Mexico: Siglo XXI-CIIH; Crespo, J.A. (1991). Derechos políticos y transición democrática. *Justicia y Paz.* No. 22, Edición especial sobre derechos políticos: 2–9. April–June; Aguayo Quezada, S. (1993). The Inevitability of Democracy in Mexico. In Roett, R. Ed. *Political and Economic Liberalization in Mexico: At a Critical Juncture?* Boulder: LynneRienner; Acosta, M. (1992). The Democratization Process in Mexico: A Human Rights Issue. In Cavanagh, J., Gershman, J., Baker, K., and Helmke, G. Eds. *Trading Freedom. How Free Trade Affects Our Lives, Work and Environment.* San Francisco: Institute for Food and Development Policy-Food First; Centro de Derechos Humanos "Miguel Agustín Pro Juárez." (1992b). Los derechos humanos: nuevo campo de la lucha social en México. In Aziz Nassif, A., Tamayo, J., and Alonso, J. Eds. *El nuevo Estado mexicano.* II. Estado y Política. Mexico: CIESAS; Concha Malo, M. Ed. (1994b). *Los derechos políticos como derechos humanos.* Mexico: La Jornada Ediciones, CIICH-Unam; Maldonado, J. (1995) *Historia de los primeros años de trabajo del Comité de Derechos Humanos Miguel Agustín Pro Juárez AC.* Internal Document. Mexico. See a comprehensive list of transition to democracy intellectuals in: Zermeño, S. (2005). *La desmodernidad mexicana y las alternativas a la violencia y a la exclusión en nuestros días.* Mexico: Océano.
5. The idea of rights in Mexico, as in most Latin American countries, dates back to nineteenth-century liberalism, more specifically the type of liberalism that emerged from the French Revolution that intellectually inspired Independence movements in the region. In the specific case of Mexico, liberalism became a strong constitutionalism that made rights legal entitlements rather than the moral basis for the restriction

of State power. In the Constitution of 1917, which emerged from the 1910 Social Revolution, rights became "individual guarantees" and the language of rights practically disappeared. Consequently, by the 1980s the international discourse of human rights had little to do with domestic rights that were understood as constitutional entitlements. Human rights were, in fact, part of diplomatic terminology.
6. These ideas were also reproduced by the Academia in its early writings concerning democracy—the articles included in *El Boletín* (The Bulletin) from 1988 to 1990 (issues 1 to 18). An editorial article published in 1990 served to wrap up the human rights situation around the world, Latin America, and Mexico during the 1980s, celebrated the fall of the Berlin Wall and military dictatorships in the Southern Cone, and at the same time drew attention to increasing poverty and unemployment in Mexico and Latin America. It stated that the fact that there were clean elections in many countries did not mean there was "political democracy," which must include respect for civil and political rights, acknowledgment of difference and tolerance. "Political democracy does not ensure enjoyment of economic, social and cultural rights, which are also human rights. On the contrary, while economic structures and processes continue to generate huge social inequalities and injustice, while the majority does not find their basic needs satisfied, while vast sectors of the population are victims of discrimination and marginalization, political democracy will remain a fiction." Academia Mexicana de Derechos Humanos. (1990b). Editorial. *El Boletín* No. 17: 1–3. March–April.
7. For an interesting discussion of how and why liberation theologians rejected ideas of democracy and human rights throughout the 1970s, see "The Development of Liberation Theology: the Marxist Phase," in: Sigmund, P.E. (1990). *Liberation Theology at the Cross Roads. Democracy or Revolution?* New York: Oxford University Press. In this chapter, Sigmund provides a characterization of the most important representatives of Marxist liberation theology, such as Gustavo Gutiérrez, Juan Luis Segundo, José Miguez Bonino, Hugo Assmann, and Enrique Dussel. See also Berryman, P. (1987). *Liberation Theology. Essential Facts about the Revolutionary Movement in Latin America and Beyond*. London: I.B. Tauris; Aguayo Quezada, S. and Parra Rosales, L.P. (1997). *Las organizaciones no gubernamentales de derechos humanos en México: entre la democracia participativa y la electoral*. Mexico: Academia Mexicana de Derechos Humanos; Grugel, J. (2002). *Democratization: A Critical Introduction*. New York: Palgrave.
8. According to Dominican priest Miguel Concha, the reason for this is the mostly conservative nature of the Mexican Catholic Church, which persecuted and repressed those priests who became sympathetic with social causes after the 1968 student massacre. For his part, Roderic Ai Camp argues that liberation theology was not very

successful in Mexico because state-led violence was not as prevalent; there was little experience in accompanying social processes; there was a minimal presence of foreign clergy; and there were few religious orders. In spite of these limitations, *comunidades eclesiales de base* (grassroots organizations organized by priests) multiplied from 1967 to the late 1970s, especially in Morelos, Veracruz, and Coahuila states, and Mexico City. See: Camp, R.A. (1997). *Crossing Swords. Politics and Religion in Mexico.* Oxford: Oxford University Press; Concha Malo, M., González Gari, O., Salas, L.F., and Bastian, J.-P. (1986). *La participación de los cristianos en el proceso popular de liberación en México.* Mexico: Siglo XXI

9. Organizations dealing with human rights issues existed in Mexico before that, but before this human rights work was not systematic and no international human rights framework was used because legal defense of liberty was constitutional rather than based on legal naturalism. Only at this time does human rights discourse develop locally and a human rights movement becomes established. Scholarly research argues that organizations dealing with human rights issues have existed in Mexico since 1964—the National Centre for Social Communication (CENCOS, Spanish Acronym for Centro Nacional de Comunicación Social)—but states that the first organization dealing with human rights material was the National Front against Repression (FNCR, the Spanish acronym for Frente Nacional Contra la Repression), set up on August 6, 1977. In the 1970s, the persecution of guerrilla groups and critics of the PRI—localized in Mexico City, Nuevo León, and Guerrero states—led to forced disappearances, killings, and torture. Relatives of the victims founded the FNCR, but in their work did not see these practices as human rights issues but as either "repression" or "crimes against humanity." The FNCR, which changed its name to Eureka in 1978, dealt with these issues but used political rather than specifically human rights tools at that time—hunger strikes and demonstrations rather than courts and conventions. The Mexican branch of Amnesty International was set up in 1971 by a group of relatives of political prisoners headed by academic Héctor Cuadra, but according to Amnesty's by-laws it could not deal with issues of the home country.

10. Up until 1988 these organizations did not address increasing governmental violence in Mexico. For instance, the Vitoria Centre focused on denouncing political violence in Guatemala, El Salvador, Honduras, Nicaragua, and Costa Rica. They addressed issues related to individual physical and psychological integrity. In November 1984 they set up the bulletin *Justicia y Paz* (Justice and Peace), which included information and analysis about human rights in Central America and the Caribbean. The bulletin became a magazine in January 1985 but failed to include systematic information about Mexico. An important attempt to address issues properly concerning

Mexico was: Stavenhagen, R. (1987). México y los derechos humanos. *Justicia y Paz* No. 1: 15–21. November 1987. For its part, it was not until 1988 that the Academia started to publish a bulletin providing information about advances in human rights policy in Latin America, such as the fall of dictatorships in the Southern Cone, increasing violence in Central America, and human rights violations in Mexico.

11. See for instance: Centro de Derechos Humanos "Fray Francisco de Vitoria." (1993). La situación de los derechos humanos en México (diciembre 1992–octubre 1993). *Justicia y Paz* No. 32: 4–64. October–December. There were some attempts to analyze ESCRs, but they failed. For instance, in *Justicia y Paz* the Vitoria Centre addressed the right to decent housing, but rather than using human rights criteria, it deals with the demands of urban movements and the problems of governmental subsidies. See: Abarca Chávez, C. (1987). La vivienda como Derecho del Hombre. *Justicia y Paz* No. 2: 3–24. February 1987. Also, in *Justicia y Paz* there was a special report on "the environment and human rights," but it deals with general issues of pollution and technological expansion. See: Centro de Derechos Humanos "Fray Francisco de Vitoria." (1990a). Editorial. *Justicia y Paz* No. 19, Medio ambiente y derechos humanos: 2. July–September 1990. Again, in the same magazine there is analysis of the right to health that deals with the effects of structural adjustment programs on housing, water, food, work, and the environment that ended up impacting negatively on the right to health. Produssep and Centro de Derechos Humanos "Fray Francisco de Vitoria." (1990). El derecho a la salud en México: una mirada desde la sociedad civil. *Justicia y Paz* No. 18, Los derechos humanos a la salud: 13–19. April–June 1990. At the same time, when there is human rights analysis in social fields, there is analysis of violations of civil rights in the economic or social arenas. For instance, in *El Boletín* No. 6, of March 1989, the Academia deals with the problems of farmer land ownership in terms of the repression of leaders. In *El Boletín* No. 16, the Academia deals with trade union issues from the perspective of "union democracy." Academia Mexicana de Derechos Humanos. (1990d). Various articles. *El Boletín* No. 17: 1–3. March–April; Academia Mexicana de Derechos Humanos. (1990c). Various articles. *El Boletín* No. 16: 15. January–February.

12. Earlier that year, a group of workers contacted father Jesús Maldonado seeking help to avoid violence and intimidation in their union elections. Previously, in 1990, the corporatist trade union had killed a worker and wounded several others during a referendum in which employees were to vote for the trade union that was to negotiate the collective labor agreement—the choices were the corporatist union and an independent union set up by workers after the corporatist union agreed with the employer to a reduction of workers' benefits.

The independent union lodged a complaint with the labor authorities, which ruled against workers. They appealed, but the company delayed the procedures for a year, providing the Ford Motor Company with the opportunity to fire 800 workers supporting the independent union. In the end, and because the case became publicized, labor authorities ruled in favor of workers' demands for a new vote. It was then that they sought help from human rights defenders, who demanded that elections be carried out again. See pp. 43–54 in Centro de Derechos Humanos "Miguel Agustín Pro Juárez." (1992a). *Informe anual 1991. Los derechos humanos en México*. Mexico: Centro Prodh. See also Fuentes, M. (1991a). El caso 'Ford': ¿Modelo de relación laboral en el futuro? *Justicia y Paz*. No. 23, Número especial sobre derechos laborales y libre comercio: 3–8. July–September; Comité de Observadores Independientes. (1991). *Ford Motor Company. Recuento 3. Informe Resolutivo COI*. Report of the Committee. Mexico.

13. Up to this point, electoral issues in human rights NGOs had been addressed from the point of view of mainstream political analysis. See, for instance, a rational choice analysis of individual political participation in: Crespo, J.A. (1991). Derechos políticos y transición democrática. *Justicia y Paz*. No. 22, Edición especial sobre derechos políticos: 2–9. April–June.

14. Aguayo centered the Academia's agenda on the promotion of free elections until the new chairperson changed this in 1997. In the Academia's activities report from 1990 to 1997, there is an emphasis on research and education in the field of elections: there was even a department dealing with political rights and the right to information. Under Aguayo, the Academia was probably the human rights NGO participating most closely in observation activities; he was one of the cofounders of Civic Alliance, an NGO network set up in 1994 for the invigilation of presidential elections. Academia Mexicana de Derechos Humanos. (1991). *Memoria de actividades 1990*. Mexico: Academia Mexicana de Derechos Humanos. Academia Mexicana de Derechos Humanos. (1993). *Memoria de actividades 1992*. Mexico: Academia Mexicana de Derechos Humanos. Academia Mexicana de Derechos Humanos. (1994). *Memoria de actividades 1993*. Mexico: Academia Mexicana de Derechos Humanos. Academia Mexicana de Derechos Humanos. (1996). *Memoria de actividades 1994–1995*. Mexico: Academia Mexicana de Derechos Humanos. Academia Mexicana de Derechos Humanos. (1997). *Memoria de actividades 1996*. Mexico: Academia Mexicana de Derechos Humanos.

15. In its 1992 annual report, the Prodh dedicated a section to repression within the context of elections—other contexts were labor, urban popular movements, and land issues. See: Centro de Derechos Humanos "Miguel Agustín Pro Juárez." (1993a). *Informe anual de derechos humanos 1992. Volumen I. Represión y movimiento de*

Derechos Humanos en México. Mexico: Centro de Derechos Humanos "Miguel Agustín Pro Juárez."
16. For instance, Concha Malo, M. (1991). El papel de la sociedad civil en la defensa de los derechos políticos. *Justicia y Paz* No. 22, Political Rights: 10–12. April–June.

3 THE EXHAUSTION OF TRANSITION TO DEMOCRACY DISCOURSE: HUMAN RIGHTS DISCOURSE ENTERS ANTI-FREE TRADE STRUGGLES

Some parts of this chapter appeared in the article "La transición a la democracia en el TLACAN: un significante vacío," in *Perfiles Latinoamericanos. Revista de la Facultad Latinoamericana de Ciencias Sociales* (29), January–June 2007 (ISSN: 0188-7653). They are reproduced here with their permission.

1. This trend dramatically took off after the Zapatista uprising. National NGOs started to focus on collaboration with international NGOs (mostly based in the United States) and started to use international instruments in order to create awareness of the human rights situation in Mexico. For the first time they started to lodge complaints and communicate with international organizations. Their initial approach was to the Inter-American Commission on Human Rights (ICHR), where they denounced the illegal nature of militarization in Chiapas, human rights violations (arbitrary detentions, house break-ins, intimidations and threats, torture, forced disappearances, killings of civilians in unclear circumstances, and extra-judicial executions), and specific cases (Red Nacional De Organismos Civiles De Derechos Humanos "Todos Los Derechos Para Todos." 1994c). In March of 1994, supported by international NGOs, they went to the UN Human Rights Commission where they denounced these violations but also called on United Nations parties and NGOs from other countries to support them in their appeal to the Mexican government to punish the perpetrators, ratify covenants, and remove reservations from others, but more importantly, they invited a delegation from the Commission to visit the country in order to assess the national human rights situation. They claimed that "We know that the Mexican government, which via its foreign policy promotes international application and respect for human rights, will not reject such an argument" (Red Nacional De Organismos Civiles De Derechos Humanos "Todos Los Derechos Para Todos" 1994b:9). This statement would form the basis of an international strategy to improve the human rights situation in the country, especially in Chiapas, based on the increasing importance of international human rights and the Mexican State's history of supporting human rights abroad.

Part of this strategy was pressuring the government to request or accept the visit of UN and OAS reporters. Consequently, from July 15–24, 1996, the ICHR made its first visit first to Mexico, visiting Mexico City, Chiapas, Guerrero, and Baja California and conducting interviews with authorities as well as NGO members.These were the first of a long list of reporters and representatives that visited Mexico during the Zedillo administration.This visit was followed by that of the Special Rapporteur on Torture and other Cruel, Inhuman and Degrading Treatment, Nigel S. Roadley, from August 7–16, 1997; the Special Rapporteur on Child Trafficking, Prostitution and Pornography, Ofelia Calcetas-Santos, in November of the same year; the Special Rapporteur on Extra-Judicial, Summary and Arbitrary Executions, from July 11–24; and the High Commissioner on Human Rights, Mary Robinson, in November 1999, with the purpose of consultancy and technical cooperation. See: Acosta, M. (2002). Lessons Learned from Relations between Mexican and US Human Rights Organizations. In Brooks, D. and Fox, J. Eds. *Cross-Border Dialogues: US-Mexico Social Movement Networking*. San Diego: Center for US Mexican Studies; Culebro Bahena, R. (2004). *Interview*. Mexico, Red Nacional de Organismos Civiles de Derechos Humanos "Todos los Derechos para Todos." (1994b). Informe que presentó la Red Nacional de Organismos Civiles de Derechos Humanos "Todos los Derechos para Todos" a la Comisión Interamericana de Derechos Humanos en Washington DC, el 10 de febrero de 1994. In Monroy, M.B. Ed. *Pensar Chiapas, repensar México. Reflexiones de las ONG mexicanas sobre el conflicto*. Mexico: Converegencia de Organismos Civiles por la Democracia-Impretei.

2. The demands of the Zapatistas were initially formulated in the First Declaration of the Selva Lacandona (January 1, 1994), which placed emphasis on demands for a change of government. They were further elaborated in a communiqué released by the Indigenous Clandestine Revolutionary Committee-General Command of the EZLN, dated March 1, 1994. The latter also detailed the historical causes of the indigenous rebellion and a list of indigenous women's demands, which included construction of maternity clinics and nurseries in their communities, community cafeterias for children, self-employment, agricultural projects, and so on. Ejército Zapatista de Liberación Nacional. (1994a). *Declaración de la Selva Lacandona* [online]. EZLN. Available from: http://www.ezln.org/documentos/1994/199312xx.es.htm. (March 3, 2004). Ejército Zapatista de Liberación Nacional (1994b). Pliego de Demandas del EZLN; las razones y las causas de la sublevación. Comunicado del Comité Clandestino Revolucionario Indígena-Comandancia General del Ejército Zapatista de Liberación Nacional, México. *Justicia y Paz* No. 33, Chiapas, democracia y derechos humanos: 63–67. January–March. See also: Molina, I. (2000). *El pensamiento del EZLN*. Mexico: Plaza y Valdés.

3. For the participation of human rights NGOs during the first six months of the conflict see: Monroy B.M. Ed. (1994). *Pensar Chiapas, repensar México. Reflexiones de las ONGs mexicanas sobre el conflicto.* Mexico: Convergencia de Organismos Civiles por la Democracia/ Impretei.
4. From 1994 to 2000, the administration of President Ernesto Zedillo ordered increased militarization of Chiapas and other states. In 2000 the new president, PAN-militant Vicente Fox, ordered the withdrawal of most troops from Chiapas. Monroy B.M. Ed. (1994). *Pensar Chiapas, repensar México. Reflexiones de las ONGs mexicanas sobre el conflicto.* Mexico: Convergencia de Organismos Civiles por la Democracia/ Impretei. (2004a) *Historia del EZLN* [online]. CCD-Utopia. Available from: http://www.geocities.com/ccd-utopia/ezln/historia_ezln/. (March 10th, 2004). Red Nacional de Organismos Civiles de Derechos Humanos "Todos Los Derechos Para Todos." (1994a). *Chiapas: una política de violación a los derechos humanos e impunidad.* Document presented at the United Nations Human Rights Commission. Geneva.
5. See for instance: Stavenhagen, R. (1986). Derechos Humanos y Derechos Indios. *Justicia y Paz* No. 2: 9–16. February. Also in Centro de Derechos Humanos "Fray Francisco de Vitoria." (1989). Los derechos indígenas: nuevo enfoque del sistema internacional. *Justicia y Paz.* No. 3–4, Derechos de los Pueblos Indios 9–26. July–December 1989; Academia Mexicana de Derechos Humanos. (1989b). Various articles. *El Boletín* No. 12–13: 1–12. September–October; Centro de Derechos Humanos "Miguel Agustín Pro Juárez." (1992a). *Informe anual 1991. Los derechos humanos en México.* Mexico: Centro Prodh; Centro de Derechos Humanos "Miguel Agustín Pro Juárez." (1993c). *Informe anual de derechos humanos 1992.* II. Los derechos humanos de los Pueblos Indios. Mexico: Centro Prodh; Academia Mexicana de Derechos Humanos. (1989a). Various articles. *El Boletín* No. 9–10: 3–10. June–July; Matos, J. (1992). Indigenismo, legislación y estados nacionales. *Justicia y Paz* No. 25: 5–7. January–May.
6. On April 9, 1995, the EZLN and the government signed the San Miguel Joint Declaration, which established a protocol for peace talks. It included discussion tables on indigenous culture and rights; democracy and justice; welfare and development; conciliation and the rights of women in Chiapas; and the cessation of hostilities. The table on indigenous culture and rights was the first to be installed, in October 1995. In February 1996, the parties signed the San Andrés Accords on Indigenous Rights and Culture, which established indigenous autonomy and constitutional acknowledgment of their existence as collective entities. However, the bill Zedillo sent to Congress ignored the most important issues agreed, for example indigenous autonomy. When Fox assumed power in 2000 he sent the original bill but failed to lobby it and was rejected by his own party.

Another version, ignoring autonomy and indigenous rights to natural resources, was passed in 2001. This is the reason why the EZLN has yet to sign a peace accord with the government. Chronicle of the San Andrés Accords in Molina, I. (2000). *El pensamiento del EZLN.* Mexico: Plaza y Valdés. See also a brief analysis of the accords in Moguel, J. (2004). *Las claves del zapatismo* [online]. Fractal. Available from: http://www.fractal.com.mx/F8Moguel.html. (March 10, 2004). For a Zapatista view of indigenous rights according to the San Andrés Accords, see: Ejército Zapatista de Liberación Nacional (1998) *Quinta Declaración de la Selva Lacandona* [online]. Nodo50. Available from: http://www.nodo50.org/pchiapas/documentos/selva.htm. (March 11, 2004).

7. The first UN top officer Fox invited, in December 2000, was Mary Robinson, who came to the country to sign the first stage of the technical cooperation accord. She was followed by Dato Param Cumaraswamy, UN Human Rights Commission Special Rapporteur for Judge and Magistrate Independence, May 13–23, 2001; Claudio Grossman, chairperson of the ICHR, July 2–5, 2001; Alejandro González Poblete and Ole Vedel Rasmussen from the UN Committee against Torture, August 23–September 12, 2001; Martha Altolaguirre, Special Rapporteur for Women's Issues, at the Inter-American Commission of Human Rights (ICHR), February 9–12, 2002; Miloon Kothari, UN Special Rapporteur for the Right to Housing, March 4–15, 2002; Juan Mendez, ICHR Special Rapporteur for Migrant Workers, July 25–31, 2002; Gabriela Rodríguez Pizarro, UN Special Rapporteur for the Rights of Migrants, March 7–18, 2002; Mary Robinson, who visited from June 30 to July 2, 2002 in order to sign an agreement to establish a UN office in Mexico; Francis M. Deng, UN Representative for Displaced Persons, August 18–28, 2002; Louis Joinet, chairperson of the UN Arbitrary Detentions Work Group, October 27–November 10, 2002; Rodolfo Stavenhagen, UN Human Rights Commission Special Rapporteur for the Situation of the Rights and Fundamental Liberties of Indigenous Peoples, July 2–13, 2002; and Eduardo Bertoni, ICHR Special Rapporteur for Freedom of Expression, August 18–26, 2003. Maza, M. (2004) *Visitas de los Mecanismos Internacionales de Derechos Humanos.* Prodh Internal Document. Mexico.

8. Notably, two cases. The first was that of General Francisco Gallardo, an Army general who was incarcerated in 1995 for proposing in his masters degree dissertation the setting up of a national military ombudsman. The ICHR had recommended his liberation since 1996. His case was publicized by the CMDPDH, but received support from the entire NGO community. Second, the so called ecologist farmers, Rodolfo Montiel and Teodoro Cabrera, two farmers who were tortured and incarcerated by the local government in 1999. Their crime: organizing their fellow farmers in La Montaña region of Guerrero state in order to resist and denounce deforestation by a Canadian timber-trading corporation.

This case was defended by the "Miguel Agustín Pro Juárez" Human Rights Center (Prodh Center) but was also widely supported by human rights and environmentalist NGOs. Both cases were considered to be paradigmatic in terms of the rights violated, the circumstances in which they occurred, and the authorities involved.

9. When Fox won, the Zapatistas demanded three signs of goodwill to restart dialogue: enforcement of the San Andrés accords, freedom for Zapatista political prisoners, and the removal of seven Army positions in Zapatista areas. Fox answered by sending the original San Andrés Accords bill to Congress. From January to March 2001 the Zapatistas carried out a lobbying campaign for approval of the bill, sending a Zapatista delegation to address Congress, but legislators refused to receive them. In April the Senate passed a bill that ignored the central demands of the San Andrés Accords, such as indigenous autonomy. It was finally passed by all 32 state congresses and became law. During this time, from January to August 2001, human rights NGOs like the Prodh and those affiliated to the Red TDT began their own lobbying campaign, producing documents arguing in favor of Fox's proposal, providing information about indigenous autonomy and rights for legislators, and comparing the final bill with the San Andrés Accords. From August 2001 to the end of 2002 they lodged complaints with national and international courts and produced information on the issue. It was hard work, but it was of almost no use in defining the role of NGOs in the new scenario. Centro de Derechos Humanos "Miguel Agustín Pro Juárez." (2004). *Cronología narrativa. Proceso de la reforma constitucional en materia indígena* [online]. Centro Prodh. Available from: http://www.sjsocial.org/PRODH/especiales/cronologia. (March 10, 2004).

10. In December 2000, during her second visit to Mexico, Mary Robinson and President Fox signed an accord to establish a Technical Cooperation Accord. In order to discuss the agenda and activities with the government during the first stage of the accord—which focused on training for the forensic and medical documentation of torture and the organization of workshops on indigenous rights for indigenous groups, a committee formed by representatives of the most important national NGOs was set up—the Link Committee. The second stage of the accord was launched in April 2002. It was signed together with an agreement to establish a Mexican branch of the High Commissioner's Office and consisted of the elaboration of a national human rights diagnosis. Oficina Del Alto Comisionado de las Naciones Unidas para los Derechos Humanos en México. (2003). *Diagnóstico sobre la Situación de los Derechos Humanos en México.* Mexico: ONU.

11. Encouraged by the World Conference against Racism, Racial Discrimination, Xenophobia and Related Forms of Intolerance held in Durban, South Africa, in 2001, organizations prioritizing

the cultural rights of certain groups, such as indigenous people and women, oriented their work toward discrimination. Notably, in 2000 the Mexican Academy of Human Rights (Academia) organized a Mexico and Central America-wide forum for the discussion of discrimination and intolerance in the region. Most of the Mexicans attending were migrant and indigenous representatives, as well as academics, but some human rights workers involved in indigenous rights were present. Academia Mexicana de Derechos Humanos. (2000). *Foro Regional de México y Centroamérica sobre Racismo, Discriminación e Intolerancia. Organizaciones No Gubernamentales.* Mexico Academia Mexicana de Derechos Humanos.

12. This clash of perspectives was evident in the preparation process of the First Dialogue between Civil Society and the EU and Mexico, in November 2002, and in a workshop held in Brussels in 2003 with the purpose of discussing methodologies for the work of the social observatory and the citizen committee.

13. For an account of the civil resistance in San Luis Potosí after the 1991 state elections, see: Acosta, M. (1994). Elecciones en México: la sociedad civil y la defensa de los derechos humanos. In Concha Malo, M. Ed. *Los derechos políticos como derechos humanos.* Mexico: La Jornada Ediciones-CIICH-UNAM. For the participation of women, see the participation of activist Patricia Palacios in: Red Mexicana de Acción Frente al Libre Comercio. (1991b). *La opinión pública y las negociaciones del Tratado de Libre Comercio: Alternativas ciudadanas* C-0024 (2) TLC. Zacatecas: RMALC.

14. This view of the role of NAFTA in transition to democracy contradicts or conflicts with what the RMALC indicates in the section "Processing consensus" of the Red Mexicana de Acción Frente al Libre Comercio. (1991c). *Memoria de Zacatecas. 25, 26 y 27 de octubre de 1991. La opinión pública y las negociaciones del Tratado de Libre Comercio: Alternativas ciudadanas.* Mexico: RMALC. p 24. Here, the RMALC states that "The struggle for union, electoral and social democracy is a domestic issue that calls for solidarity and support, but not interventionism; neither can it be imposed from outside under pressure with alleged trade concessions." This position is understandable given the centrality of sovereignty in the RMALC. However, it seems that when other social actors joined the RMALC in Zacatecas, different strategies were adopted—conditionality of human rights and democracy is a widely used strategy used in human rights movements. See Keck, M.E. and Sikkink, K. (1998a). Human Rights Advocacy in Latin America. In *Activists beyond Borders.* Ithaca: Cornell University Press.

15. See also: the speeches of intellectuals Adolfo Aguilar Zínser, and José Antonio Crespo; journalists and researchers Abraham Nuncio, Miguel Basáñez, Jorge Eugenio Ortiz, Javier Livas; PRD members Jorge Calderón and Graco Ramírez, who talk about the need to

make democracy a condition for signature of the trade agreement if the Mexican "transition" was to work; and the summary of discussions of the Democracy, Human Rights and Women group; and the Development, Sovereignty and Debt group, in: Red Mexicana de Acción Frente al Libre Comercio. (1991b). *La opinión pública y las negociaciones del Tratado de Libre Comercio: Alternativas ciudadanas* C-0024 (2) TLC. Zacatecas: RMALC.
16. The idea of citizen participation was widely developed during a meeting held in Washington from March 25–27, 1993, organized by the Alliance for Responsible Trade, the Citizen Trade Campaign, the RMALC, and the Action Canada Network. During this meeting the delegations of the three countries drafted a document outlining the "principles for fair and sustainable development": respect for basic human rights, promotion of sustainability, reduction of inequality, promotion of democracy, and participation. See: Red Mexicana de Acción Frente al Libre Comercio. (1994a). *Mesa de medio ambiente. Propuesta de discusión. Comisión ambiental. RMALC.* C-0022(2) RMALC Medio ambiente 1988–1994. Mexico: RMALC.
17. *Subcomandante* Marcos expressed this view on January 1, 1994, when he sustained a dialogue with people assembled in the main square of San Cristóbal de la Casas. Centro Potosino de Derechos Humanos. (1994). *El estallido que estremece a México* [online]. Native-L. Available from: http://listserv.tamu.edu/cgi/wa?A2=ind9401b&L=native-l&D=0&P=2641. (June 16, 2006).
18. For Zapatista ideas on democracy see: Moguel, J. (2004). *Las claves del zapatismo* [online]. Fractal. Available from: http://www.fractal.com.mx/F8Moguel.html. (March 10, 2004).
19. It is not within the scope of this research to analyze the role of the Zapatistas in the global movement against neoliberal globalization. This can be found elsewhere. See for instance: Molina, I. (2000). *El pensamiento del EZLN*. Mexico: Plaza y Valdés. *Subcomandante* Marcos. (1997a). *7 piezas sueltas del rompecabezas mundial (El neoliberalismo como rompecabezas: la inútil unidad mundial que fragmenta y destruye naciones)* [online]. EZLN. Available from: http://palabra.ezln.org.mx/comunicados/1997/1997_06_b.htm. (June 15, 2006). Ejército Zapatista de Liberación Nacional. (1996). *1a-2a Declaración de la Realidad* [online]. IdeaSapiens. Available from: http://www.ideasapiens.com.../primera_%20segunda%20declaracion%20realidad.%20ezln.htm. (March 11, 2004). Centro de Investigaciones Económicas y Políticas de Acción Comunitaria. (2001). *La Agenda Social Mundial contra la Globalización Neoliberal* [online]. CIEPAC. Available from: http://ciepac.org/bulletins/200-300/bolec252.htm. (March 11, 2004). Ejército Zapatista de Liberación Nacional. (1997). *Convocatoria al Segundo Encuentro por la Humanidad y contra el Neoliberalismo* [online]. Nodo50. Available from: http://www.nodo50.org/encuentro/convocatoria.htm. (March 11, 2004).

Subcomandante Marcos. (1997b). *Carta del Subcomandante Marcos a los organizadores y asistentes al Segundo Encuentro Intercontinental por la Humanidad y contra el Neoliberalismo* [online]. EZLN. Available from: http://www.ezln.org/documentos/1997/19970727.es.htm. (March 11, 2004). (1997b). *Mundialización y nuevas desigualdades. Mesa de Ruesta* [online]. II Encuentro Intercontinental por la Humanidad y contra el Neoliberalismo. Available from: http://chiapas.solidaridaragon.org/mesas/mesa2-1htm. (June 17, 2006).
20. (2001a). *Declaración de la Segunda Cumbre de los Pueblos de las Américas* [online]. RMALC. Available from: http://www.rmalc.org.mx/tratados/alca/alca.htm. (March 12, 2006).

Part II Introduction

1. The notion of nodal point is also taken from Laclau and Mouffe's work (Laclau and Mouffe: 2001). The concept of nodal points disappears from Laclau's theoretical work and it is apparently replaced by the idea of empty signifier. In their early work, Laclau and Mouffe defined nodal points as privileged language points that partially fix meaning in an articulation. Howarth argues that it remains unclear whether the concept of empty signifier is a continuation of the work of nodal points thus understood. However, he does point out that while Laclau and Mouffe seem to refer to a variety of nodal points, Laclau refers to one single empty signifier achieving articulation. Nodal points did not carry the totalizing connotations of an empty signifier; they seemed to coexist with other nodal points, which is why the term can be used in this context. See the work on nodal points in: Laclau, E. and Mouffe, C. (2001). *Hegemony and Socialist Strategy. Towards a Radical Democratic Politics.* London: Verso. See the work on empty signifier in: Howarth, D. (2004). Hegemony, Political Subjectivity, and Radical Democracy. In Critchley, S. and Marchart, O. Eds. *Laclau: A Critical Reader.* London: Routledge; Laclau, E. (2000a). Constructing Universality. In Butler, J., Laclau, E., and Zizek, S. Eds. *Contingency, Hegemony, Universality. Contemporary Dialogues on the Left.* London: Verso; Laclau, E. (1993). Discourse. In Goodin, R.E. and Pettit, P. Eds. *A Companion to Contemporary Political Philosophy.* London: Blackwell; Laclau, E. (1996). *Emancipation (s).* London: Verso; Laclau, E. (2000b). Identity and Hegemony: The Role of Universality in the Constitution of Political Logics. In Butler, J., Laclau, E., and Zizek, S. Eds. *Contingency, Hegemony, Universality. Contemporary Dialogues on the Left.* London: Verso; Laclau, E. (2006). *Las identidades políticas en un mundo globalizado.* Mexico: Colegio de México; Laclau, E. (1990). *New Reflections on the Revolution of Our Time.* London: Verso; Laclau, E. (2005). *On Populist Reason.* London: Verso; Laclau, E. (1994). Why Do Empty Signifiers Matter

to Politics? In Weeks, J. Ed. *The Lesser Evil and the Greater Good. The Theory and Politics of Social Diversity.* Cornwall: Rivers Oram Press; Laclau, E. and Mouffe, C. (1987). Post-Marxism without Apologies. *New Left Review.* I (166): 79–106; Laclau, E. and Zac, L. (1994). Minding the Gap: The Subject of Politics. In Laclau, E. Ed. *The Making of Political Identities.* London: Verso.
2. For discussions on SMOs see: Eschle, C. and Stammers, N. (2004). Taking Part: Social Movements, INGOs and Global Change. *Alternatives: Global, Local, Political.* 29 (3): 333–372; Mcadam, D., Mccarthy, J.D. and Zald, M.N. Eds. (1996) *Comparative Perspectives on Social Movements. Political Opportunities, Mobilizing Structures, and Cultural Framings.* Cambridge: Cambridge University Press; Kaldor, M. and Kavan, Z. (2001). Democracy and Civil Society in Central and Eastern Europe. In Axtmann, R. Ed. *Balancing Democracy.* London: Continuum; Cohen, J. and Arato, A. (1992). *Civil Society and Political Theory.* Cambridge, Mass: MIT Press; Smith, J. (1997). Characteristics of the Modern Transnational Social Movement Sector. In Smith, J., Chatfield, C., and Pagnucco, R. Eds. *Transnational Social Movements and Global Politics. Solidarity beyond the State.* New York: Syracuse University Press; Smith, J., Pagnucco, R. and Chatfield, C. (1997). Social Movements and World Politics. In Smith, J., Chatfield, C., and Pagnucco, R. Eds. *Transnational Social Movements and Global Politics. Solidarity beyond the State.* New York: Syracuse University Press. For discussions on NGOs, see: Chalmers, D.A. and Piester, K. (1996). Nongovernmental Organizations and the Changing Structures of Mexican Politics. In Randall, L. Ed. *Changing Structure of Mexico: Political, Social and Economic Prospects.* New York: ME Sharpe; Fisher, W. (1997). Doing Good? The Politics and Antipolitics of NGO Practices. *Annual Review of Anthropology.* 26: 439–464; Eschle, C. and Stammers, N. (2004). Taking Part: Social Movements, INGOs and Global Change. *Alternatives: Global, Local, Political.* 29 (3): 333–372; Kaldor, M. (2003). *Global Civil Society: An Answer to War.* Cambridge: Polity Press; Cohen, R. and Shirin, M.R. (2000). Global Social Movements. Towards a Cosmopolitan Politics. In Cohen, R. and Shirin, M.R. Eds. *Global Social Movements.* London: The Athlone Press.

4 Constructing Free Trade Worldviews with Human Rights Discourse

Some parts of this chapter appeared in the book article "Libre comercio y acción colectiva internacional: un enfoque desde los derechos humanos," in Yamín, Alicia, *Derechos económicos, sociales y culturales: del invento a la herramienta*, Plaza y Valdés, 2006 (ISBN: 970-722-524-6) (ISBN: 1-55250-323-2/ e-book). The excerpts are reproduced here with the permission of APRODEH.

Notes

1. The RMALC claims that the first international protest against free trade was the struggle against NAFTA (Arroyo 2004). Broader international coordination is believed to have started in 1996, when the EZLN held the First Inter-Continental Meeting for Humanity and Against Neoliberalism, which took place July 27–August 3, in La Realidad, Chiapas. Three thousand people from 43 countries attended the meeting and discussed alternatives to neoliberal economics. The meeting had two sequels: Summer 1997 in Spain, and Summer 1998 in Brazil. Those meetings became the precursors and inspiration for subsequent meetings for global movements opposing free trade, among many other issues related to economic globalization. The first major global protest against free-trade related issues was the campaign against the Multilateral Agreement on Investment (MAI). For the Zapatista influence in global civil society, see: Molina, I. (2000). *El pensamiento del EZLN*. Mexico: Plaza y Valdés; Ejército Zapatista de Liberación Nacional. (1996). *1a-2a Declaración de la Realidad* [online]. IdeaSapiens. Available from: http://www.ideasapiens.com.../primera_%20segunda%20declaracion%20realidad.%20ezln.htm. (March 11, 2004); Centro de Investigaciones Económicas y Políticas de Acción Comunitaria. (2001). *La Agenda Social Mundial contra la Globalización Neoliberal* [online]. CIEPAC. Available from: http://ciepac.org/bulletins/200-300/bolec252.htm. (March 11, 2004); Ejército Zapatista de Liberación Nacional. (1997). *Convocatoria al Segundo Encuentro por la Humanidad y contra el Neoliberalismo* [online]. Nodo50. Available from: http://www.nodo50.org/encuentro/convocatoria.htm. (March 11, 2004); Subcomandante Marcos. (1997b). *Carta del Subcomandante Marcos a los organizadores y asistentes al Segundo Encuentro Intercontinental por la Humanidad y contra el Neoliberalismo* [online]. EZLN. Available from: http://www.ezln.org/documentos/1997/19970727.es.htm. (March 11, 2004); (1997b). *Mundialización y nuevas desigualdades. Mesa de Ruesta* [online]. II Encuentro Intercontinental por la Humanidad y contra el Neoliberalismo. Available from: http://chiapas.solidaridaragon.org/mesas/mesa2-1htm. (June 17, 2006).
2. Antecedents for the academic study of human rights and free trade are to be found in the fields of Development and International Relations. On the one hand, in the field of development, use was made of a human rights perspective to build theoretical approaches to the obligation of the state in terms of social policy after an evaluation of the impact of structural adjustment programs in the 1980s. On the other hand, from the peak of studies of globalization as an economic, political, cultural, and social process in international relations, in the mid-1990s the relation between globalization and human rights began to be considered in terms of the internationalization of their normativity. Concerning the first point see: Claude, R.P. and Weston, B.H. (1992). Basic Needs, Security Rights, and Humane Governance. In Claude, R.P. and

Burns, H.W. Eds. *Human Rights in the World Community: Issues and Action.* Philadelphia: University of Pennsylvania. Concerning the second see: Held, D., Mcgrew, A., Goldblatt, D., and Perraton, J. (1999). *Global Transformations. Politics, Economics and Culture.* London: Polity Press.

3. For a review of the evolution of the link between labor, human rights, and international trade, see: Compa, L.A. and Diamond, S.F. Eds. (1996) *Human Rights, Labor Rights, and International Trade.* Philadelphia: University of Pennsylvania Press.

4. A more or less general agreement exists that the economic and social impact of corporations is negative. See: Jochnick, C. (1999). Confronting the Impunity of Non-State Actors: New Fields for the Promotion of Human Rights. *Human Rights Quarterly.* 21 (1): 56–79; Forsythe, D.P. (2000). *Human Rights in International Relations.* Cambridge: Cambridge University Press. Nevertheless, there are those who claim there is empirical evidence demonstrating that corporations are positive for development. For an interesting discussion see: Meyer, W.H. (1998). *Human Rights and International Political Economy in Third World Nations. Multinational Corporations, Foreign Aid and Repression.* Westport: Praeger Publishers.

5. More recently the discussion has focused on whether it would be pertinent to establish minimum labor standards within the WTO. The debate divided the academic community and activists into two camps: those who maintained that the so-called social clause would only promote protectionism on the part of rich countries, and those who saw the need to establish labor on the same level as other services and goods converted into merchandise and therefore subject to commercial normativity (Pangalangan 2002). Today there exists a more or less general consensus to the effect that trade bodies, in particular the WTO, should take human rights into consideration. Nevertheless, there exists debate as to whether human rights cases arising within the WTO should be fought internally, with a view to widening the areas of implementation in detriment to, or complementarily with, universal and regional bodies for the implementation of human rights. In the discussion it is noteworthy that there exists a marked contrast between those who see trade as essentially good but with certain faults, and those who see it as a permanent threat if there is repeated insistence on leaving it unregulated. This difference is epistemological, for while the supporters of trade (almost always a priori) consider that a market economy, from its theoretical precepts, protects economic and political freedoms with the impulse to economic growth through the free market, its opponents prioritize human dignity to argue that the primacy of human rights should be defended before that of trade and for this reason it is necessary to force the WTO to respect them and not implement them. The responsibility for implementing them resides fundamentally with the state and only later falls to multilateral and regional human rights bodies. In the group of those privileging commercial legislation can be found: Lim, H.

(2001). Trade and Human Rights, What's at Issue? *Journal of World Trade.* April 2001. 35 (2): 275–300; Salman, B. (2001). International Free Trade Agreements and Human Rights: Interpreting Article XX of the GATT. *Minnesota Journal of Global Trade.* Winter 2001. 10 (1): 62–108; Petersman, E.-U. (2002). Time for a United Nations "Global Compact" for Integrating Human Rights into the Law of Worldwide Organizations: Lessons from European Integration. *European Journal of International Law.* September 2002. 13 (3): 621–650. The group of those privileging a human rights vision includes: Alston, P. (2002). Resisting the Merger and Acquisition of Human Rights by Trade Law: A Reply to Petersman. *European Journal of International Law.* September 2002. 13 (4): 815–844; Marceau, G. (2002). WTO Dispute Settlement and Human Rights. *European Journal of International Law.* September 2002. 13 (4): 753–814; Dommen, C. (2002). Raising Human Rights Concerns in the World Trade Organization: Actors, Process and Possible Strategies. *Human Rights Quarterly.* 24 (1): 1–50. There also exists a debate concerning the usefulness of safeguards established in Article XX of the GATT for the defense of human rights. This article establishes that exceptions can be made to free trade legislation for the protection of public morals; human, animal, or vegetable life; health; and the conservation of nonrenewable natural resources. The discussion focuses on whether the safeguards should be interpreted through a human rights framework and therefore use the WTO mechanism for dispute settlement for the litigation of human rights cases. There are some who agree and others who believe it is for states to respect these safeguards and for UN bodies to say whether states have met their obligations. See: Marceau, G. (2002). WTO Dispute Settlement and Human Rights. *European Journal of International Law.* September 2002. 13 (4): 753–814.

6. Before the norms were first drafted in 2001, the UN started to address the issues of the responsibility of corporations toward human rights with the Global Compact, a platform of action agreed between the UN and a group of corporations in order to promote sound corporate practices based on human rights principles. According to the Compact, which is not legally binding, firms subscribe to the Compact by sending a letter to the UN General Secretary, and are required to submit periodical reports of their compliance with the eight human rights principles established in the Compact—respect for civil rights, noncomplicity in violations of individual freedoms perpetrated by governments, trade union freedom and recognition of collective bargaining, eradication of forced labor and child labor, nondiscrimination, respect for the environmental precaution principle, environmental responsibility, and use of environmentally friendly technologies.

7. The UN used as its basis at least four previous documents: the Tripartite Declaration of Principles Governing Multinational Companies and the Social Policy of the ILO (binding); the Global Compact (2000); the

Directives of the OECD (from 1976 but reformed in 2000 to include matters related to labor rights and the environment, and to establish mechanisms for dispute settlement); and the Project of Fundamental Human Rights Principles for Companies (2001). These include ESCRs and CPRs in areas that vary according to the document.

8. In 2004, during the 60th session of the Commission there was a heated debate about the convenience of the norm, and some countries and corporations tried to get the UN to abort the project altogether, but an NGO caucus managed to get the Commission to keep the issue of corporate responsibility in its future agenda and it committed to produce a report on the scope of corporate legal responsibility toward human rights—it was agreed that the Norms could not yet be legally binding. In 2005, during its 61st session, the Commission requested the secretary general to appoint a special representative for human rights and corporations, and establish the extent of those responsibilities. For a critical analysis of the norms see: Deva, S. (2004). *UN's Human Rights Norms for Transnational Corporations and Other Business Enterprises: An Imperfect Step in Right Direction?* [online]. The Berkeley Electronic Press. Available from: http://law.bepress.com/expresso/eps/112 (January 1, 2007).

9. Article 14(1) of the Convention points out: "The rights of ownership and possession of the peoples concerned over the lands which they traditionally occupy shall be recognized. In addition, measures shall be taken in appropriate cases to safeguard the right of the peoples concerned to use lands not exclusively occupied by them, but to which they have traditionally had access for their subsistence and traditional activities. Particular attention shall be paid to the situation of nomadic peoples and shifting cultivators in this respect." International Labor Organization (1989) *Convention No. 169 Concerning Indigenous and Tribal Peoples in Independent Countries* [online]. United Nations. Available from: http://www.unhchr.ch/html/menu3/b/62.htm. (June 16, 2006).

10. Frade's intellectual work is developed in: Frade Rubio, L. (2001). *Las implicaciones de la globalización económica y la internacionalización del Estado en las mujeres.* Mexico: Milenio Feminista.

5 THE CONSTRUCTION OF IDENTITIES AND SPECIFIC AGENDAS WITH HUMAN RIGHTS DISCOURSE

1. However, the farmers' movement does not mix farmer and indigenous identities because many farmers are mixed race or do not identify with any particular ethnic group.
2. In 2003, the Prodh Center invited certain farmers' leaders to collaborate in a report on farmers' rights, which built on a manifesto signed

by the leaders of the important farmers' coalition, Agriculture Can Take no More, entitled "Dialogue for a State Policy and a National Agreement on Agriculture: Where Are We and What Is Next?." The Prodh document dealt with the rights to land, territory, and natural resources; food; work; a clean environment; and liberty, physical integrity, and participation. Farmers' leaders especially welcomed the formulation of the "right to be a farmer." See: Centro de Derechos Humanos "Miguel Agustín Pro Juárez." (2003). *Pensar el Campo desde los Derechos Humanos.* Mexico: Centro Prodh.
3. Article 1(2) of the Declaration on the Right to Development states: The human right to development also implies the full realization of the right of peoples to self-determination, which includes, subject to the relevant provisions of both International Covenants on Human Rights, the exercising of their inalienable right to full sovereignty over all their natural wealth and resources. United Nations Commission of Human Rights. (1986). *Declaration on the Right to Development* [online]. United Nations. Available from: http://www.unhchr.ch/html/menu3/b/74.htm. (June 16, 2006).
4. United Nations Committee On Economic, S.A.C.R. (1999). *General Comment 12, The Right to Adequate Food.* UN Doc. E/C.12/1999/5 (1999), reprinted in Compilation of General Comments and General Recommendations Adopted by Human Rights Treaty Bodies, UN Doc. HRI/GEN/1/Rev.6 at 62 (2003). Available at: http://www1.umn.edu/humanrts/gencomm/escgencom12.htm. Geneva: United Nations.

6 Articulating Anti-free Trade Struggles with Human Rights Discourse

1. The text of the *Final Declaration of the Trade Union Inter-American Summit on Trade and Labor Rights,* Denver, June 29, 1995, was not available, therefore it was necessary to rely on summaries of the critiques, demands and proposals, in Osorio, V. (1998). *Reinventando el continente. Agenda social y libre comercio en las Américas.* Mexico: RMALC.
2. Excerpts of the *Final Declaration of the Second Labor Forum "Workers and Integration,"* Cartagena, March 1996, in Osorio, V. (1998). *Reinventando el continente. Agenda social y libre comercio en las Américas.* Mexico: RMALC.
3. *Final Declaration of the Third Labor Forum "Workers and Integration,"* Belo Horizonte, May 1997, in Alianza Social Continental. (2000). *Carpeta informativa básica.* Mexico: ASC.
4. *Declaración de Belo Horizonte, Brasil,* in Alianza Social Continental. (2000). *Carpeta informativa básica.* Mexico: ASC.
5. *Final Declaration of the Colloquium on the Americas' Solidarity "Building Sustainable and Democratic Americas, with Solidarity and*

without Poverty," Montreal, September 1997, in Osorio, V. (1998). *Reinventando el continente. Agenda social y libre comercio en las Américas.* Mexico: RMALC.

6. The text of the *Final Declaration of the Colloquium on the Americas' Solidarity "Building Sustainable and Democratic Americas, with Solidarity and without Poverty,"* Montreal, September 1997 was not available anywhere, therefore I had to rely on summaries of the basic critiques, demands, and proposals, in Osorio, V. (1998). *Reinventando el continente. Agenda social y libre comercio en las Américas.* Mexico: RMALC.

7. *Final Declaration of the First Peoples' Summit, Santiago de Chile, April 18, 1998*, in Alianza Social Continental. (2000). *Carpeta informativa básica.* Mexico: ASC.

8. *Declaración de la Cumbre de los Pueblos de las Américas, Santiago de Chile, April 1998*, in Alianza Social Continental. (2000). *Carpeta informativa básica.* Mexico: ASC.

9. In the interview, Herrera said: "In real terms a thorough discussion during the negotiations was difficult and much escaped us, such as the forms and wording, but we knew it was a reaction—it was also perhaps a matter of presence, leadership and quotas concerning who entered the conversation first. We did recognize that human rights organisms had not arrived first and that we did not have the same time and trajectory invested in the process of organization and articulation around economic integration. For example, if, after the meeting in Costa Rica when the HSA was established, we had called on the other participants from Santiago to attend and offer a follow-up on discussions, as well as to become involved in the different activities organized in order for responsibility of the movement to be shared, we would have been able to present our proposals in a timely fashion. However, the organizations present in Santiago were involved in other matters related to their own agendas and those that did follow up were the unions, while in Mexico it was the RMALC and not the Human Rights Network. Therefore these organizations demanded the right to continue with their arguments and their proposals, and in the final wording it was they who had followed up and maintained their presence in the discussions."

10. These types of strategies have been conceptualized by Keck and Sikkink as "boomerang" and "spiral" effects. In the sociopolitical study of human rights these terms are widely used. See: Keck, M.E. and Sikkink, K. (1998b). Transnational Advocacy Networks in International Politics: Introduction. In *Activists beyond Borders.* Ithaca: Cornell University Press; Keck, M.E. and Sikkink, K. (1998a). Human Rights Advocacy in Latin America. In *Activists beyond Borders.* Ithaca: Cornell University Press; Khagram, S., Riker, J.V., and Sikkink, K. (2002). *Restructuring World Politics. Transnational Social Movements, Networks, and Norms.* 14. Minnesota: University

of Minnesota Press; Risse, T., Ropp, S.C., and Sikkink, K. (1999). *The Power of Human Rights. International Norms and Domestic Change*. Cambridge: Cambridge University Press; Risse, T. (2000). The Power of Norms versus the Norms of Power: Transnational Civil Society and Human Rights. In Florini, A. Ed. *The Third Force. The Rise of Transnational Civil Society*. Washington DC: Japan Center for International Exchange-Carnegie Endowment for International Peace.

11. For instance, the representative of the Copenhagen Initiative for Central America, Luis Guillermo Pérez-Casas said: "We agree that multilateral and intra-regional systems for the protection of human rights need to be strengthened according to their own dynamic and that any follow-up initiative cannot hope to replace internal tribunals. However, the scope of obligations assumed by parties with respect to the Rule of Law, democratic governance, transparency in public administration, respect for human rights, the eradication of poverty, environmental protection, etc. require a level of continuity that moves beyond questions of whether a company from the European Union violates labor rights somewhere in Mexico or bribes a public servant in bidding for a contract. The democratic clause, or human rights clause, is to be applied in the reciprocal sense and therefore it is not a question of whether it serves as a 'colonial vision' of the North toward the South. The commitments assumed by States via the clause should not be limited to writing and we therefore need to be imaginative in order to establish adequate follow-up measures and ensure that society itself demands the compliance of States." Centro de Derechos Humanos "Miguel Agustín Pro Juárez" and Iniciativa de Copenhague para Centroamérica y México. (2002). *Email Conversation between Representatives from Centro Prodh and CIFCA Regarding the Scope of Human Rights Observation in the Democratic Clause Project*. Mexico-Brussels.

Bibliography

(1997a). *Masstricht Guidelines on Violations of Economic Social and Cultural Rights* [online]. International Commission of Jurists, the Urban Morgan Institute on Human Rights, and the Centre for Human Rights of the Faculty of Law of Maastricht University. Available from: http://www1.umn.edu/humanrts/instree/Maastrichtguidelines_.html (June 14, 2006).

(1997b). *Mundialización y nuevas desigualdades. Mesa de Ruesta* [online]. II Encuentro Intercontinental por la Humanidad y contra el Neoliberalismo. Available from: http://chiapas.solidaridaragon.org/mesas/mesa2-1htm (June 17, 2006).

(1998). Declaración del Foro de Derechos Humanos de la Cumbre de los Pueblos de América. Santiago de Chile 15, 16, 17 y 18 de abril de 1998. In Corporación de Promoción y Defensa de los Derechos del Pueblo—CODEPU. *Foro de Derechos Humanos de la Cumbre de los Pueblos de América. Recopilación de las Exposiciones, Debates y Conclusiones.* Santiago de Chile: CODEPU.

(2001a). *Declaración de la Segunda Cumbre de los Pueblos de las Américas* [online]. RMALC. Available from: http://www.rmalc.org.mx/tratados/alca/alca.htm (March 12, 2006).

(2001b). *Declaración del Foro sobre los Derechos Humanos.* Segunda Cumbre de los Pueblos de las Américas. Quebec: Centro Prodh.

(2004a). *Historia del EZLN* [online]. CCD-Utopia. Available from: http://www.geocities.com/ccd-utopia/ezln/historia_ezln/ (March 10, 2004).

(2004b). *Pronunciamiento social de Guadalajara frente a la Cumbre Unión Europea-América Latina y el Caribe "Los derechos de los pueblos están primero."* Guadalajara.

Abarca Chávez, C. (1987). La vivienda como Derecho del Hombre. *Justicia y Paz* No. 2: 3–24. February.

Academia Mexicana de Derechos Humanos. (1989a). Various articles. *El Boletín* No. 9–10: 3–10. June–July.

———. (1989b). Various articles. *El Boletín* No. 12–13: 1–12. September–October.

———. (1990a). Avisos. *El Boletín* No. 16: 14. January–February.

———. (1990b). Editorial. *El Boletín* No. 17: 1–3. March–April.

———. (1990c). Various articles. *El Boletín* No. 16: 15. January–February.

———. (1990d). Various articles. *El Boletín* No. 17: 1–3. March–April.

230 BIBLIOGRAPHY

Academia Mexicana de Derechos Humanos. (1991). *Memoria de actividades 1990*. Mexico: Academia Mexicana de Derechos Humanos.
———. (1993). *Memoria de actividades 1992*. Mexico: Academia Mexicana de Derechos Humanos.
———. (1994). *Memoria de actividades 1993*. Mexico: Academia Mexicana de Derechos Humanos.
———. (1996). *Memoria de actividades 1994–1995*. Mexico: Academia Mexicana de Derechos Humanos.
———. (1997). *Memoria de actividades 1996*. Mexico: Academia Mexicana de Derechos Humanos.
———. (2000). *Foro Regional de México y Centroamérica sobre Racismo, Discriminación e Intolerancia. Organizaciones No Gubernamentales*. Mexico: Academia Mexicana de Derechos Humanos.
Aceves, R. (2000). *Derechos humanos y derechos laborales*. Mexico: Sindicato Mexicano de Electricistas.
Acosta, M. (1992). The Democratization Process in Mexico: A Human Rights Issue. In Cavanagh, J., Gershman, J., Baker, K., and Helmke, G. Eds. *Trading Freedom. How Free Trade Affects Our Lives, Work and Environment*. San Francisco: Institute for Food and Development Policy-Food First. pp. 82–85.
———. (1994). Elecciones en México: la sociedad civil y la defensa de los derechos humanos. In Concha Malo, M. Ed. *Los derechos políticos como derechos humanos*. Mexico: La Jornada Ediciones-CIICH-UNAM.
———. (2002). Lessons Learned from Relations between Mexican and US Human Rights Organizations. In Brooks, D. and Fox, J. Eds. *Cross-border Dialogues: US-Mexico Social Movement Networking*. San Diego: Center for US Mexican Studies. pp. 293–302.
Addo, M.K. (1999a). The Corporation as a Victim of Human Rights Violations. In Addo, M.K. Ed. *Human Rights Standards and the Responsibility of Transnational Corporations*. The Hague: Kluwer Law International. pp. 187–197.
———. (1999b). Human Rights and Transnational Corporations, an Introduction. In Addo, M.K. Ed. *Human Rights. Standards and the Responsibility of Transnational Corporations*. The Hague: Kluwer Law. pp. 3–37.
Aguayo Quezada, S. (1993). The Inevitability of Democracy in Mexico. In Roett, R. Ed. *Political and Economic Liberalization in Mexico: At a Critical Juncture?* Boulder: LynneRienner.
Aguayo Quezada, S. and Parra Rosales, L.P. (1997). *Las organizaciones no gubernamentales de derechos humanos en México: entre la democracia participativa y la electoral*. Mexico: Academia Mexicana de Derechos Humanos.
Aldana, J.C. and Vázquez Ortega, J.J. (2005). La ilegalidad de la legalidad: el discurso de los derechos humanos a fiscalización. In López Gutiérrez, C., Vázquez Ortega, J.J., and Uribe Patiño, F.J. Eds. *Globalización, violencia y derechos humanos. Entre lo manifiesto y lo oculto*. Mexico: UAM-Itaca.

Alianza Social Continental. (2000). *Carpeta informativa básica*. Mexico: ASC.
———. (2001a). *Alternativas para las Américas*. Quebec: RMALC.
———. (2001b). *Declaración de la II Cumbre de los Pueblos de las Américas* [online]. Alianza Social Continental. Available from: http://www.asc-hsa.org/quebec.html (May 22, 2003).
———. (2003). *Proceso ALCA* [online]. asc. Available from: http://www.asc-hsa.org/quebec.html (May 22, 2003).
Alliance for Responsible Trade (Art-Estados Unidos), Common Frontiers/Fronteras Comunes (Canadá), Red Chile Por Una Iniciativa De Los Pueblos (Rechip-Chile), Red Mexicana De Acción Frente Al Libre Comercio (Rmalc-México), and Réseau Québécois Sur L'intégration Continentale (Rqic-Québec). (1998). *Alternativas para las Américas. Hacia la Construcción de un Acuerdo Hemisférico de los Pueblos*. Ontario: RMALC.
Alston, P. (2002). Resisting the Merger and Acquisition of Human Rights by Trade Law: A Reply to Petersman. *European Journal of International Law*. September. 13 (4): 815–844.
Alvarez Díaz, R. (1996). De la resistencia a la propuesta: las ONG's de derechos humanos en México. In Meza, A. and Chamberline, M. Eds. *La integralidad de los derechos humanos. Primer paquete didáctico*. II. Mexico: Red TDT.
Alvarez Enríquez, L. (2002). *La sociedad civil en la Ciudad de México: proceso de conformación a la vertiente de izquierda*. PhD. UNAM.
An-Na'im, A.A. Ed. (1995). *Human Rights in Cross-cultural Perspectives: A Quest for Consensus*. Philadelphia: University of Pennsylvania Press.
Andersen, N.A. (2003). *Discursive Analytical Strategies. Understanding Foucault, Koselleck, Laclau, Luhmann*. Bristol: Policy Press.
Arditi, B. (1991). *Conceptos: Ensayos sobre teoría política, democracia y filosofía*. Asunción: CDE and RP.
Arroyo Picard, A. and Monroy, M. (1996). *Red Mexicana de Acción Frente al Libre Comercio. 5 años de lucha (1991–1996)*. Mexico: RMALC.
Arroyo Picard, A. and Peñaloza Méndez, A. Eds. (2000). *Derechos Humanos y Tratado de Libre Comercio México-Unión Europea*. Mexico: RMALC.
Arroyo Picard, A., Gómez Cruz, M.A., Schwentesius Rindermann, R., Ranney, D., Dillon, J., and Hansen Kuhn, K. (2003). *Lessons from NAFTA: The High Cost of "Free" Trade*. Mexico: ASC.
Aziz, N. (1995). The Human Rights Debate in an Era of Globalization: Hegemony of Discourse. *Bulletin of Concerned Asian Scholars*. 4 (27): 9–23.
Balkin, J.M. (2005). Deconstruction's Legal Career. *Cardozo Law Review*. 27 (2): 101–122.
Baxi, U. (2002). *The Future of Human Rights*. New Delhi: Oxford University Press.
———. (2003). *The Politics of Reading Human Rights*. The Legalization of Human Rights. London: UCL.

Bejarano González, F. (2003). El conflicto del basurero tóxico de Metalclad en Guadalcázar, San Luis Potosí. In Carlsen, L., Wise, T., and Salazar, H. Eds. *Enfrentando la globalización. Respuestas sociales a la integración económica de México.* Mexico: GDAE-Tufts University-RMALC-Porrúa. pp. 27–54.

Berryman, P. (1987). *Liberation Theology. Essential Facts about the Revolutionary Movement in Latin America and Beyond.* London: I.B. Tauris.

Beuchot, M. (1993). *Filosofía y derechos humanos.* Mexico: Siglo XXI Editores.

———. (2000). *Filosofía social de los pensadores novohispanos.* México: IMDOSOC.

———. (2005). *Interculturalidad y derechos humanos.* México: Siglo XXI : UNAM, Facultad de Filosofía y letras.

Bizberg, I. (2003). Estado, organizaciones corporativas y democracia. In *México al inicio del siglo XXI. Democracia, ciudadanía y desarrollo.* Mexico: CIESAS-Porrúa. pp. 183–229.

Brysk, A. (2002). Introduction. In Brysk, A. Ed. *Globalization and Human Rights.* California: University of California Press. pp. 1–16.

———. (2005). *Human Rights and Private Wrongs: Constructing Global Civil Society.* New York: Routledge.

Buechler, S.M. (1995). New Social Movement Theories. *The Sociological Quarterly.* 36 (3): 441–464.

Butler, J., Laclau, Ernesto, and Zizek, Slavoj. (2000). *Contingency, Hegemony, Universality. Contemporary Dialogues on the Left.* London: Verso.

Calderón, F., Piscitelli, A., and Reyna, J.L. (1992). Social Movements: Actors, Theories, Expectations. In Escobar, A. and Alvarez, S.E. Eds. *The Making of Social Movements in Latin America: Identity, Strategy, and Democracy.* Boulder: Westview Press. pp. 19–36.

Calderón Rodríguez, J.M. (1988). La ruptura del colaboracionismo de clases y las perspectivas de la democracia. In Gutiérrez Garza, E. Ed. *La crisis del Estado de Bienestar.* II. Mexico: Siglo XXI-UNAM. pp. 85–128.

Camp, R.A. (1996). *Politics in Mexico.* 2nd. New York: Oxford University Press.

———. (1997). *Crossing Swords. Politics and Religion in Mexico.* Oxford: Oxford University Press.

Carozza, P.G. (2003). From Conquest to Constitutions. *Human Rights Quarterly.* May. 25 (2): 281–313.

Casasbuenas, C. (1997). *Informe de viaje por Bruselas y Holanda, 18–31 de julio.* Carpeta C-0027(5) TLCUEM. Relaciones UE-México 95–97. Mexico: RMALC.

Castañeda, J.G. (1993). *Utopia Unarmed. Latin America Left after the Cold War.* New York: Alfred A. Knop.

Centro de Derechos Humanos "Fray Francisco de Vitoria." (1989). Los derechos indígenas: nuevo enfoque del sistema internacional. *Justicia y Paz* No. 3–4, Derechos de los Pueblos Indios 9–26. July–December.

———. (1990a). Editorial. *Justicia y Paz* No. 19, Medio ambiente y derechos humanos: 2. July–September.

———. (1990b). Información sobre derechos humanos. *Justicia y Paz* No. 18, Los derechos a la salud: 32–43. April–June.

———. (1990c). Información sobre derechos humanos. *Justicia y Paz* No. 20, Memoria de cinco años: 34–40. October–December.

———. (1990d). Memoria de cinco años. *Justicia y Paz* No. 20: 3–5. October–December.

———. (1990e). Metodología para la investigación de casos y situaciones de violación a los derechos humanos (Experiencia de una Organización No Gubernamental). *Justicia y Paz* No. 20: 7–12. October–December.

———. (1991). Información sobre derechos humanos. *Justicia y Paz* No. 23, Derechos laborales y TLC: 29–35. July–September.

———. (1992). La situación de los derechos humanos en México (diciembre 1991–noviembre 1992). *Justicia y Paz* No. 28: 4–43. October–December.

———. (1993). La situación de los derechos humanos en México (diciembre 1992–octubre 1993). *Justicia y Paz* No. 32: 4–64. October–December.

———. (1994). La situación de los derechos humanos en México (diciembre 1993–octubre 1994). *Justicia y Paz* No. 35–36: 4–69. October–November 1994.

———. (1997). Consideraciones acerca del papel del Centro Vitoria como centro de derechos humanos en la sociedad mexicana actual. *Justicia y Paz* No. 44/45: 39–43. January–August 1997.

Centro de Derechos Humanos "Miguel Agustín Pro Juárez." (1991). *La concepción de los derechos humanos y el Tratado de Libre Comercio*. Statement. Mexico.

———. (1992a) *Informe Anual 1991. Los derechos humanos en México*. Mexico: Centro Prodh.

———. (1992b). Los derechos humanos: nuevo campo de la lucha social en México. In A. Aziz Nassif, J. Tamayo, and J. Alonso. Eds. *El nuevo Estado mexicano*. II. Estado y Política. Mexico: CIESAS. pp. 225–271.

———. (1993a) *Informe Anual de Derechos Humanos 1992. Volumen I. Represión y movimiento de Derechos Humanos en México*. Mexico: Centro de Derechos Humanos "Miguel Agustín Pro Juárez."

———. (1993b) *Informe Anual de Derechos Humanos 1992. Volumen III. Los derechos político-electorales*. Mexico: Centro de Derechos Humanos "Miguel Agustín Pro Juárez."

———. (1993c). *Informe Anual de Derechos Humanos 1992*. II. Los derechos humanos de los Pueblos Indios. Mexico: Centro Prodh.

———. (1993d). *Informe Anual de Derechos Humanos 1992*. IV. Los derechos laborales y sindicales/ V. Los derechos sociales y el derecho a un medio ambiente sano. Mexico: Centro Prodh.

———. (2002). *Defensa de la postura frente a la cláusula democrática*. Mexico. NGO Internal Communication.

Centro de Derechos Humanos "Miguel Agustín Pro Juárez." (2003). *Pensar el Campo desde los Derechos Humanos.* Mexico: Centro Prodh.

———. (2004). *Cronología narrativa. Proceso de la reforma constitucional en materia indigena* [online]. Centro Prodh. Available from: http://www.sjsocial.org/PRODH/especiales/cronologia (March 10, 2004).

Centro de Derechos Humanos "Miguel Agustín Pro Juárez" and Iniciativa de Copenhague para Centroamérica y México. (2002). *Email Conversation between Representatives from Centro Prodh and CIFCA regarding the Scope of Human Rights Observation in the Democratic Clause Project.* Mexico-Brussels.

Centro de Investigaciones Económicas y Políticas de Acción Comunitaria. (2001). *La Agenda Social Mundial contra la Globalización Neoliberal* [online]. CIEPAC. Available from: http://ciepac.org/bulletins/200-300/bolec252.htm (March 11, 2004).

Centro Potosino de Derechos Humanos. (1994). *El estallido que estremece a México* [online]. Native-L. Available from: http://listserv.tamu.edu/cgi/wa?A2=ind9401b&L=native-l&D=0&P=2641 (June 16, 2006).

Centro Prodh, RMALC and Equipo Pueblo. (2002). *Towards a Positive Dimension of the Democratic Clause.* First Forum "European Union—Mexico Civil Society Dialogue." Brussels: RMALC.

Chalmers, D.A. and Piester, K. (1996). Nongovernmental Organizations and the Changing Structures of Mexican Politics. In Randall, L. Ed. *Changing Structure of Mexico: Political, Social and Economic Prospects.* New York: ME Sharpe. pp. 253–261.

Chand, V.K. (2001). *Mexico's Political Awakening.* Indiana: University of Notre Dame Press.

Chang, H.-J. (2002). Una perspectiva institucional sobre el papel del Estado: hacia una política económica institucional. In Basave, J., Dabat, A., Morera, C., Rivera Ríos, M.Á., and Rodríguez, F. Eds. *Globalización y alternativas incluyentes para el siglo XXI.* Mexico: Facultad de Economía-UAM-I. pp. 541–565.

Chinkin, C. (1999). Gender Inequality and International Human Rights Law. In Hurrell, A. and Woods, N. Eds. *Inequality, Globalization, and World Politics.* Oxford: Oxford University Press.

Chinkin, C.M., Gardner, J.P., and British Institute of International and Comparative Law. (1997). *Human Rights as General Norms and a State's Right to Opt Out: Reservations and Objections to Human Rights Conventions.* London: BIICL.

Cienfuegos, E. and Carlsen, L. (2003). Un caso de derechos humanos, ecología e integración económica: los campesinos ecologistas de la Sierra de Petatlán y Coyuca de Catalán. In Carlsen, L., Wise, T., and Salazar, H. Eds. *Enfrentando la globalización. Respuestas sociales a la integración económica de México.* Mexico: RMALC-GDAE. pp. 55–77.

Clapham, A. (1993). *Human Rights in the Private Sphere.* Oxford: Clarendon Press.

Clarke, S. (1988). *Keynesianism, Monetarism and the Crisis of the State.* Aldershot: Edward Elgar Publishing Limited.
Claude, R.P. and Weston, B.H. (1992). Basic Needs, Security Rights, and Humane Governance. In Claude, R.P. and Burns, H.W. Eds. *Human Rights in the World Community: Issues and Action.* Philadelphia: University of Pennsylvania.
Cohen, J. and Arato, A. (1992). *Civil Society and Political Theory.* Cambridge, Mass.: MIT Press.
Cohen, R. and Shirin, M.R. (2000). Global Social Movements. Towards a Cosmopolitan Politics. In Cohen, R. and Shirin, M.R. Eds. *Global Social Movements.* London: Athlone Press. pp. 1–17.
Comblin, J. (1979). *The Church and the National Security State.* New York: Orbis Books.
Comisión Mexicana de Defensa y Promoción de Los Derechos Humanos. (1992). *Intercambio Trinacional. Perspectivas Continentales de Derechos Humanos. Septiembre 11–13, Reynosa, Tamaulipas.* RMALC C-0002(2) ALCA-ASC 1992–2001. Mexico: RMALC.
Comité De Observadores Independientes. (1991). *Ford Motor Company. Recuento 3. Informe Resolutivo COI.* Report of the Committee. Mexico.
Compa, L.A. and Diamond, S.F. Eds. (1996). *Human Rights, Labor Rights, and International Trade.* Philadelphia: University of Pennsylvania Press.
Concha Malo, M. (1991). El papel de la sociedad civil en la defensa de los derechos políticos. *Justicia y Paz* No. 22, Political Rights: 10–12. April–June.
———. (1994a). Las organizaciones civiles y la lucha por la democracia. *Justicia y Paz* No. 33: 17–19. January–March.
———. Ed. (1994b). *Los derechos políticos como derechos humanos.* Mexico: La Jornada Ediciones, CIICH-UNAM.
Concha Malo, M. and Centro de Derechos Humanos "Fray Francisco de Vitoria." (1989). Las violaciones a los derechos humanos individuales en México (periodo 1971–1986). In González Casanova, P. and Cadena Roa, J. Eds. *Primer informe sobre la democracia: México 1988.* Mexico: Siglo XXI-CIICH-UNAM. pp. 115–187.
Concha Malo, M., González Gari, O., Salas, L.F. and Bastian, J.-P. (1986). *La participación de los cristianos en el proceso popular de liberación en México.* Mexico: Siglo XXI.
Convergencia de Organismos Civiles por la Democracia. (2005). *Campo de acción político-social* [online]. Convergencia de Organismos Civiles por la Democracia. Available from: http://www.convergenciacivil.org.mx/campos/politico.html (April 15, 2005).
Craven, M. (1995). *The International Covenant on Economic, Social and Cultural Rights. A Perspective on its Development.* Oxford: Clarendon Press.

Crespo, J.A. (1991). Derechos políticos y transición democrática. *Justicia y Paz* No. 22, Edición especial sobre derechos políticos: 2–9. April–June.
Cruz Ramón, B.A. (1994). Grupos indígenas y su relación con la tierra. *Justicia y Paz* No. 34, Derechos humanos y campo: 5–10. April–June 1994.
Culebro Bahena, R. (2004). Interview. Mexico.
Czerny, M.F. (1992). Liberation Theology and Human Rights. In Bauzon, K.E. Ed. *Development and Democratization in the Third World. Myths, Hopes, and Realities.* London: Crane Russak. pp. 135–147.
Dasgupta, B. (1998). *Structural Adjustment, Global Trade and the New Political Economy of Development.* New York: Zed Books.
Davidson, S. (1993). *Human Rights.* Buckingham: Open University Press.
De la Cruz, C., Tamayo, G., and Antolín, L. (2001). *Globalización y derechos económicos y sociales de las mujeres.* Córdoba: Universidad de Córdoba.
De la Torre Rangel, J.A. (1994). El reconocimiento del "otro": raíz de una concepción integral e histórica de los derechos humanos. *Anuario Mexicano de la Historia del Derecho.* 6:263–273.
Deva, S. (2004). *UN's Human Rights Norms for Transnational Corporations and Other Business Enterprises: An Imperfect Step in Right Direction?* [online]. The Berkeley Electronic Press. Available from: http://law.bepress.com/expresso/eps/112 (January 1, 2007).
Dommen, C. (2002). Raising Human Rights Concerns in the World Trade Organization: Actors, Process and Possible Strategies. *Human Rights Quarterly.* 24 (1): 1–50.
Donnelly, J. (2002). *Universal Human Rights in Theory and Practice.* 2nd. Ithaca: Cornell University Press.
Douzinas, C. (1996). Justice and Human Rights in Posmodernity. In Georty, G. and Tomkins, A. Eds. *Understanding Human Rights.* London: Pinter. pp. 115–137.
———. (2000). *The End of Human Rights.* Portland, Oregon: Hart Publishing.
Durán de Huerta, M. (1999). An interview with *Subcomandante* Marcos, Spokesperson and Military Commander of the Zapatista National Liberation Army (EZLN). *International Affairs.* 1999. 2 (75): 269–279.
Durán Juárez, J.M. and Partida, R. (1992). Modelo económico, regionalización y nuevo Estado mexicano (1940–1990). In Alonso, J., Aziz Nassif, A., and Tamayo, J. Eds. *El nuevo Estado mexicano.* I. Estado y economía. Mexico: Nueva Imagen. pp. 241–251.
Dussel, E. (2006). *Ética de la liberación en la edad de la globalización y la exclusión.* 5a. Madrid: Trotta.
———. (2007). *La originalidad de la filosofía latinoamericana.* Facultad de Filosofía y Letras: UNAM.
Dussel, E. and Senent de Frutos, J.A. (2001). *Hacia una filosofía política crítica.* Bilbao: Desclée de Brouwer.

Einhorn, B., Kaldor, M., and Kavan, Z. (1996). *Citizenship and Democratic Control in Contemporary Europe.* Cheltenham: Brookfield US/Edward Elgar.

Ejército Zapatista de Liberación Nacional. (1994a). *Declaración de la Selva Lacandona* [online]. EZLN. Available from: http://www.ezln.org/documentos/1994/199312xx.es.htm (March 3, 2004).

———. (1994b). Pliego de Demandas del EZLN; las razones y las causas de la sublevación. Comunicado del Comité Clandestino Revolucionario Indígena-Comandancia General del Ejército Zapatista de Liberación Nacional, México. *Justicia y Paz* No. 33, Chiapas, democracia y derechos humanos: 63–67. January–March.

———. (1996). *1a-2a Declaración de la Realidad* [online]. IdeaSapiens. Available from: http://www.ideasapiens.com…/primera_%20segunda%20declaracion%20realidad.%20ezln.htm (March 11, 2004).

———. (1997). *Convocatoria al Segundo Encuentro por la Humanidad y contra el Neoliberalismo* [online]. Nodo50. Available from: http://www.nodo50.org/encuentro/convocatoria.htm (March 11, 2004).

———. (1998). *Quinta Declaración de la Selva Lacandona* [online]. Nodo50. Available from: http://www.nodo50.org/pchiapas/documentos/selva.htm (March 11, 2004).

Ellacuría, I. (1990). Historización de los derechos humanos desde los pueblos oprimidos y las mayorías populares. *Estudios Centroamericanos* August 1990. 45 (502): 589–596.

Eschle, C. and Stammers, N. (2004). Taking Part: Social Movements, INGOs and Global Change. *Alternatives: Global, Local, Political.* 29 (3): 333–372.

Escobar, A. (1992). Culture, Economics and Politics in Latin American Social Movements Theory and Research. In Escobar, A. and Alvarez, S. Eds. *The Making of Social Movements in Latin America: Identity, Strategy, and Democracy.* Boulder: Westview Press. pp. 62–85.

Facio, A. (2000). Viaje a las estrellas: las nuevas aventuras de las mujeres en el universo de los derechos humanos (a manera de prefacio). In Bunch, C., Hinojosa, C., and Reilly, N. Eds. *Los derechos de las mujeres son derechos humanos.* Mexico: Edamex-Center for Women's Global Leadership. pp. 19–44.

Falk, R.A. (2000). *Human Rights Horizons: The Pursuit of Justice in a Globalizing World.* New York: Routledge.

Fields, A.B. and Narr, W. (1992). Human Rights as a Holistic Concept. *Human Rights Quarterly.* 14 (1): 1–20.

Fisher, W. (1997). Doing Good? The Politics and Antipolitics of NGO Practices. *Annual Review of Anthropology.* 26: 439–464.

Fix-Zamudio, H. (1982). *La protección jurídica y procesal de los derechos humanos ante las jurisdicciones nacionales.* Madrid: Universidad Nacional Autónoma de México, Civitas.

Forsythe, D.P. (2000). *Human Rights in International Relations.* Cambridge: Cambridge University Press.

Foucault, M. (1977). *Madness and Civilization. A History of Insanity in the Age of Reason*. 3rd. London: Tavistock Publications.
———. (1985). *The Use of Pleasure*. The History of Sexuality II. Middlesex: Viking Penguin Books Ltd.
———. (1988). *The Care of the Self.* The History of Sexuality III. London: Allen Lane The Penguin Press.
———. (1998). *The Will to Knowledge*. The History of Sexuality I. London: Penguin.
Foweraker, J. (1989). Popular Movements and the Transformation of the System. In Cornelius, W.A., Gentleman, J., and Smith, P.H. Eds. *Mexico's Alternative Political Futures*. California: Center for US-Mexican Studies. pp. 109–129.
———. Ed. (1990). *Popular Movements and Political Change in Mexico*. London: Lynne Rienner Publishers.
Foweraker, J. and Landman, T. (2000). *Citizenship Rights and Social Movements—A Comparative and Statistical Analysis*. Oxford: Oxford University Press.
Fox, J. (1995). Mexico's Difficult Democracy: Grassroots Movements, NGOs, and Local Government. In Reilly, C.A. Ed. *New Paths to Democratic Development in Latin America. The Rise of NGO-Municipal Collaboration*. Boulder: Lynne Rienner. pp. 179–210.
Frade Rubio, L. (2001). *Las implicaciones de la globalización económica y la internacionalización del Estado en las mujeres*. Mexico: Milenio Feminista.
Friedman, M. and Friedman, R. (1981). *Free to Choose*. New York: Penguin Books.
Fuentes, M. (1991a). El caso "Ford": ¿Modelo de relación laboral en el futuro? *Justicia y Paz* No. 23, Número especial sobre derechos laborales y libre comercio: 3–8. July–September.
———. (1991b). El caso "Ford": ¿Modelo de relación laboral en el futuro? *Justicia y Paz* No. 23, Número especial sobre derechos laborales y libre comercio: 3–8. July–September.
Gabardi, W. (2001). *Negotiating Postmodernism*. Minnesota: University of Minnesota Press.
García Alba, P., Gutiérrez, L., and Torres Ramírez, G. Eds. (2004). *El Nuevo Milenio Mexicano. México y el Mundo I*. Mexico: UAM Azcapotzalco.
Gilpin, R. (2001). *Global Political Economy. Understanding the International Economic Order*. New Jersey: Princeton University Press.
González Casanova, P. (1989). Pensar la democracia. In González Casanova, P. and Cadena Roa, J. Eds. *Primer informe sobre la democracia: México 1988*. Mexico: Siglo XXI-CIICH. pp. 11–35.
González, O. (1997). *Propuesta para una Agenda de la Academia Mexicana de Derechos Humanos 1997–2000*. Mexico: Academia Mexicana de Derechos Humanos.
Gray, J. (1998). *Hayek on Liberty*. 3rd. London: Routledge.

Gready, P. (2003). The Politics of Human Rights. *Third World Quarterly.* 24 (4): 745–757.
———. (2004). Introduction. In Gready, P. Ed. *Fighting for Human Rights.* London: Routledge. pp. 1–32.
Green, D. (1995). *Silent Revolution: The Rise of Market Economics in Latin America.* London: Cassell: LAB.
Grugel, J. (2002). *Democratization: A Critical Introduction.* New York: Palgrave.
Gutiérrez Garza, E. (1988). Introducción. In Gutiérrez Garza, E. Ed. *La crisis del Estado de Bienestar.* Testimonios de la crisis II. Mexico: Siglo XXI-UNAM.
———. (1990). La crisis laboral y la flexibilidad del trabajo. México 1983–1988. In Gutiérrez Garza, E. Ed. *Los saldos del sexenio (1982–1988).* Testimonios de la crisis IV. Mexico: Siglo XXI Editores. pp. 178–220.
Haber, P.L. (1997). ¡Vamos por la dignidad de Durango! Un estudio del poder sociopolítico. In Zermeño, S. Ed. *Movimientos sociales e identidades colectivas. México en la década de los noventa.* México: La Jornada-CIICH. pp. 55–108.
Hale, C.A. (2005). *El liberalismo mexicano en la época de Mora.* México: Siglo XXI.
Harvey, D. (1989). *The Condition of Postmodernity.* Oxford: Blackwell.
Hayek, F. (1960). *The Constitution of Liberty.* London: Routledge & Kegan Paul.
Held, D. (2000). *A Globalizing World? Culture, Economics and Politics.* London: Routledge-Open University.
Held, D. and Mcgrew, A. (2003). The Great Globalization Debate: An Introduction. In Held, D. and McGrew, A. Eds. *The Global Transformations Reader.* 2nd. Cambridge: Polity Press. pp. 1–50.
Held, D., Mcgrew, A., Goldblatt, D., and Perraton, J. (1999). *Global Transformations. Politics, Economics and Culture.* London: Polity Press.
Hellman, J.A. (1994). Mexican Popular Movements, Clientelism and the Process of Democratization. *Latin American Perspectives.* Spring. 21 (2): 124–142.
Heredia, C. (1991). *Las ONGs y el Tratado de Libre Comercio.* Paper presented at the II National Meeting of the Convergencia de Organismos Civiles por la Democracia, Tlaxcala, México, May 27–28. Mexico.
Hernández Navarro, L. (1994). Organizaciones No Gubernamentales y Democracia Emergente. *Justicia y Paz* No. 33: 17–19. January–March.
Hernández, L. and Fox, J. (1995). Mexico's Difficult Democracy: Grassroots Movements, NGOs, and Local Government. In Reilly, C.A. Ed. *New Paths to Democratic Development in Latin America. The Rise of NGO-Municipal Collaboration.* Boulder: Lynne Rienner. pp. 179–228.
Houtzager, P. (2006). *Society-State Relations; Civil Society, Social Movements and the Quality of Democracy.* Latin America in the Spotlight. Brighton: University of Sussex.

Howarth, D. (2000). *Discourse*. Buckingham: Open University Press.
———. (2004). Hegemony, Political Subjectivity, and Radical Democracy. In Critchley, S. and Marchart, O. Eds. *Laclau: A Critical Reader*. London: Routledge. pp. 256–276.
Hunt, A. (1990). Rights and Social Movements: Counter-Hegemonic Strategies. *Journal of Law and Society*. 17 (3): 309–328.
Ibargüengoitia, A. (1994). *Filosofía social en México, siglos XVI al XX*. México: Universidad Iberoamericana.
Inegi. (2006). *Encuesta nacional de ocupación y empleo* [online]. Gobierno de México. Available from: http://www.inegi.gob.mx/est/default.asp?c=5213 (January 20, 2006).
International Commission of Jurists, Faculty of Law of the University of Limburg and Urban Morgan Institute for Human Rights. (1986). *Limburg Principles on the Implementation of the International Covenant on Economic Social and Cultural Rights* [online]. Available from: http://shr.aaas.org/thesaurus/instrument.php?insid=94 (June 14, 2006).
International Labor Organization. (1989). *Convention No. 169 Concerning Indigenous and Tribal Peoples in Independent Countries* [online]. United Nations. Available from: http://www.unhchr.ch/html/menu3/b/62.htm (June 16, 2006).
Isin, E.F. and Wood, P.K. (1999). *Citizenship & Identity*. London: Sage.
Jochnick, C. (1999). Confronting the Impunity of Non-State Actors: New Fields for the Promotion of Human Rights. *Human Rights Quarterly*. 21 (1): 56–79.
Johnson, E.S. and Johnson, H.G. (1978). *The Shadow of Keynes. Understanding Keynes, Cambridge and Keynesian Economics*. Oxford: Basil Blackwell.
Kaldor, M. (2003). *Global Civil Society: An Answer to War*. Cambridge: Polity Press.
Kaldor, M. and Kavan, Z. (2001). Democracy and Civil Society in Central and Eastern Europe. In Axtmann, R. Ed. *Balancing Democracy*. London: Continuum. pp. 239–254.
Kaplan, M. (2002). El Estado latinoamericano: crisis y reformas. In Basave, J., Dabat, A., Morera, C., Rivera Ríos, M.Á., and Rodríguez, F. Eds. *Globalización y alternativas incluyentes para el siglo XXI*. Mexico: Facultad de Economía-UAM-I. pp. 679–699.
Kaufman, R.R. and Trejo, G. (1997). Regionalism, Regime Transformation and Pronasol: The Politics of the National Solidarity Programme in Four Mexican States. *Latin American Perspectives*. October 1997. 29 (3): 717–745.
Kay, C. (1989). *Latin American Theories of Development and Underdevelopment*. London: Routledge.
Keck, M.E. and Sikkink, K. (1998a). Human Rights Advocacy in Latin America. In Keck, M.E. and Sikkink, K. *Activists beyond Borders*. Ithaca: Cornell University Press. pp. 79–120.

———. (1998b). Transnational Advocacy Networks in International Politics: Introduction. In Keck, M.E. and Sikkink, K. *Activists beyond Borders.* Ithaca: Cornell University Press. pp. 1–38.

Khagram, S., Riker, J.V., and Sikkink, K. (2002). *Restructuring World Politics. Transnational Social Movements, Networks, and Norms.* Vol. 14. Minnesota: University of Minnesota Press.

Kirzner, I.M. (1992). *The Meaning of Market Process. Essays in the Development of Modern Austrian Economics.* New York: Routledge.

Kitching, G. (1990). *Development and Underdevelopment in Historical Perspective. Populism, Nationalism and Industrialization.* London: Routledge.

Korey, W. (1998). *NGOs and the Universal Declaration of Human Rights: A Curious Grapevine.* New York: St. Martin's Press.

Kusý, M. (1985). Chartism and "Real Socialism": Citizens against the State in Central-Eastern Europe. In Keane, J. Ed. *The Power of the Powerless.* London: Hutchinson. pp. 152–177.

La Neta. (2005). *Campaña para solicitar re-examen de patente* [online]. La Neta-Ambiente. Available from: http://www.laneta.apc.org/ambiente/acciones3.htm (January 23, 2005).

Laclau, E. (1977). Politics as the Construction of the Unthinkable. Article. The Department of Government, University of Essex.

———. (1990). *New Reflections on the Revolution of Our Time.* London: Verso.

———. (1993). Discourse. In Goodin, R.E. and Pettit, P. Eds. *A Companion to Contemporary Political Philosophy.* London: Blackwell. pp. 431–437.

———. (1994). Why Do Empty Signifiers Matter to Politics? In Weeks, J. Ed. *The Lesser Evil and the Greater Good. The Theory and Politics of Social Diversity.* Cornwall: Rivers Oram Press. pp. 167–177.

———. (1996). *Emancipation (s).* London: Verso.

———. (2000a). Constructing Universality. In Butler, J., Laclau, E., and Zizek, S. Eds. *Contingency, Hegemony, Universality. Contemporary Dialogues on the Left.* London: Verso. pp. 281–307.

———. (2000b). Identity and Hegemony: The Role of Universality in the Constitution of Political Logics. In Butler, J., Laclau, E., and Zizek, S. Eds. *Contingency, Hegemony, Universality.* pp. 44–87.

———. (2005). *On Populist Reason.* London: Verso.

———. (2006). *Las identidades políticas en un mundo globalizado.* Mexico: Colegio de México.

Laclau, E. and Mouffe, C. (1987). Post-Marxism without Apologies. *New Left Review.* 1 (166): 79–106.

———. (2001). *Hegemony and Socialist Strategy. Towards a Radical Democratic Politics.* London: Verso.

Laclau, E. and Zac, L. (1994). Minding the Gap: The Subject of Politics. In Laclau, E. Ed. *The Making of Political Identities.* London: Verso. pp. 11–37.

Lefort, C. and Thompson, J.B. (1986). *The Political Forms of Modern Society: Bureaucracy, Democracy, Totalitarianism.* Cambridge: Polity Press.

Lesgart, C. (2003). *Usos de la transición a la democracia.* Santa Fe, Argentina: Homo Sapiens Ediciones.

Lim, H. (2001). Trade and Human Rights, What's at Issue? *Journal of World Trade.* April. 35 (2): 275–300.

Luján, B.E. (2002). Citizen Advocacy Networks and the NAFTA. In Brooks, D. and Fox, J. Eds. *Cross-Border Dialogues: U.S.-Mexico Social Movement Networking.* San Diego: Center for US-Mexican Studies University of California. pp. 211–226.

Mabey, N. (1999). Defending the Legacy of Rio: The Civil Society Campaign against the MAI. In Picciotto, S. and Mayne, R. Eds. *Regulating International Business. Beyond Liberalism.* London: Macmillan. pp. 60–81.

MacPherson, C.B. (1977). *The Life and Times of Liberal Democracy.* Oxford: Oxford University Press.

Maldonado, J. (1995). *Historia de los primeros años de trabajo del Comité de Derechos Humanos Miguel Agustín Pro Juárez AC.* Internal document. Mexico.

Malloy, J.M. (1977). Authoritarianism and Corporatism in Latin America: The Modal Pattern. In Malloy, J.M. Ed. *Authoritarianism and Corporatism in Latin America.* Pittsburgh: University of Pittsburgh Press. pp. 3–19.

Marceau, G. (2002). WTO Dispute Settlement and Human Rights. *European Journal of International Law.* September. 13 (4): 753–814.

Margier, A.M. (1997). El gobierno mexicano intervino para que la Comisión Europea no financiara proyectos de la Conai y la AMDH. *Proceso* No. 1056: 49–51. January 25, 1997.

Marmor, A. (1997). *Law and Interpretation: Essays in Legal Philosophy.* Oxford: Clarendon Press.

Matos, J. (1992). Indigenismo, legislación y estados nacionales. *Justicia y Paz* No. 25: 5–7. January–May.

Maza, M. (2004). *Visitas de los Mecanismos Internacionales de Derechos Humanos.* Prodh internal document. Mexico.

Mcadam, D., Mccarthy, J.D., and Zald, M.N. Eds. (1996). *Comparative Perspectives on Social Movements. Political Opportunities, Mobilizing Structures, and Cultural Framings.* Cambridge: Cambridge University Press.

Meyer, W.H. (1998). *Human Rights and International Political Economy in Third World Nations. Multinational Corporations, Foreign Aid and Repression.* Westport: Praeger.

Moguel, J. (2004). *Las claves del zapatismo* [online]. Fractal. Available from: http://www.fractal.com.mx/F8Moguel.html (March 10, 2004).

Molina, I. (2000). *El pensamiento del EZLN.* Mexico: Plaza y Valdés.

Mondragón Pérez, Y. (1997). La recomposición neocorporativa entre Estado y sindicatos: los límites a los proyectos sindicales de interlocución, el caso del STRM. In Zermeño, S. Ed. *Movimientos sociales e identidades colectivas. México en la década de los noventa*. Mexico: La Jornada-CIICH. pp. 281–311.

Monroy B.M. Ed. (1994). *Pensar Chiapas, repensar México. Reflexiones de las ONGs mexicanas sobre el conflicto*. Mexico: Convergencia de Organismos Civiles por la Democracia/ Impretei.

Monshipouri, M., Welch, C.E.J., and Kennedy, E. (2003). Multinational Corporations and the Ethics of Global Responsibility: Problems and Possibilities. *Human Rights Quarterly*. November. 25 (4): 965–989.

Monsiváis, C. (2000). Prólogo. Lo marginal en el centro. In Monsiváis, C. Ed. *Entrada libre. Crónicas de la sociedad que se organiza*. Mexico: Era. pp. 11–15.

Morris, S.D. (1992). Political Reformism in Mexico: Salinas at the Brink. *Journal of Interamerican Studies and World Affairs*. Spring. 34 (1): 27–57.

Muchlinski, P.T. (2001). Human Rights and Multinationals: Is There a Problem? *International Affairs*. 1 (77): 31–48.

Novelo Urdanivia, F. (2004). Balance y Desafíos del TLCAN. In García Alba, P., Gutiérrez, L., and Torres Ramírez, G. Eds. *El Nuevo Milenio Mexicano. T. México y el Mundo I*. Mexico: UAM Azcapotzalco. pp. 207–236.

Nyamu-Musembi, C. (2002). *Towards an Actor-Oriented Perspective on Human Rights*. IDS Working Papers. Brighton: Institute of Development Studies.

Oficina del Alto Comisionado de las Naciones Unidas para los Derechos Humanos en México. (2003). *Diagnóstico sobre la Situación de los Derechos Humanos en México*. Mexico: ONU.

Oloka-Onyango, J. and Udagama, D. (1999). *The Realization of Economic, Social and Cultural Rights. Human Rights as the Primary Objective of International Trade, Investment and Finance Policy and Practice*. E/CN.4/Sub.2/1999/11. Geneva: United Nations Commission of Human Rights.

Organización de Las Naciones Unidas. (1995). *Plataforma de Acción de la IV Conferencia Mundial sobre la Mujer (Selección)*. Mexico: Comité Promotor por una Maternidad sin Riesgos en México.

Ortega, M. and Solís, A.A. (1990). Estado, Capital y Sindicatos, México 1983–1988. In Gutiérrez Garza, E. Ed. *Los saldos del sexenio (1982–1988)*. Testimonios de la crisis IV. Mexico: Siglo XXI. pp. 221–236.

Osorio, V. (1998). *Reinventando el continente. Agenda social y libre comercio en las Américas*. Mexico: RMALC.

Palan, R. Ed. (2000). *Global Political Economy. Contemporary Theories*. London: Routledge.

Pangalangan, R.C. (2002). Sweatshops and International Labor Standards. Globalizing Markets, Localizing Norms. In Brysk, A. Ed. *Globalization and Human Rights*. California: University of California Press. pp. 98–112.

Paredes Olguín, J. (2004). Hacia una definición politológica de los derechos humanos. In Van Beuren, I. and Soto Badillo, O. Eds. *Derechos Humanos y Globalización Alternativa: una Perspectiva Iberoamericana.* Puebla: Universidad Iberoamericana. pp. 103–123.

Peces-Barba, G. and Universidad Carlos III de Madrid. (1995). *Curso de derechos fundamentales teoría general.* Madrid: Universidad Carlos III BOE.

Peces-Barba, G., Asís Roig, R.D., and Barranco Avilés, M.D.C. (2004). *Lecciones de derechos fundamentales.* Madrid: Dykinson.

Petersman, E.-U. (2002). Time for a United Nations "Global Compact" for Integrating Human Rights into the Law of Worldwide Organizations: Lessons from European Integration. *European Journal of International Law.* September. 13 (3): 621–650.

Potter, D. (2000). Explaining Democratization. In Potter, D., Goldblatt, D., Kiloh, M., and Lewis, P.G. Eds. *Democratization.* Cambridge: Open University Press. pp. 1–39.

Produssep and Centro de Derechos Humanos "Fray Francisco de Vitoria." (1990). El derecho a la salud en México: una mirada desde la sociedad civil. *Justicia y Paz* No. 18, Los derechos humanos a la salud: 13–19. April–June 1990.

Programa de Las Naciones Unidas Para el Desarrollo. (2002). *Informe sobre Desarrollo Humano Mexico 2002.* Mexico-Madrid-Barcelona: UNDP.

Promotora de la Unidad Nacional contra el Neoliberalismo. (2002). *Primera Declaración.* Public document. Mexico.

Quintana, V. (2003). El derecho a ser campesino. Speech. Pensar el Campo desde los Derechos Humanos. Mexico: Centro Prodh.

Ramírez Saiz, J.M. (2003). Organizaciones cívicas, democracia y sistema político. In Aziz Nassif, A. Ed. *México al inicio del siglo XXI. Democracia, ciudadanía y desarrollo.* Mexico: CIESAS-Porrúa. pp. 133–229.

Ramsay, M. (1997). *What's Wrong with Liberalism? A Radical Critique of Liberal Political Philosophy.* Leicester: Leicester University Press.

Rawls, J. (1999). *The Law of Peoples* Cambridge, Mass.: Harvard University Press.

Red Género y Economía, Alianza Social Continental, and Oxfam Internacional. (2003). *Memoria del Foro Internacional "Los derechos de las mujeres en los tratados de libre comercio y la organización mundial del comercio."* Mexico: RMALC.

Red Mexicana de Acción Frente al Libre Comercio. (1991a). *Founding Document of the Mexican Action Network on Free Trade.* Internal Document. Mexico.

———. (1991b). *La opinión pública y las negociaciones del Tratado de Libre Comercio: Alternativas ciudadanas* C-0024 (2) TLC. Zacatecas: RMALC.

———. (1991c). *Memoria de Zacatecas. 25, 26 y 27 de octubre de 1991. La opinión pública y las negociaciones del Tratado de Libre Comercio: Alternativas ciudadanas.* Mexico: RMALC.

BIBLIOGRAPHY

———. (1992). *Impactos democráticos en el proceso de integración del continente americano.* C-0024(3) TLC 1991–1994. Mexico: RMALC.

———. (1993a). *Agenda Social. Propuestas en materia laboral, medio ambiente y derechos humanos.* Mexico: RMALC.

———. (1993b). *Los acuerdos paralelos y la agenda social frente al TLC. Documento RMALC para la revista Coyuntura Marzo de 1993.* Lobbying Document. Mexico.

———. (1994a). *Mesa de medio ambiente. Propuesta de discusión. Comisión ambiental. RMALC.* C-0022(2) RMALC Medio ambiente 1988–1994. Mexico: RMALC.

———. (1994b). *Promesas a cumplir. La agenda inconclusa para los derechos humanos y la justicia económica en las Américas. Declaración y recomendaciones de los organismos comprometidos con la sociedad civil para la Cumbre de las Américas.* NGO Declaration. Miami.

———. (1997). *Espejismo y realidad: el TLCAN tres años después. Análisis y propuesta desde la sociedad civil.* Mexico: RMALC.

Red Mexicana de Acción Frente al Libre Comercio, Centro de Derechos Humanos "Miguel Agustín Pro Juárez," and Deca-Equipo Pueblo. (2002a). *Proyecto de incidencia 2002–2005 ante el Acuerdo Global México-Unión Europea.* Lobbying document. Mexico/Brussels.

Red Mexicana de Acción Frente al Libre Comercio, Centro de Derechos Humanos "Miguel Agustín Pro Juárez," Deca-Equipo Pueblo, and Iniciativa de Copenhague Para Centroamérica y México. (2002b). *Towards a Positive Dimension of the Democratic Clause.* Lobbying Document. Mexico.

Red Mexicana de Acción Frente al Libre Comercio, Deca-Equipo Pueblo, and Centro de Derechos Humanos "Miguel Agustín Pro Juárez." (2002c). *Propuesta hacia el Consejo Conjunto México / Unión Europea sobre mecanismos de participación y consulta de las organizaciones civiles en el Acuerdo Global Unión Europea-México.* Lobbying document. Mexico.

Red Mexicana de Acción Frente al Libre Comercio, Deca-Equipo Pueblo, Centro de Derechos Humanos "Miguel Agustín Pro Juárez," Red Género y Economía, and Incide Social. (2005). *Postura de las Organizaciones Civiles Mexicanas en el II Foro de Diálogo de las sociedades civiles y las instituciones de Gobierno de México y la Unión Europea.* Mexico: RMALC.

Red Mexicana de Acción Frente al Libre Comercio and Iniciativa de Copenhague Para Centroamérica y México. (2002). *Memoria.* Primer Foro de Diálogo con la Sociedad Civil México-Unión Europea en el Marco del Acuerdo de Asociación Económica, Concertación Política y Cooperación entre la Unión Europea y México (Acuerdo Global). Brussels: RMALC-CIFCA.

———. (2003). *Propuestas para la Implementación de la Cláusula Democrática, Mecanismos de Participación de la Sociedad Civil y Observatorio Social en el Marco del Acuerdo Global México-Unión Europea.* Lobbying Document. Mexico.

Red Mexicana de Acción Frente al Libre Comercio and Iniciativa de Copenhague Para Centroamérica y México. (2005). *Propuestas Conjuntas de la RMALC y CIFCA*. *Segundo Foro de Diálogo entre las Sociedades Civiles y las Instituciones del Gobierno de México y de la Unión Europea (28 de febrero–1 de marzo)*. Lobbying Document. Mexico.

Red Mexicana de Acción Frente al Libre Comercio, Iniciativa de Copenhague para Centroamérica y México, Deca-Equipo Pueblo, and Cncd/Bélgica. (2001). *Memoria*. Encuentro de Organizaciones Sociales y Civiles de México y la Unión Europea en el Marco del Acuerdo Global UE-México. Mexico: Fundación Heinrich Böll.

Red Nacional de Organismos Civiles de Derechos Humanos "Todos Los Derechos Para Todos. (1994a). *Chiapas: una política de violación a los derechos humanos e impunidad*. Document Presented at the United Nations Human Rights Commission. Geneva.

———. (1994b). Informe que presentó la Red Nacional de Organismos Civiles de Derechos Humanos "Todos los Derechos para Todos" a la Comisión Interamericana de Derechos Humanos en Washington DC, el 10 de febrero de 1994. In Monroy, M.B. Ed. *Pensar Chiapas, repensar México. Reflexiones de las ONG mexicanas sobre el conflicto*. Mexico: Converegencia de Organismos Civiles por la Democracia-Impretei. pp. 133–142.

Red Nacional Género Comercio y Derechos Humanos, Alianza Chilena Por Un Comercio Justo y Responsable, Red Latinoamericana Mujeres Transformando La Economía, and Red Internacional Género y Comercio. (2002). *Encuentro Internacional sobre Género, Comercio y Derechos Humanos*. Santiago de Chile: Género y Economía.

Regional Coordination Committee of the Hemispheric Social Alliance. (1999). *Actas de la Reunión del 12–14 de marzo de 1999*. Internal Document. San José, Costa Rica.

Reyes Heroles, J. (1978). *México. Historia y Política*. Madrid: Tecnos.

Risse, T. (2000). The Power of Norms versus the Norms of Power: Transnational Civil Society and Human Rights. In Florini, A. Ed. *The Third Force. The Rise of Transnational Civil Society*. Washington DC: Japan Center for International Exchange-Carnegie Endowment for International Peace. pp. 177–209.

Risse, T., Ropp, S.C., and Sikkink, K. (1999). *The Power of Human Rights. International Norms and Domestic Change*. Cambridge: Cambridge University Press.

Rist, G. (1997). *The History of Development. From Western Origins to Global Faith*. London: Zed Books.

Rodríguez Castañeda, R. (1990). Antidemocracia y violación de derechos humanos, en aras de salvaguardar el proyecto económico. *Proceso* No. 669: 14–17. March 26.

Roitman Rosenmann, M. (2005). *Las razones de la democracia en América Latina*. Mexico: Siglo XXI.

Román Morales, L.I. (1992). *¿Qué es el ajuste estructural?* Mexico: ITESO y Proyecto CONACYT-SIMORELOS.
Rosenfeld, M. (1998). *Just Interpretations: Law between Ethics and Politics.* Berkeley: University of California Press.
Ruiz Contardo, E. (2004). La desconocida y manipulada relación entre ciencia social e ideología. In Sánchez Ramos, I. and Sosa Elízaga, R. Ed. *América Latina: los desafíos del pensamiento crítico.* I. Mexico: Siglo XXI-UNAM. pp. 50–73.
Rupp, H. (2002). *Propuestas para la instrumentalización de la cláusula democrática (con fuentes y observaciones).* Internal Communication. Brussels.
Salman, B. (2001). International Free Trade Agreements and Human Rights: Interpreting Article XX of the GATT. *Minnesota Journal of Global Trade.* Winter. 10 (1): 62–108.
Scott, A. (1995). Political Culture and Social Movements. In Allen, J. Ed. *Political and Economic Forms of Modernity.* London: Open University Press. pp. 127–165.
Schmitz, H.P. and Sikkink, K. (2002). International Relations Theory and Human Rights. In Carlsnaes, W., Risse-Kappen, T., and Simmons, B.A. Eds. *Handbook of International Relations.* London: Sage.
Scholte, J.A. (2001). The Globalization of World Politics. An Introduction to International Relations. In Baylis, J. and Smith, S. Eds. *The Globalization of World Politics.* Oxford: Oxford University Press. pp. 13–32.
Secretaría de Economía. (2006a). *Acuerdos y Negociaciones* [online]. Gobierno de México. Available from: http://www.economia.gob.mx (January 18, 2006).
———. (2006b). *Estadísticas de Comercio e IED. Tabla de Exportaciones y Tabla de Importaciones* [online]. Gobierno de México. Available from: http://www.economia.gob.mx/?P=2261 (January 25, 2006).
Sen, A. (1999). Human Rights and Economic Achievements. In Baver, J.R. and Bell, D.A. Eds. *The East Asian Challenge to Human Rights.* Cambridge: Cambridge University Press. pp. 88–99.
Shand, A.H. (1990). *Free Market Morality.* London: Routledge.
Shue, H. (1980). *Basic Human Rights. Subsistence, Affluence, and US Foreign Policy.* New Jersey: Princeton University Press.
Sigmund, P.E. (1990). *Liberation Theology at the Cross Roads. Democracy or Revolution?* New York: Oxford University Press.
Skilling, H.G. (1981). *Charter 77 and Human Rights in Czechoslovakia.* London: Allen & Unwin.
Skogly, S.I. (1999). Economic and Social Rights, Private Actors and International Obligations. In Addo, M.K. Ed. *Human Rights Standards and the Responsibility of Transnational Corporations.* The Hague: Kluwer Law. pp. 239–257.
Smith, A.M. (1994a). *New Right Discourse on Race and Sexuality: Britain 1968–1990.* Cambridge: Cambridge University Press.

Smith, A.M. (1994b). Rastafari as Resistance and the Ambiguities of Essentialism in the "New Social Movements." In Laclau, E. Ed. *The Making of Political Identities*. London: Verso. pp. 171–204.

Smith, J. (1997). Characteristics of the Modern Transnational Social Movement Sector. In Smith, J., Chatfield, C., and Pagnucco, R. Eds. *Transnational Social Movements and Global Politics. Solidarity beyond the State*. New York: Syracuse University Press. pp. 42–58.

Smith, J., Pagnucco, R., and Chatfield, C. (1997). Social Movements and World Politics. In Smith, J., Pagnucco, R., and Chatfield, C. Eds. *Transnational Social Movements and Global Politics. Solidarity beyond the State*. New York: Syracuse University Press. pp. 59–77.

Snow, D.A. (1992). Master Frames and Cycles of Protest. In Morris, A.D. and McClurg Mueller, C. Eds. *Frontiers in Social Movement Theory*. London: Yale University Press.

Soria, V.M. (1988). La crisis de la protección social en México. Un análisis de largo plazo con énfasis en el periodo 1971–1985. In Gutiérrez Garza, E. Ed. *La crisis del Estado de Bienestar*. II. Mexico: Siglo XXI-UNAM. pp. 174–203.

Stammers, N. (1993). Human Rights and Power. *Political Studies*. March. 41 (1): 70–82.

Stavenhagen, R. (1986). Derechos Humanos y Derechos Indios. *Justicia y Paz* No. 2: 9–16. February.

———. (1987). México y los derechos humanos. *Justicia y Paz* No. 1: 15–21. November.

Stephen, L. (1995). The Zapatista Army of National Liberation and the National Democratic Convention. *Latin American Perspectives*. Fall. 22 (4): 88–99.

Stevens, E.P. (1977). Mexico's PRI: The Institutionalization of Corporatism? In Malloy, J.M. Ed. *Authoritarianism and Corporatism in Latin America*. Pittsburgh: University of Pittsburgh Press. pp. 227–258.

Subcomandante Marcos. (1997a). *7 piezas sueltas del rompecabezas mundial (El neoliberalismo como rompecabezas: la inútil unidad mundial que fragmenta y destruye naciones)* [online]. EZLN. Available from: http://palabra.ezln.org.mx/comunicados/1997/1997_06_b.htm (June 15, 2006).

———. (1997b). *Carta del Subcomandante Marcos a los organizadores y asistentes al Segundo Encuentro Intercontinental por la Humanidad y contra el Neoliberalismo* [online]. EZLN. Available from: http://www.ezln.org/documentos/1997/19970727.es.htm (March 11, 2004).

Taggart, P. (2000). *Populism*. Buckingham: Open University Press.

Talbott, W.J. (2005). *Which Rights Should be Universal?* Oxford: Oxford University Press.

Tamayo, J. (1990). Neoliberalism Encounters *Neocardenism*. In Foweraker, J. and Craig, A.L. Eds. *Popular Movements and Political Change in Mexico*. Boulder: Lynne Rienner. pp. 121–136.

Tarrow, S. (1992). Mentalities, Political Cultures, and Collective Action Frames: Constructing Meanings through Action. In Morris, A.D. and McClurg Mueller, C. Eds. *Frontiers in Social Movement Theory.* London: Yale University Press.

Thomas, D.C. (2001). *The Helsinki Effect: International Norms, Human Rights, and the Demise of Communism.* New Jersey: Princeton University Press.

Tilly, C. (1978). *From Mobilization to Revolution.* Massachusetts: Addison-Wesley Publications.

Torfing, J. (1999). *New Theories of Discourse.* Oxford: Blackwell.

Toye, J. (1993). *Dilemmas of Develpment.* 2nd. Oxford: Blackwell.

Trebilcock, M. and Howse, R. (1999). *The Regulation of International Trade.* 2nd. London: Routledge.

Trubek, David (1984). "Economic, Social and Cultural Rights in the Third World: Human Rights Law and Human Needs Programs." In Meron T. Ed. *Human Rights in International Law: Legal and Policy Issues.* Oxford: Claredon Press.

Tuda Rivas, R. (2005). *The Role of International Factors in Democratization: A Comparison of the Spanish and Mexican Transitions.* PhD. University of Sussex.

Tussie, D. and Woods, N. (2000). Trade, Regionalism and the Threat to Multilateralism. In Woods, N. Ed. *The Political Economy of Globalization.* Hong Kong: Macmillan. pp. 54–75.

United Nations Commission of Human Rights. (1986). *Declaration on the Right to Development* [online]. United Nations. Available from: http://www.unhchr.ch/html/menu3/b/74.htm (June 16, 2006).

———. (2003). *Norms on the Responsibilities of Transnational Corporations and Other Business Enterprises with Regard to Human Rights.* E/CN.4/Sub.2/2003/12/Rev.2 [online]. Available from: http://www1.umn.edu/humanrts/links/norms-Aug2003.html (July 11, 2006).

United Nations Committee on Economic, S.A.C.R. (1999). *General Comment 12, the Right to Adequate Food.* UN Doc. E/C.12/1999/5 (1999), reprinted in Compilation of General Comments and General Recommendations Adopted by Human Rights Treaty Bodies, UN Doc. HRI/GEN/1/Rev.6 at 62 (2003). Available at: http://www1.umn.edu/humanrts/gencomm/escgencom12.htm (January 14, 2007). Geneva: United Nations.

United Nations Development Program. (2005). *Human Development Report 2005. International Cooperation at a Crossroads. Aid, Trade and Security in an Unequal World.* New York: United Nations.

Villarreal, R. (1993). *Liberalismo social y reforma del Estado. México en la era del capitalismo moderno.* México: FCE-NAFIN.

Wetherell, M. and Potter, J. (1992). *Mapping the Language of Racism: Discourse and the Legitimation of Exploitation.* London: Harvester Wheatsheaf.

Williams, H.L. (2001). *Social Movements and Economic Transition. Markets and Distributive Conflict in Mexico.* Cambridge: Cambridge University Press.

Wilson, R. (1997). Human Rights, Culture and Context: An Introduction. In Wilson, R. Ed. *Human Rights, Culture & Context. Anthropological Perspectives.* London: Pluto Press.

Woldenberg, J. (1989). La negociación político-social en México. In González Casanova, P. Ed. *Primer informe sobre la democracia: México 1988.* Mexico: Siglo XXI-CIIH. pp. 188–208.

Woodiwiss, A. (2002). Human Rights and the Challenge of Cosmopolitanism. *Theory, Culture and Society.* February–April. 19 (1–2): 139–155.

———. (2003). *Making Human Rights Work Globally.* London: GlassHouse.

Woodroffe, J. (1999). Regulating Multinational Corporations in a World of Nation States. In Addo, M.K. Ed. *Human Rights Standards and the Responsibility of Transnational Corporations.* The Hague: Kluwer Law. pp. 131–142.

Zald, M.N. and McCarthy, J.D. (1979). *The Dynamics of Social Movements: Resource Mobilization, Social Control, and Tactics.* Cambridge, Mass.: Winthrop Publishers.

Zermeño, S. (2005). *La desmodernidad mexicana y las alternativas a la violencia y a la exclusión en nuestros días.* Mexico: Océano.

Interviews

Aceves, Ramón. (2003). Member of the International Relations Office at the Mexican Electricians' Union. Mexico City. December 2003.

Aguayo, Sergio. (2004). Academic, political commentator, and cofounder and former chairperson of the Mexican Academy of Human Rights. Mexico City. January 2004.

Arroyo, Alberto. (2004). Researcher and member of the Mexican Free Trade Action Network coordination committee. Mexico City. March 2004.

Canto, Manuel. (2004). Chairperson of the NGO network Citizen Movement for Democracy. Mexico City. February 2004.

Carriquiriborde, Alicia. (2004). Member of the Food International Action Network, Mexican branch. Mexico City. February 2004.

Concha, Leonor Aída. (2003). Chairperson of the women's groups network Gender and Economy. Mexico City. November 2003.

Concha, Miguel. (2004). Dominican priest. Founder and current chairperson of the "Fray Francisco de Vitoria" Human Rights Centre. Mexico City. January 2004.

Cortez, Edgar. (2003). Former chairperson of the "Miguel Agustín Pro Juárez" Human Rights Centre (1998–2004). Mexico City. November 2003.

Culebro, Rocío. (2004). Former member of the Mexican Academy of Human Rights and the Mexican Commission of Defence and Promotion of Human Rights. Former chairperson of the Civil Organisations Network "All Rights for Everyone." Mexico City. January 2004.

Fernández, David. (2003). Jesuit priest and former chairperson of the "Miguel Agustín Pro Juárez" Human Rights Centre (1994–1998). Mexico City. December 2003.

Herrera, Carmen. (2004). Former coordinator of the Advocacy Office at the Prodh Centre, and representative of the Civil Organisations Network "All Rights for Everyone" at the Second People's Summit, Quebec, 2001. Mexico City. March 2004.

Maldonado, Jesús. (2004). Jesuit priest, former chairperson of the "Miguel Agustín Pro Juárez" Human Rights Centre (1988–1994). Mexico City. March 2004.

Rangel, Gabriela. (2004). Mexican Free Trade Action Network representative at the Mexican Alliance for People's Self-Determination. Mexico City. March 2004.

Sandoval, Areli. (2003). Coordinator of the ESCR Programme at DECA-Equipo Pueblo. Mexico City. November 2003.

Suárez, Víctor. (2004). Chairperson of farmers' group National Association of Agricultural Producer Enterprises. Mexico City. January 2004.

Villalba, Antonio. (2004). Member of the coordination committee at the Authentic Labour Front. Mexico City. February 2004.

Villamar, Alejandro. (2004). Researcher, consultant, and Mexican Free Trade Action Network representative for environmental issues. Mexico City. March 2004.

Index

Absolute Advantage, Theory of, 106
Academia, 63–66, 72–73, 83, 202n, 209n, 211n, 212n, 218n
Aceves, Ramon, 123–24, 138
Acosta, Mariclaire, 66, 76, 81
Advocacy Group for the National Unity against Neoliberalism (Promotora), 94
Agreement on Economic Partnership, Political Co-ordination and Co-operation between the Mexican Government and the European Union. *See* Global Agreement
agriculture, 109–10, 119, 150
   employment in, 8
   environmental protection and, 9
   free trade policy's effect on, 1, 5, 7–8, 10, 83, 114, 163, 198n
   human rights and, 139–42, 149–51, 167
   "modernization" of, 46–47
   right to development and, 144
   right to food and, 146
   and right to be a farmer, 141–43, 191, 226n
   subject position in, 135, 139–42, 163
   See also farmers' movement
Agriculture Can Take No More (farmers network), 94, 151
agricultural reform, 160
Aguayo Quezada, Sergio, 52–53, 68, 72, 212

Alliance for Progress, 56
Alternatives for the Americas, 165–67
Alternatives 2001, 168–69
Alternatives 2002, 169
Alvarez Enríquez, L., 46, 48
American Convention of Human Rights, 72
American Declaration of the Rights and Duties of Man, 114
American School of Social Movements, 3, 195n
Americas Solidarity Forum, 158, 165
antidescriptivism, 23
Argentina, 2, 59, 62, 158
Arroyo, Alberto, 6–8, 86, 125, 129–30
Asia-Pacific Economic Cooperation, 110
Assmann, Hugo, 62
Austrian liberalism (Austrian School), 36–37, 203n
Authentic Labor Front (FAT), 89, 102, 177
Authentic Party of the Mexican Revolution (PARM), 44

basic rights, 20, 68, 139
Baxi, Upendra, 13–21, 191, 198n
Beuchot, M., 12–13
Boff, Clodovis, 62, 63
Boff, Leonardo, 62, 63
Boise Cascade, 9
Bolivia, 15, 62

Index

Bonino, José Miguel, 62
Brazil, 15, 62, 101, 157–58
Bretton Woods Institutions, 109
bureaucratic-authoritarian systems, 56–57

Cabrera, Teodoro, 9
caciques, 41, 43
Camacho, Manuel Avila, 39
Camp, Roderic Ai, 209–10n
Canto, Manuel, 125–27
capitalism, cycles of, 57
capitalism, late, 1, 23, 200n
capitalism, monopoly, 207n
Cárdenas, Cuauhtémoc, 44–46, 48, 50, 58, 80
Cárdenas, Lázaro, 15, 39
Carozza, P. G., 12
Carriquiriborde, Alicia, 120–21, 134, 139, 146–47
Castañeda, Jorge, 88, 205n
Catholic Church, 49, 52, 61, 206n, 209n
Centre for Border Studies and Human Rights Promotion AC (Cefrodhac), 76–77
Chang, H. -J., 38
Chávez, Hugo, 15
Chile, 15, 59, 62, 157, 158, 159, 162, 166, 203n
China, 6, 196n
Citizen Movement for Democracy (MCD), 49, 82, 102
citizen participation, 86–91, 145–46, 161, 164, 219n
  democracy and, 90–91
  NAFTA and, 86–90
  NGO and, 84, 133, 135, 152, 171–84
  RMALC and, 86–89
citizenship, 111, 133–37, 140–41, 144, 153, 185
  construction of, 3
  farmers and, 140–44
  focus on, 2
  NGOs and, 102–3, 152
  SMOs and, 152
  subject position of, 140–44, 150, 162, 170, 179, 184
citizenship discourse, 133–35
citizenship rights, 3, 21, 68, 140–41, 152, 162–63, 170, 185
Civic Alliance, 49, 73, 212n
civil and political rights (CPRs)
  ESCRs and, 63, 67–68, 73, 92–92, 136, 148, 152
  as first generation of rights, 69
  prioritization of, 70, 76, 78, 193
  transition to democracy and, 171
  violations of, 66, 69–71, 73, 78, 139, 175, 182
civil society, 5, 42, 48, 57, 90, 101, 140, 169, 174–84
Civil Society Mexico-European Union, 178–80, 184
clientelism, 40, 43, 46, 48
Clinton, Bill, 156, 165
Cold War, 56
Comblin, José, 62
Committee for Popular Defense (CDP), 47
communism, 4, 51
Comparative Advantage, Theory of, 106
comparative advantages, 5–6, 10, 106
Concha, Leonor Aída, 136–37, 143, 148–49
Concha, Miguel, 92, 209–10n
Constitution, Mexican, 12, 44, 61, 204n, 209n
constitutional (fundamental), rights, 12, 31, 33, 55, 66, 164
constitutionalism, 16, 31, 33, 36, 208–9n
contractualism, French, 12
convenios de concertación (consensus agreements), 47
Convention for the Elimination of All Forms of Discrimination against Women (CEDAW), 17

Index

Convergence of Civic Organizations for Democracy (Convergencia), 49, 82–83
corporate responsibility, 14, 113–18, 128, 130, 194, 225n
corporatism, 8, 33, 38–48, 51–53, 55–56, 111, 189, 204n, 205n, 206n, 211n
Cortez, Edgar, 82
Critical Legal Studies, 17, 191, 198n, 199n
Cuadra, Héctor, 210n
Cuba, 15, 56
Cuéllar, Benjamín, 60–61, 63
Cuéllar, Roberto, 60–61, 63
Czechoslovakia, 199n

De la Madrid, Miguel, 41, 44, 47, 52
De las Casas, Fray Bartolomé, 11–12
De Piedra, Rosario Ibarra, 44–45
De Quiroga, Vasco, 11–12
De Vitoria, Francisco, 11–12
Declaration of Rights and Fundamental Principles in the Workplace (ILO), 112–13
decolonization, 15, 111
deforestation, 9, 216n
democracy, transition to, 48, 55, 66–68, 141, 157
  citizen participation and, 86, 88–89
  clean elections and, 72–73, 87–91
  exhaustion of, 85, 88, 92, 94
  free trade linked to, 85–88, 95
  hegemonic project of, 75, 78, 81, 160, 173
  history of in Latin America, 56–60
  human rights discourse and, 26, 61, 74, 157, 171–74, 177, 187–89
  liberation theology and, 69–70
  NAFTA and, 77–78, 86–90, 218n
  and neglect of socioeconomic rights, 76–80
  observation of elections and, 82
Democratic Clause Project (DCP), 27, 155, 170–78, 183, 185, 192
"Democratic Spring," 52
dependency theory, 56, 61, 207n
developmentalism, 34, 40
discourses, 16–17, 24–25
domestic violence, 14, 124, 136, 163
domestic work, 7
Douzinas, Costas, 19–20, 135
drug trafficking, 67, 68, 77
Dussel, Enrique, 12–13, 15–16, 21–22

earthquake, Mexico City (1985), 41–43
Echeverría, Luis, 205n
economic, social, and cultural rights (ESCRs), 1, 14, 18, 65, 115, 118–19, 211n, 225n
  CPRs and, 63, 66–71, 73–74, 76, 84, 136, 152, 175
  globalization and, 111
  institutional negligence of, 31
  limitations of NGOs approach to, 92–93
  as a nodal point, 143, 148–52, 174–75
  Prodh Center analysis of, 71
  religious NGOs and, 73, 76
  and second-generation approach to human rights, 68–69, 71
  state duty and, 123, 125–27
  strategy change needed for, 151, 193
  violations of, 66, 69, 78, 126, 173
  women's, 136, 148–49
  Zapistas and, 78–80
Economic Commission for Latin America and the Caribbean (ECLAC), 34
Ecuador, 15

256 INDEX

El Salvador, 59–63, 158, 210n
electoral democracy, 55, 67, 82, 218n
electoral fraud, 46, 50–52, 59, 66, 69, 72, 80, 88, 91, 95, 175
"electoral machinery" of the PRI, 39
electoral observations, 72–73, 80, 88
electoral reforms, 47–48, 51–52, 73
electoral rights, 72–73, 82
electoral system, 44–53, 58–59, 76, 80–81, 88–91, 204n, 212n
Ellacuría, Ignacio, 62–63
emancipatory politics, 20, 23
empty signifiers, 23–24, 118, 220n
human rights as, 25, 75–76, 99–100, 119, 129, 151, 153, 164, 176–81
transition to democracy as, 76
Enola beans, 10
Eschle, C., 101
exports, 4–5, 196–97n

Factor Proportions Hypothesis, 106
farmers and farming. *See* agriculture
Farmers' Democratic Front (FDC), 102, 177
farmers' movement, 39–42, 46–50, 59, 64, 76, 93–94, 119–23, 139–43, 225–26n
Farmers' National Confederation (CNC), 39, 40, 44, 46–47
feminism, 14, 129, 135–37
Final Declaration, 157–66, 180, 226n, 227n
First People's Summit, 159–60, 165–66
fixing meaning, 99–100, 122, 127, 142, 150–53, 164–65, 176–82, 185
Food First and Informational and Action Network (FIAN International), 139
food industry, 6
Ford Motor Company, 8–9, 71, 212n
Foreign Direct Investment (FDI), 8, 108, 110–11, 116

Foucault, Michel, 16–17, 24
foundationalism, 13, 22
Foweraker, J., 3, 43
Fox, J., 40, 47
Fox, Vicente, 81, 91, 215n, 216n, 217n
Fray Francisco de Vitoria Human Rights Center, 41, 63–66, 71, 92, 102, 202n, 210n, 211n
Free Trade Area of the Americas (FTAA), 26, 91, 115, 155–60, 164–68, 174, 191
free trade discourse, 105, 111
Freire, Paulo, 50
Friedman, Milton, 36–38, 106, 203n

Gallardo, Francisco, 216n
García Urrutia, Manuel, 89
Gender and Economy (GyE), 102, 119, 122, 124, 136–37, 177
genealogy of human rights discourse, 16–17, 22–25
General Agreement on Trade and Tariffs (GATT), 34, 107, 109, 224n
German Continental Tires ((Hulera Euzkadi), 9
Global Agreement, 27, 79, 84, 127, 155, 170–78, 183, 191
globalization, 90, 124, 160, 194, 222n
  consequences for nation-state, 113
  corporate responsibility in, 130
  discourses of, 128–30, 145, 187
  ESCRs in, 111, 148–49
  human rights and, 2–3, 112
  labor rights and, 138
  Mexico's reduced bargaining power in, 128
  neoliberal, 219n
  NGOs and, 48, 85, 94, 118, 126
González Casanova, Pablo, 61, 64, 85, 208n
Gorbachev, Mikhail, 4

INDEX

Gray, J., 36–37
Guatemala, 59, 158, 210n
Gutiérrez, Father Gustavo, 61–62, 209n

Hayek, Friedrich von, 36–37, 203n
Heckscher-Olin Theorem, 106
hegemonic articulation, 23–25, 27, 99–100, 122, 135, 148–50, 170, 191
hegemonic project, human rights as, 118–22, 130, 160, 166
hegemonic project, transition to democracy as, 75, 78, 81, 160, 173
hegemonic projects, 99–100, 155, 185, 188, 193
hegemonic relationships, 94
Hellman, J. A., 43
Hemispheric Social Alliance (HSA), 7, 26, 91, 119, 155, 156–70, 184–85, 192, 227n
Heredia, Carlos, 86–87
Herrera, Carmen, 127–28, 227n
holistic human rights discourse, 26, 55, 61, 66–68, 73–75, 168
Houtzager, Peter, 101
Howse, R., 106
human dignity, 1, 12–13, 119, 122, 133–42, 148–53, 156–66, 188
human nature, universal, 12–14, 19
human rights
  actor-oriented perspective of, 18–19
  contemporary, 11, 192–94, 198n
  corporations' claim to, 20
  as a discursive formation, 16–17
  hegemonic project of, 118–22, 130, 160, 166
  as an "insurrectionary practice," 15, 17–19, 22–27, 155, 187–92, 194
  modern vs. contemporary, 13–16, 198n
  political potentiality of, 2, 76, 92–95, 128, 187, 190–92, 194
  universal, 20, 31, 198n

human rights law, 20, 119–22, 127, 135, 147, 163–69, 173, 192, 199n
human rights proper, 20

import-substitution, 34, 38, 202n
imports, neoliberal free trade policy's effect on, 7–8, 106, 109, 114, 196–97n
Income Tax Law, 49
income, 6–7, 110, 116, 125, 147, 163. *See also* wages
income, distribution of, 6
income tax, 38
Indigenous and Tribal Peoples in Independent Countries, 121
indigenous peoples
  excluded from NAFTA, 79, 90
  identity of, 90, 225n
  land rights and, 121, 134, 145–46
  as nodal point of meaning, 170
  rebellion of, 214n
  right to natural resources of, 10, 121, 144–46, 152, 216n
  rights of, 15, 21, 66, 71, 77–78, 83, 92, 144, 163, 170, 215–16n, 217n, 218n
  subject position of, 139–40, 167, 185
Indigenous Rights for the San Andrés Accords, 79, 82, 215n, 217n
indirect expropriation, 107–8, 116
"individual," understandings of, 14
individualism, 14, 18, 63, 203n
Institutional Revolutionary Party (PRI), 39–40, 43–48, 51–53, 58–59, 72–73, 183, 204n, 205n, 206n, 210n
Inter-American Commission for Human Rights (ICHR), 72, 213–14n, 216n
International Bill of Rights, 13, 21, 70, 111, 114

International Covenant on Civil
    and Political Rights (ICCPRs),
    70, 111
International Covenant on
    Economic, Social and Cultural
    Rights (ICESCRs), 70, 111
International Federation of Human
    Rights (IFHR), 84–85, 162
international financial institutions
    (IFIs), 33, 111, 129, 149, 161
International Monetary Fund
    (IMF), 35, 38, 109
interpretative repertoires, 22,
    24–25, 99–100, 114, 122
intertextuality of human rights
    discourse, 16–22, 191–94, 199n

Keck, M. E., 2–3, 227n
Kennedy, J. F., 56
Keynesianism, 34, 35, 37, 111

labor agreements, 8, 211n
labor, child, 157, 224n
labor discourses, 158–59
labor flexibility, 46, 197n
Labor Party (PT), 47
labor rights, 71, 78, 83, 165, 197n,
    225n, 228n
    FDI and, 110–11
    Final Declaration and, 158, 165
    FTAA and, 156–60, 167–68
    as human rights, 149–51
    "labor standards" substituted for,
        113
    NGOs and, 67, 78, 182
    subject position of workers and,
        137–40
    Zacatecas Forum, and, 87
labor standards and regulations,
    113, 124, 156, 173, 223n
labor unions, 8–9, 39–42, 46–49,
    70–71, 83, 86–87, 117, 150,
    156, 165, 208n, 211–12n, 227n
Laclau, E., 22–24, 99, 200n, 201n,
    220n

laissez-faire doctrine, 35
Latin American Council for Social
    Sciences (CLACSO), 56, 61
Latin American human rights
    discourse, 10–16, 18–22
law enforcement
    Arroyo on, 125, 129–30
    definition of, 12
    of ESCRs, 125–26, 175
    "existing reality" contrasted with,
        125
    fixing of meaning with, 128,
        165, 179, 191
    human rights discourse and,
        129–30, 161, 169–72, 174
    NGOs and, 121–22, 125–27,
        130, 147, 161, 169–72,
        179–80, 185
    as nonidealogical form, 121–22
    SMOs and, 122, 130, 169, 179,
        185
    state duty and, 123, 169–70,
        179–80, 183, 185
liberal democracy, 39, 56, 73, 75
liberalism, 12, 36–37, 190, 198n,
    208n. *See also* neoliberalism
liberation theology, 16, 26, 60–64,
    69, 70, 75, 206–7n, 209n
Limburg Principles, 114–15
López Portillo, José, 51–52

Maastricht Guidelines, 114–15
Maldonado, Father Jesús, 59,
    65–66, 71, 211n
manufacturing industry, 7–8
maquiladora industry, 5–6
March against Structural
    Reforms, 94
Marcos, *Subcomandante*, 90,
    219n
Marxism and Marxist discourses,
    23, 56, 62, 187, 189–90, 200n,
    201n, 203n, 208n, 209n
McAdam, D., 101
Metalclad, 9

Mexican Academy of Human
    Rights (Academia), 63–66,
    72–73, 83, 202n, 209n, 211n,
    212n, 218n
Mexican Action Network on Free
    Trade (RMALC), 5, 79, 102n,
    155, 160, 174, 197n, 202n,
    222n, 227n
  citizen participation and, 86, 89,
    219n
  creation of, 49, 76, 85
  transition to democracy and, 86,
    88–89, 218n
  NAFTA and, 83
Mexican Commission for the
    Defense and Promotion of
    Human Rights (CMDPDH),
    66, 76, 81, 94, 102, 216n
Mexican League, 102
Mexican Revolution (1910), 44, 58,
    78, 208n
Mexican Workers' Confederation
    (CTM), 8–9, 39–40, 44
"Miguel Agustín Pro Juárez"
    Human Rights Center (Prodh
    Center), 63–67, 71, 84–85, 94,
    102, 141, 173–74, 202n, 212n,
    217n, 225–26n
military, 37, 39, 56–58, 68, 77–78,
    129, 207n, 208n, 209n, 216n
Mises, Ludwin von, 36, 203n
Monsiváis, Carlos, 42–43
Montiel, Rodolfo, 9, 216n
Morales, Evo, 15
Morales, Román, 204n
Most Favored Nation principle, 107
Mouffe, C., 23, 200n, 220n
Multilateral Agreement on
    Investment (MAI), 112, 222n

National Action Party (PAN), 39,
    45, 52, 58, 72, 81, 87, 173,
    183, 204n
National Confederation of Popular
    Organizations (CNOP), 39, 40

National Democratic Front (FDN),
    45
National Human Rights
    Commission (CNDH), 67
National Network of Civil
    Organizations "All Rights for
    All" (Red TDT), 49, 66, 72,
    85, 217n
national security doctrine, 56, 62,
    207n
National Solidarity Program
    (Pronasol), 47–48, 206n
National Treatment principle, 107,
    116
National Union of Farmer
    Organizations (UNORCA), 47
neoclassical liberal economic
    discourse, 35–36
neoliberal discourse, 33–38,
    43–44, 105
neoliberal policies, 38, 40–45, 48,
    52, 81, 137
neoliberalism, 38–43, 55, 85, 187,
    189
new conservatism, 34–35, 190
New Social Movement Theory
    (NSM), 196n, 200n
NGO activists, 87, 102, 124, 133–35,
    140, 142, 151, 161, 177, 193
Nicaragua, 60, 210n
Nietzsche, Friedrich, 16
nodal points of meaning, 23, 100,
    143, 220n
  ESCRs as, 148, 152–53, 174
  human rights as, 152–53, 159,
    163, 179, 182, 184
  indigenous people's rights as, 170
  right to development as, 144–46,
    148, 153
  right to food as, 131, 142,
    144–48, 153
  women's rights as, 170
  workers' rights as, 158, 170
nondiscrimination, 107–8, 111,
    163, 224n

Index

nongovernmental organizations (NGOs)
  activists, 87, 102, 124, 133–35, 140, 142, 151, 161, 177, 193
  citizen participation and, 84, 133, 135, 152, 171–84
  citizenship and, 102–3, 152
  ESCRs and, 73, 76, 92–93
  globalization and, 48, 85, 94, 118, 126
  labor rights and, 67, 78, 182
  law enforcement and, 121–22, 125–27, 130, 147, 161, 169–72, 179–80, 185
  SMOs and, 65, 94, 101, 102, 193
  state duty and, 125–27, 130, 135, 147, 169, 175, 180
normative theory in international relations, 4
North America Free Trade Agreement (NAFTA), 4, 49, 67, 83, 107, 108, 115, 165
  agriculture under, 7
  citizen participation under, 89
  environmental vulnerability and, 9
  establishment of, 86–88, 196n
  FTAA and, 155, 156, 165
  as geographical network, 110
  indigenous people excluded from, 79, 90
  protests against, 222n
  transition to democracy and, 76–77, 88, 90, 218n
Nyamu-Musembi, Celestine, 18

Organization for Economic Cooperation and Development (OECD), 112, 225n
Osorio, V., 159
overproduction of rights, 20–21

Party of the Democratic Revolution (PRD), 59, 80, 87, 91, 218n
"pastoral practices" of the Catholic Church, 61–62
Peces-Barba, G., 11

Pérez-Casas, Luis Guillermo, 228n
Permanent Agrarian Council (CAP), 46
Perón, Juan, 15
petroleum industry, 5, 34, 39, 44
Pinochet, August, 203n
Pod-Ners, 10
political democracy, 57–58, 209n
poor, rights of the, 62–63, 73, 76, 119
poor countries (periphery), 23, 109, 112, 194, 207n
popular movements, 3, 40–48, 52, 205n, 212n
postmodernism, 1, 15
Potter, J., 24, 99
poverty, 6, 9, 50, 82–83, 124, 135, 159, 168, 177, 209n, 228n
Proctor, Larry, 10
Prodh Center, 63–57, 71, 84–85, 94, 102, 141, 173–74, 202n, 212n, 217n, 225–26n
Promotora, 94
Pronasol (National Solidarity Program), 47–48, 206n
protectionism, 106, 110, 223n
public and private spheres, 14, 116, 136
Public Opinion and Negotiation of the Free Trade Agreement: Citizen Alternatives, 77–78, 87–88
Puebla-Panama Plan, 126, 147

Quintana, Victor, 140–43

Rangel, Gabriela, 121, 146–47, 151–52
Reagan, Ronald, 38
Red TDT, 49, 66, 72, 85, 217n
relativism, 12, 13, 22
Ricardo, David, 106
right to a clean environment, 83, 144–45, 226n
right to a dignified life, 123, 143, 161

right to association, 51, 70, 86–87, 145, 164
right to be a farmer, 141–43, 191, 226n
right to collective bargaining, 156, 157, 164
right to consultation, 89, 146, 163
right to culture, 141, 191
right to determination, 21
right to development, 21, 115, 117, 130, 143–48, 152–53, 191, 226n
right to education, 117, 137
right to food sovereignty, 120, 150
right to food, 71, 100, 117, 120, 131, 137, 142–49, 152–53, 191
right to freedom, 12, 66, 226n
right to freedom of expression, 51
right to freedom of thought, 117
right to health, 117, 122, 136, 137, 211n
right to housing, 117, 211n
right to industrial safety, 157
right to information, 51, 89, 144–46, 163, 212n
right to life, 12, 63, 64, 66, 73, 76, 123, 143, 144, 150
right to natural resources, indigenous people's, 10, 121, 144–46, 152, 216n
right to participation, 144, 146, 185, 226n
right to personal security, 66, 68, 157, 163
right to physical integrity, 66, 68, 163, 226n
right to privacy, 117
right to property, 12, 226n
right to strike, 86, 164
right to unionize, 70, 87, 157
right to water, 117, 144–45
right to welfare, 137
right to work, 114, 141, 143, 191, 226n
rights of peoples, 69
Rio Declaration, 90

Rivas, Tuda, 41
Robinson, Mary, 216n, 217n
Rosenfeld, M., 198n
Rupp, Helen, 180

Salinas de Gortari, Carlos, 45–49, 59, 67, 78, 90, 206n
sameness, 24, 25, 133, 191
Sandinista revolution, 15
Sandoval, Areli, 126, 134, 144–45, 148
Second Americas Summit, 159, 165
Second People's Summit, 163, 166
sexual violence, 14, 136
Sikkink, K., 2–3, 227n
Smith, Adam, 35, 37, 106
Sobrino, Jon, 63
social movement organizations (SMOs)
  agendas of, 143
  citizenship and, 152
  law enforcement and, 122, 130, 169, 179, 185
  NGOs and, 65, 94, 101, 102, 193
  political approach of, 122–25
  state duty and, 122–25, 130, 169, 179
  women's rights and, 122–24, 143, 185
social movements, 2, 60, 112, 191, 193–94
  agendas of, 20, 31
  as agents of change, 4, 187
  in civil society, 140
  contesting of liberal understandings of rights by, 13
  corporate power and, 111, 114, 118
  focus on state duty, 114, 118, 125, 127–28
  Foweraker on, 3, 43
  human rights discourse of, 25
  Mexico City earthquake and, 42
  neoliberalism and, 107, 189
  "new" and "old," 200n
  NGOs and, 65, 94, 101, 102, 193
  SMOs and, 101, 102, 149

social movements—*continued*
  state's relationship with, 43, 46, 128, 130
  strategies of, 2, 5
  symbolic features of, 188, 200n
  transnational, 3
  urban, 45
  See also New Social Movement Theory
stabilization, 38, 197n, 198n
Stammers, N., 101
state duty
  definitions of, 37, 120–21
  Final Declaration and, 165
  fixed meaning with, 128, 146, 165, 191
  human rights discourse and, 4, 105, 114–15, 120–21, 128–31, 147, 159, 193
  law enforcement and, 123, 169–70, 179–80, 183, 185
  NGOs and, 125–27, 130, 135, 147, 169, 175, 180
  as nonideological form, 121–22
  Sandoval on, 126, 144–45
  SMOs and, 122–25, 130, 169, 179
  social movements' focus on, 114, 118, 125, 127–28
  woman and, 124
state intervention, 36–38, 120–21
structural adjustment, 7, 38, 44, 135–36, 197n, 211n, 222n
structuralism, 11, 17, 22–26, 56, 187
Structuralist School of Development, 34
Suarez, Victor, 120, 123, 140–42, 150
subject positions, 23–26, 99–100, 152, 185
  citizen, 162, 170, 177, 179, 184–85
  construction of, 25, 139, 142, 151, 180, 188, 192–93
  of farmers, 135, 139–41
  human rights-related, 143–44, 150, 152, 163
  indigenous, 139–40, 167, 185
  of NGO activists, 134–35, 170, 177–78, 184
  of women, 135–37
  of workers, 135, 137–39
subjectivism in economics, 36–37, 203n

Tamayo, J., 44
tariff reduction, 4, 7, 34–35, 86, 109
Telmex, 206n
textile industry, 6, 42, 109
Thatcher, Margaret, 38, 203n
Thomas, D. C., 4
three-generation approach to human rights, 69–73, 129
timber industry, 9, 216n
trade liberalization, 38, 107, 109, 110, 164, 197n
trade unions. *See* labor unions
transition theory, 57, 61
transnational collective action, 2–4, 174–78, 181–84, 189, 194
transnational corporations, 109–10, 114, 116–17, 168, 207n
Trebilcock, M., 106

unemployment, 6–8, 125, 128, 197n, 209n
United Nations
  Charter, 180–81
  human rights discourse and, 31, 77, 81, 92, 198n
  NGOs and, 14, 82, 117, 126; state obligation and, 112, 115, 120
  Norms Governing the Responsibilities of.... Human Rights, 117–18
United Nations Development Program (UNDP), 5–6
Universal Declaration of Human Rights (UDHR), 13, 17, 60, 70, 79, 111, 117, 162, 168, 170–71, 183

Venezuela, 15, 190
Vienna World Human Rights Conference, 136
Villalba, Antonio, 139, 149
Villamar, Alejandro, 127, 145–47
Vitoria Center. *See* Fray Francisco de Vitoria Human Rights Center

wages, 6, 8, 34, 38, 40, 83, 124, 136, 156, 197n. *See also* income
welfare state, 34
Westphalian state, 113
Wetherell, M., 24, 99
Williams, H. L., 3
women, indigenous, 214n, 218n
women, subject position of, 135–37, 148–49
women's groups, 50, 88
women's movement, 17
women's rights, 17, 83, 92, 129
  domestic violence and, 14
  employment conditions and, 6–7
  FTAA and, 159–64, 167
  health and, 122
  as human rights, 14, 136–39, 149
  neoliberalism and, 189
  as nodal point, 152, 169
  poverty and, 82–83
  San Miguel Joint Declaration and, 215n
  separation of public and private spheres and, 14
  SMOs and, 122–24, 143, 185
  subject position and, 134–37, 143, 185
  trade policy and, 6–7, 93, 114, 119, 159–60
Women's World March, 136
Woodiwiss, A., 31–32, 198n
Workers' Confederation of Mexico (CTM), 8–9, 39, 40, 44, 100
Workers' Inter-American Organization (ORIT), 156–57, 165
Workers' Revolutionary Party (PRT), 45
World Bank (WB), 35, 38, 109
World Campaign for the Rights of Women, 136
world philosophy, 15
World Trade Organization (WTO), 115, 129, 149
  agreement on patents and copyright, 10
  creation of, 109
  human rights and, 112, 137, 144, 161, 223–24n
  liberalization and, 107, 109
World War II, 17, 203n

Zacatecas Forum, 77–78, 87–88
Zapatista Army for National Liberation (EZLN), 78, 90, 214n, 215–16n, 222n
Zapatista uprising/movement, 15, 78–80, 90, 213n, 214n, 216n, 217n, 219n, 222n